MAOIST MOVEMENT IN NEPAL
A Sociological Perspective

MAOIST MOVEMENT IN NEPAL
A Sociological Perspective

Uddhab P. Pyakurel

ADROIT

Published by
ADROIT PUBLISHERS
4675/21, Ganpati Bhawan, Ansari Road,
Daryaganj, New Delhi-110 002
Phones : 011-23266030

Distributors
AKHIL BOOK DISTRIBUTORS
e-mail: akhilbooks@yahoo.com
akhilbooks@hotmail.com

ISBN : 81-87392-78-9

Layout
Sudhir Vatsa

Laser Typeset by
Arpit Printographers
E-mail : arpitprinto@yahoo.com

Printed in India on behalf of M/s Adroit Publishers
by Arpit Printographers
Phones : 09350809192, 011-22825424

Dedicated To

My Late Grand Mother

Tara Devi Pyakurel,

And

Those Innocents Who Lost Their Lives during the Clash between the Security Force and the Maoist

CONTENTS

Acknowledgements 9
Acronyms and Abbreviations 11

Chapter 1 : Introduction **13–26**
1.1. Background 13
1.2. Objectives 15
1.3. Chapterisation 16
1.4. Understanding the Maoist struggle in Nepal 16
1.5. Defining the Maoist movement as social movement 23
1.5.1. Social/political debate 25

Chapter 2 : Process of Hinduization and Nepalization in Nepal **27–59**
2.1. Pre-Unification 28
2.2. Post-Unification 35
2.2.1. Shah Regime (1769–1846) 35
2.2.2. Rana Regime (1846–1951) 41
2.2.3. Pseudo-democratic period (1951–60) 47
2.2.4. Panchayat regime (1960–1990) 51
2.2.5. Democratic system (1990–2002) 54

Chapter 3 : Origin, Growth and Spread of the Maoist Movement in Nepal **60–126**
3.1. Communists history in Nepal 60
3.2. Some elements of the Maoist movement 67
3.3. Origin, growth and spread of the Maoist movement in Nepal 102

Chapter 4 : Summary and Conclusion **127–135**

Annexes **137–209**

References **211–222**

Index **223-228**

LIST OF TABLES

Table 1:	Human Development by Caste and Ethnicity, 1996	73
Table 2:	Integrated National Index of Governance (INDH), 1999	74
Table 3:	Share of Caste/Ethnic Groups in Prestigious Occupations	75
Table 4:	Caste/Ethnic Composition of HOR and Party Central Committees	76
Table 5:	Land Holding Position of Caste/Ethnic and Religious Groups	77
Table 6:	Educational Status of the Caste/Ethnic and Regional Groups	79
Table 7:	Gender Participation in Economic and Political Activities	80
Table 8:	Constitutional Provision for the Different Communities in 1990 Constitution	81–82
Table 9:	Election Manifestas of the Parties in the Elections 1991, 1994 and 1999 (on Caste/Ethnicity and Regional Groups)	84-88
Table 10:	Caste/Ethnic Composition in the 24 Districts with the Maoist Influence	90
Table 11:	Caste/Ethnic and Region-based Frontier Organization of the Maoist and its Leadership	91
Table 12:	The CPN (Maoist) Regional Autonomous Government	92
Table 13:	Killing by the State and the Maoist	113
Table 14:	Killing by the State and the Maoist (after Assumption of the Power by the King)	116

ACKNOWLEDGEMENTS

I am grateful to Prof. Virginius Xaxa, without whose support and encouragement the study would never have been undertaken; without whose meticulous editing it would have been considerably less readable; and without whose guidance I would not have joined at the Department of Sociology, Delhi School of Economics, University of Delhi. I have received regular support from him since I met him in Kathmandu in January 2005. His critical suggestion and sympathetic support helped me to complete this work within my limited time constraint. For all this, I am immensely indebted to him. I am thankful to Prof. Aneeta A. Minocha, Prof. Nandini Sundar, Dr. Rabindra Ray, Dr. Rita Barara, Dr. Meena Radhakrishna and other faculty members of the Department of Sociology, University of Delhi, for their intellectual input and support. My thanks are also due to Vijay Pratap and Dr. Bela Bhatia for helpful comments and suggestions.

In Nepal, I am indebted to Prof. Lok Raj Baral who encouraged me for further study. Credit should go to him for his appreciative comments on the tentative framework of this research work. I am also thankful to Prof. Krishna Khanal, Dhruba Kumar and Dr. Krishna Hachhethu for their constant backing, comments and suggestions.

I express my sincere appreciation to all those seniors and friends from Nepal and India who helped the work in various ways. I am also thankful to Ms. Chameli Xaxa for her moral support and encoragement.

I owe a debt to D. K. Sharma of Adroit Publishers for accepting the manuscript for publication. I must thank Sudhir Vatsa for helping the manuscript's language and structure. This book would not have been possible without their initiative.

Thanks are also due to the authority of the Kathmandu-based NCCS Library, and Delhi-based Ratan Tata, JNU, and Teen Murti Libraries.

Lastly but not least, I would like to express my deepest gratitude to my father Krishna P. Pyakurel, mother Sita Pyakurel and mother-in-law Krishna Kumari Adhikari for their all sorts support and constant help without which the research work would not be possible. I am extremely thankful to my wife, Indra Adhikari for her constant backing. I am also thankful to my brothers and sisters for their emotional support.

This work has its own limitations and weaknesses. However, I have decided to get it published in hurry because of the speedy conversion of the Maoist Movement from "people's war" to the mainstream peaceful competitive politics. I am hopeful that all the eminent readers will forgive the weaknesses of this book considering it as my first try. I always appreciate valuable comments and suggestions which would help me with my future career. I am alone responsible for whatever errors may exist in this work.

January 12, 2007

Uddhab P. Pyakurel
Nuwakot, Nepal

ACRONYMS AND ABBREVIATIONS

APF	Armed Police Force
CA	Constituent Assembly
CPN	Communist Party of Nepal
CPN (M)	Communist Party of Nepal (Maoist)
CPN (UML)	Communist Party of Nepal (United Marxist Leninist)
CSWC	Community Study and Welfare Centre
DAO	District Administration Office
DFID	Department for International Development
FPA	Four Parties Alliance
GDP	Gross Domestic Production
HDI	Human Development Index
HMG	His Majesty of Government
ICG	International Crisis Group
IDP	Integrated Development Program
IGP	Inspector General of Police
INIG	Integrated National Index of Governance
INSEC	Informal Sector Service Center
ISRSC	Informal Sector Research and Study Centre
JM	Jana Morcha
ML	Marxist-Leninist
MP	Member of Parliament
NC	Nepali Congress
NC (D)	Nepali Congress (Democratic)
NCDN	National Committee for Development of Nationalities

NESAC	Nepal South Asia Centre
NGO	Non-governmental Organization
NSP	Nepal Sadhbhawana Party
NWPP	Nepal Worker Peasant Party
PLA	People's Liberation Army
RIM	Revolutionary Internationalist Movement
RNA	Royal Nepal Army
RPP	Rashtriya Prajatantra Party
SFDP	Small Farmers Development Program
SPA	Seven Parties Alliance
UK	United Kingdom
ULF	United Left Front
ULFA	United Liberation Front of Assam
UML	United Marxist and Leninist
UNDP	United Nations Development Program
UNPM	United National People's Movement
UPFN	United People's Front, Nepal
URPC	United Revolutionary People's Council
US	United States
VDC	Village Development Committee

1 INTRODUCTION

1.1. BACKGROUND

Nepal, a South Asian Himalayan country, has been of late suffering from a crisis of Maoist insurgency. It began with simultaneous raids on government offices, police posts and private businesses by the Maoist in the name of the 'People's War' on February 13, 1996.

The Maoist insurgency has spread all over the country in the last 11 years. At least 15,000 people have already lost their lives. The Communist Party of Nepal-Maoist (CPN [M]) has been waging a 'People's War' for establishing a communist republican state in Nepal instead of constitutional monarchy and western model parliamentary democracy. In regard to the latter (parliamentary democracy), the Maoist has, of late, changed their strategy by accepting it as a route to the ultimate objective i.e. the establishment of the so-called 'people's democracy.'

After the declaration of 'the People's War' by the Maoist, the people of Nepal have become victim not only of extra judicial killing but also of looting, kidnap or abduction, torture, disappearance, threat, rape, extortion and other forms of violence both by the security force and the Maoist. Nepal ranked first in the world in the disappearance of the persons in 2003. According to the Human Rights Commission Report of Nepal, the number of disappeared persons in Nepal stood at 717 from January 2000 to November 2003. Informal Sector Service Centre (INSEC) records show that the number of detainees that had disappeared after arrest by state forces had reached 1,000 in 2004. The Human Rights yearbook reports that 38,191 people had been displaced by the conflict and insecurity up to end of 2004. The Community Study and Welfare Center (CSWC) guess that the number of displaced people from the most affected districts comprised 12.25 per cent of the total population of Nepal till January 2004. However, the Internally

Displaced People (IDP) Project of the Norwegian Refugee Council estimates the number of people displaced as over 200,000 (Nepal: Human Rights Yearbook 2005:ix).

Nepal is loosing at Gross Domestic Production (GDP) an average rate of 1.25 percent per year compared to the pre-conflict period because of the internal violent conflict. Paul's empirical study of 93 countries covering a period of 1990–89 has shown that the annual growth generally got reduced at an average of 2.2 percent during civil war (Collier 1999). If we extend this argument, it would mean that the Nepali economy lost 22.0 percent of its GDP during the ten years long period of conflict.

There is hardly any aspect of life, which is not affected by the conflict. Tourism, the main stay of the economy has been affected by decreasing tourist flow in last ten years. The security expenditure has increased by more than 300 percent in the same period. On the one hand, militarization has increased on the pretext of curbing Maoist insurgency and on the other, the Maoist is also recruiting young people for its militia. According to the 2002 estimate, Nepal spent US$ 57.22 million, that is, 1.1 percent of GDP and 22-25 percent of its total revenue towards security. The army and the police are thus absorbing more than 16 percent of the total budget. According to another estimate, the cost of deploying security forces during the most intense phase of fighting stood at US$ 100,000 per day whereas the per capita annual income was around US$ 200 (Thapa 2003). The security forces—the Nepal Army, the Armed Police Force (APF) and the Nepal Police—had requested the government for an additional budget grant of Rs. 11 billion in 2004 for effective action plan against the Maoist (*The Kathmandu Post* August 31, 2004). All these demands were made at a time when the GDP growth rate was at its worst. For example, in 2002-03, it stood at 2.7 percent, and in 2003-04, it was 3.6 percent. The growth rate in 2001-02 was negative by 0.6 percent (*The Himalayan Times* July 16, 2004). As a result of the rampant increment of security expenditure, development expenditure in social sector especially education, health, rural drinking water and local development has rapidly slowed down.

The DFID report had estimated the total cost of destruction of the physical infrastructure and development projects until 2002 at 18 billion (DFID Report 2002). Agricultural sector has also been affected due to widespread displacement of the population due to the conflict. It is to be noted that more than 37 percent of the GDP in Nepal comes from the agriculture. No youth, especially strong male laborers are seen in the rural areas because of the fear created by both the security force and the Maoist.

In this context, I have tried to examine the social causes which helped the origin and spread of Maoist Movement in Nepal. A lot has been written on the Maoist Movement but this study tries to deal more with the social aspects.

1.2. OBJECTIVES

In the context of Nepal's Maoist Movement, one can conduct researches on various dimensions such as the role of ideology (Marxist–Leninist–Maoist), the history of the Maoist Movement, the leadership of the Maoist Party, the comparision of the authoritarian and democratic systems of government and their role in nurturing and furthering the movement etc. The study here has only focused on the social background. Indeed, one can find out some influential social causes of the movement if one examines both the social factors and the area-wise influences of the movement. Although the movement has spread to all the districts of Nepal, its strength and influence varies from place to place. Accordingly, the study has focused on the following objectives:

- To examine the discriminations in society on the basis of religion, caste, ethnicity, gender and language which directly and indirectly helped in strengthening the Maoist Movement in Nepal.
- To examine the processes of Nepalization and Hinduization in Nepal which led the social conflicts among different groups of society.

1.3. CHAPTERIZATION

Keeping the above objectives in mind, the study has been divided into four chapters, which are as follows:

The first chapter is an introduction to the topic of the study. It conceptualizes Nepal's Maoist Movement 1996-2006 as a social movement. The chapter also discusses the definitions of different social movements and their basic characteristics.

The second chapter examines the processes of Nepalization and Hinduization in Nepal. It has covered the period prior to the unification of modern Nepal to the present time. The chapter traces out the problems confronted by the Nepali state in different periods. Further, the government policies, which contributed to the marginalization of different groups is the main focus of this chapter.

The third chapter analyzes the origin, development, and spread of the Maoist Movement in Nepal. The history of the communist movement in Nepal, in general, has also been examined. It also explores the reasons for some caste/ethnic groups of Nepal not being able to get absorbed in the mainstream of Nepali state. All the social factors—gender, caste, ethnicity, class, region etc—have been examined. Moreover, this chapter has looked at how the Maoists' techniques are capable of covering up such ambiguities of the origin and development of the movement. The chapter examines the policies and programs of the different governments and the Maoist. The election manifestos of the mainstream political parties have also been examined in this chapter.

The concluding chapter focuses on the major findings of the study. It analyzes critically some of the government policies and party policies responsible for the Maoist Movement.

1.4. UNDERSTANDING THE MAOIST STRUGGLE IN NEPAL

Some of the key terms used in the study of an armed struggle against the state are 'people's war', insurgency, movement, problem, terrorist activity, conflict, and violence. This has also been the case in the context of the Maoist struggle in Nepal. Hence, attempt has been made to clarify the terms in this section.

Peoples' War: 'People's War' is a military-political strategy invented by Mao Tse Tung. The underlying meaning of the term is to ensure and maintain the support of the people and draw the enemy deep into the interior where the people will bleed them to dry through a mix of 'Mobile Warfare and Guerrilla Warfare'. However, the Maoist in Nepal used the term for their strategy of long-term armed revolutionary struggle. For Krishna Bahadur Mahara, the spokesperson of the Nepali Maoist, 'peoples' war' is a 'war of the peoples' community' (Mahara 2005:8)

The term, 'people's war' was used by Mao, when the Communist Party of China was engaged in the Chinese Revolution. The theory of Mao on 'people's war' is based upon the 'scientific proposition' that 'masses are the creators of the history.' Some basic features of the people's war are; 1) it is a small revolutionary movement with broad-based popular support. 2) It is the revolution against the state power and is carried out by a well-equipped small army. 3) Strategically, it is just a tiny battle and not a decisive war because the force is constituted of a few dozen soldiers. 4) Its objective is to get easy and successful confrontation with the state through carefully chosen battles. 5) The war starts in a remote area with mountainous or otherwise difficult terrain in which the presence of the state is weak. 6) Making and spreading the revolutionary base area (a local stronghold of the revolutionary party) in the countryside is the motto of the war. 7) For gaining popular support and making the base area, people-based agenda like land reform, peoples' court and social reform programs are launched. 8) The primary objective of the people's war is seizing the power in the whole country.

Insurgency: 'Insurgency' means an organized rebellion that engages in deliberate actions to cause the downfall of a governmental authority, through destruction of public properties and armed actions. According to the Oxford Dictionary, insurgency is 'an attempt to take control of a country by force', or 'an attempt by some of the people in a country to change their government, using violence'. Baral writes, 'An insurgent is a person or act of "rising in revolt" against an established state authority' (Baral 2006). Insurgency refers to the use of extra-constitutional and violent means aimed at achieving the goal of regime change or of bringing about qualitative transformations in the society and polity. Thus, "insurgency is 'revolutionary' in character because of its set goals and boundaries, while the objective of terrorism remains obscure" (*Ibid*). Insurgency is a 'prolonged armed struggle carried out immaculately step by step in order to achieve specific objectives leading finally to overthrow of the existing order' (Pokhem 1997:2). Insurgency is also defined "as use of armed force against an established government to achieve public purpose, which cannot, in the opinion of the insurgents, be achieved by pacific means" (Shuman 1967).

Movement: Generally, the term 'movement' refers to a group of people who share the same ideas, aims, or activities over a period of time. Movements may be social, economic, political, cultural etc. Social movement is an organized effort by a significant number of people to change (or resist change) some major aspect or aspects of society (Oxford Dictionary of Sociology 2005:615). Movements are goal-directed and purposeful activities in which people join and participate with the overt understanding that they are working with each other to accomplish one or more explicit aims (Etzioni 1991 cited in Weinstein 2005: 135).

The term was used for the first time in the Eighteenth century by Saint-Simon to characterize social protest that emerged in France and later elsewhere. There, it was applicable to the new political forces that opposed the status quo. Now, the concept of 'neo-social movement' has emerged in the study of social movement. The new social movement differs from the conventional one. According to the advocates of the neo-social movements, focus is diverted from economic grounds to cultural grounds like ethnicity, identity, environment etc (Raj and Chaudhary 1998). In fact, social movements are closely linked to social change. Movements differ from the other forms of protests, partly because of their scale; they are the largest, most organizationally complex and most permanent. They can involve millions of participants and last for generations

(Weinstein 2005: 135).

Problem: According to the Oxford Dictionary, problem is 'a thing that is difficult to deal with or to understand'. Problem refers to a situation, condition, or issue that is unresolved or undesired. Usually, the nature of a problem is such that an answer or solution is needed. In such cases, problem solving is used to understand important aspects of the problem so that an answer or solution can be found.

Arya argues, 'the roots of social movements mostly lie within the social problems, and as such, these might be assigned as the main basis of such movements' (Arya 1998:20). Merton and Nisbet write, 'the first and basic ingredient of a social problem consists of a substantial discrepancy between widely-shared social standards and actual conditions of social life' (Merton and Nisbet 1971). The politicians, diplomats and other elites are using the term 'problem' while they discuss the Maoists' struggle in Nepal. However, the Maoist leaders are against such a description of their struggle. They argue that the problem is not the movement launched by them but the state and its structures. They further argue that the 'people's war' is a solution to a 240 year old rooted problem in Nepal.

Terrorist Activity or Terrorism: Many researchers have tried to define the term 'terrorism', but no one has been able to provide a comprehensive definition that would cover all its aspects. Bassiouni tried to define terrorism by studying 36 cases all over the world but could not do so. He, ultimately, concluded that 'terrorism' has never been defined... (Bassiouni 2004:305). It is mainly because of its nature, which is always unstable. The same action can be considered differently. For some people, the person can be a terrorist and for others he/she can be a freedom fighter. Therefore, it is said, 'today's terrorist is tomorrow's freedom fighter' (Adhikari 2006).

The term 'terrorism' is based on the Latin verbs *terrere* (to frighten) and *deterrere* (to frighten from). It dates back to 1795 when it was used to describe the actions of the Jacobin Club in post-Revolutionary France, the so-called 'Reign of Terror.' Webster's New International Dictionary defines terrorism as the "act of terrorizing, or state of being terrorized by a) the system of the Reign of Terror, b) a mode of governing or of opposing government by intimidation, and c) any policy of intimidation. For Halliday (2001), the term 'terrorism' refers to forms of action-assassination, bombings, seizures of individuals as hostages and the hijacking of planes tend to be included (cited in Baral 2003:226). Malaysian Prime Minister Mahathir Muhammad opines that all attacks targeting civilians should be considered terrorism (Ghosh 2003: 177).

After 11 September 2001, U.S.A. is more concerned to destroy terrorism in the world. Therefore, every institution of the U.S. has tried to define terrorism. U.S. Code of Federal Regulations mentions terrorism as '...the unlawful use of force and violence against persons or property to intimidate or coerce a government, the civilian population, or any segment thereof, in furtherance of political or social objectives' (U.S. Code of Federal Regulation, 28 C.F.R. section 0.85). Again, according to the current U.S. national security strategy, terrorism is 'premeditated, politically motivated violence against innocents.' United States Department of Defense defines it as the 'calculated use of unlawful violence to inculcate fear; intended to coerce or intimidate governments or societies in pursuit of goals that are generally political, religious, or ideological' (http://www.homeoffice.gov.uk).

The term has been used to refer to the Maoist by the Nepali government when the first ceasefire and ongoing negotiations were called off by the Maoist. After the government of Nepal tagged the Maoist as 'terrorist,' other countries like U.S.A., U.K., and India followed the path. However, the official position of Nepali state towards the Maoist is 'confusing' (Baral 2003:226); sometimes the state considers the Maoist as a political force and sometimes as terrorist.

Conflict: Apart from the above-mentioned terms, another common term in use to describe the Maoists' activities in Nepal is conflict. Without understanding the concept of conflict, understanding of any revolution, movement and activity will be incomplete. Defining conflict, Warner states that conflict can refer to a debate or a contest; a disagreement or argument; dispute or quarrel; a struggle, battle or confrontation; or a state of unrest, turmoil, chaos and violence

(Warner 2001). Rijal and Yokota define 'conflict' as a clash of interests. They further write that conflict is real or apparent clash or struggle over political, socio-cultural, and economic power, values, and resources (Rijal and Yokota 2006:71-72). Coser writes that a conflict is a struggle between two or more people over value or competition for status, power, and scarce resources (Coser 1956).

Similarly, Buckles opines that conflict is an active stage of disagreement between people with opposing opinions, principles and practices manifested in different forms such as grievance, conflict, dispute and war. The clashes between the different social groups and individuals create antagonism that leads to conflicts in the society. Therefore, conflict sometimes creates social disorder and sometimes positive change in society.

There is always misperception in society about the nature of conflict. This misunderstanding is that conflict is always destructive in society. However, social scientists agree that not every conflict is negative. Without conflict, no society will change. Conflict can assume various forms. It can be defined as armed, peaceful, violent, or non-violent. From the perspectives of the objectives, it can be classified as political, economic, social, cultural, religious etc. From the coverage area and actors involvement point of view, it can be in-house, local, national or internal and international or external.

Lopez and Stohl (1989:429-431) have classified conflicts into four basic types —structural, perceptual, manifest and latent. For them, the 'objective' factors like race, ethnicity, religion, language, ideology can be categorized as structural conflicts because these are rooted in the very structure of the system of polity, economy, society and tend to provoke direct structural violence. For perceptual conflicts, misunderstandings that arise out of ideological, historical, religious, nationalist, racial and ethnic differences are the common sources where one believes that the other is an actual or potential source of harm to one's vital interests or primary values. For manifest conflicts, clear behavioral evidence for neglecting, ignoring, isolating, and even suppressing the opposition's views are the main causes. Lastly, the grievance of the subordinate groups against the establishment is the main source of latent conflicts.

Violence: The term 'violence' refers to physical acts—typically connotative with aggressive and criminal behavior—that intends to cause or is causing injury to human beings. Harm to non-human beings or animals may be considered violence, though this depends on the social mores related to animal cruelty, and the situational context in which such acts take place. The concept of violence can also be extended to any abuse, usually depending on severity. Damage to property is typically considered minor relative to violence against people.

Galtung writes that violence is exerted by situation, institutions, social, political and economic structures. He describes violence as urban and rural, public and private, political and non-political (Galtung 1996:157). Rijal and Yokota have categorized violence into three kinds. These are: 1) economic violent acts, which is motivated and propelled by a desire for economic power. 2) Social violent acts, which are motivated by desire to gain social power such as abuse of spouse and child, sexual assault on women etc. The category seems very narrow because the term 'social' covers more areas. 3) Political violence is one where the goal is to obtain or maintain political power. They conceptualize violence in a broader sense because the examples they mention cover all sorts of social activities. For them, insurgency, guerrilla conflict, paramilitary conflict, terrorism, separatist or secessionist movement, revolutionary movement, coup-oriented movement, political issues or personality-oriented movement, primordial such as religious and racial struggles are the examples of political violence (Rijal and Yokota 2006:73–75).

For Nieburg 'political violence' is 'acts of disruption, destruction, injury, whose propose, choice and targets or victims, surrounding circumstances, implementation, and/or effects have political significances, that is, tend to modify the behavior of others in a bargaining situation that has consequences for the social system' (Nieburg 1969:13). For Gurr, political violence is 'the use of threat or violence by any party or institution to attain ends within or outside the political order' (Gurr 1974: 4). Likewise, Apter argues that the 'political violence is disorderly but it is designated for a reordering propose i.e., to overthrough a tyrannical regime, to redefine and realize justice and equality, to achieve independence or territorial autonomy, to impose one's religious and doctrinal beliefs' (Apter 1997: 5, 26).

Political violence has been classified into various forms by social scientists. Rijal and Yozoyo (2006:77) classified political violence into anti-systemic and extra-systemic, which are somewhat similar to Phadnis's broad objectives of ethnic movements in South Asian states. Phadnis had classified movements into systemic, anti-systemic and extra-systemic (Phadnis 1990:216). Mehden divides political violence into five categories. These are: primordial (religious or racial), separatist or secessionist, revolutionary and counter revolutionary, coup-oriented, and political issue or personality oriented (Mehden 1973:7-17). Zwi and Ugalde mention four kinds of political violence and their causes. According to them, 'structural political violence' is due to the misdistribution of the resources. 'Repressive political violence' is due to state action on the basis of religion, language, caste/ethnicity and political belief. 'Reactive political violence' occurs when the above-mentioned suppressed groups react against the suppressor. In addition, 'combative political violence' takes place when force is used to preserve or gain power (Zwi and Ugalde 1991:203-217).

1.5. DEFINING THE MAOIST MOVEMENT AS SOCIAL MOVEMENT

In view of the above-mentioned description, defining ten years armed struggle of the Maoist is a difficult task. Sociologically, the Maoist movement in Nepal can be defined as a social movement. Since such a movement has multiple features, it is not possible to fit the movement in a single concept of people's war, insurgency, problem, conflict, violence and terrorism.

'People's War' is the way the Maoist cadres and their supporters define the Maoist movement, since the movement is primarily guided by Mao's ideology. For others, however, it is not a suitable characterization. Some of the features of the Maoists' struggle look similar to insurgency because its ultimate goal is to capture state power. The description of the movement as 'terrorism' by some people seems far from appropriate because all agenda raised by it, are social. According to Baral, the agenda the Maoist are related to social and economic justice but "some of its methods are similar to terrorism (Baral 2006: 185). Even the government of Nepal is in a dilemma in characterizing the Maoist struggle. Sometimes it considers it as a political struggle and some other times as a terrorist activity. Apart from the above-mentioned characterization, it is also described as 'an internal armed conflict', a social movement. Indeed almost all the agenda taken up by the Maoist are social in value.

To begin with, most of the agenda taken by the Maoist in Nepal are people's agenda. From the beginning, the Maoist has been repeatedly and consistently raising the agenda of discrimination and inequality in the society. In the course of its struggle, it has tried to enforce its ideas in society. The methods used for addressing discrimination and inequality may be debated, but credit must be given to the Maoist for radicalizing the people.

Before launching its struggle in 1996, the Maoist submitted its 40-points demands to the government. Though the submission of the demand to the government become debatable because of the Maoist's decision to begin the war before the given dateline, the demands had taken most of the socio-economic and cultural issues. Of these demands, nine were related to nationality, 17 to democracy, and the rest 14 to the livelihood issues of the people.

Wilkinson defines social movement as a 'deliberate collective endeavor to promote change in any direction and by any means' (Wilkinson 1971). It means there is no hard and fast limitation on the means of a movement. The means may be violent, peaceful, or mixed. It is a definition, which is very broad. According to Wilkinson if a movement has people's participation and its aim is to promote change, it is a social movement. According to the Blackwell Dictionary of Modern Social Thought, 'many social movements challenge institutional structures, ways of life and thinking, norms and moral codes.' The means used in the movement are not the indicators of a movement's nature; whether it is terrorist activity, war, or insurgency. Giving examples of several confrontations between British troops and Gandhi's followers during the Indian independence struggle and the struggles between police and protesters during the U.S. Civil Rights movements, Weinstein argues that even declared non-violent movements have been met with violent reactions from state authorities (Weinstein 2005:139).

For Mukherjee (1977), a social movement is a collective mobilization seeking change of structure either through institutional or non-institutional means. To Wilson (1973), social movement is a conscious, collective, and organized attempt to bring about or resist large-scale change in the social order by non-institutionalized means. Similarly, Diani argues, 'A social movement is a network of informal interactions between a plurality of individuals, groups and/or organizations, engaged in political or cultural conflict, on the basis of a shared collective identity' (Diani 2000:165).

Although the Maoist Movement meets all the criteria that the social movement writers describe in their definitions, there is a debate whether it is a political or a social movement. This raises the question as to the differences between social and political movements. An equally interesting question is that if the main concern of the Maoist is to capture the state power, why should it not be defined as a political movement?

1.5.1. Social/Political Debate

Given the fact that the Maoist is politically oriented; its primary goal is to capture state power and its main slogan is to change Nepal from a kingdom into a republican state, a question can be raised why is the movement being described as a social movement?

Earlier, the concept 'political' and 'social' was too narrowly defined. However, today, because of the multidisciplinary nature of social science, one is not able to distinguish between political and social. Postmodern theorists do not believe in the centralism of power. According to them, power is located at various levels of society. Even the liberal democrats believe that power is not solely confined to the government; it is located in the civil society, media and so on. Therefore, now, the distinction between what is social and what is political is considerably minimal. Rio, in his two volumes on Social Movements in India (1978), has described the Naxalite Movement of India as a social movement. Heberle (1951) argues that all movements have political implications even if their members do not strive for political power. Shah writes that because of the nexus of the social and political disciplines, 'political scientists, too, are not inhibited in using the term "Social Movement" '. He further writes that the book on 'social movements' by Wilkinson, published under the series 'The Concept of Political Science', is suggestive of this reality. For Shah, a 'social movement' also includes those movements, which have clear objectives of bringing about political change. The difference between social and political movements is merely semantic (Shah 2002:19-22). Accepting the complexity of social movements, Jelin writes that social movements are seen to be engaged in a significant political struggle in terms of access to the mechanisms of power but also a cultural struggle in the search for different identities (Jelin 1990:206). Polletta and Jasmer also argue that every social movement has 'combined political goals with more culturally oriented efforts' (Polletta and Jasmer 2001:287). For Habermas, Social movements are symbiotically locked to the politics of self-actualization or an emancipatory form of politics. It is the politics of life-chances because it tries to achieve liberation of the life-world from the penetration of technological, bureaucratic and economic rationality in everyday life (Habermas 1995:335-337).

The points of view of various scholars show that the concept of social movement is vaguer than that of a political movement. Even if a movement has some elements of political agenda, it can easily be accommodated under the category of social movement. Political movement gives narrow meaning to the term 'movement' but the term 'Social Movement' tends to deal with all the agenda like political, cultural, regional etc. On this ground, I would like to view the Maoist Movement as 'Social Movement' launched for specific political objective, despite some methods used by the Maoist being similar to those of other groups called 'terrorist'.

Scholars are divided in dealing the elements of social movements. Shah refers to five important, interdependent and influencing elements—objectives, ideology, programs, leadership, and organization—of social movements (Shah 2002:17). Mohanty, on the other hand, mentions four dimensions. These are: environments, ideology, organization and strategy (Mohanty 1977: 6-14). This study confines to explain ideology, strategy, organization and objectives of the Maoist Movement in Nepal as essential elements.

2 PROCESS OF HINDUIZATION AND NEPALIZATION IN NEPAL

The term 'Hinduization' is a common term in countries where the Hindus form the dominant majority. The term Hinduization means the process whereby one accepts the Hindu religion and cultures either by choice or by coercion by the political authority. 'Nepalization' is a broader term than the term Hinduization. It indicates not only the religious process of Hinduization but also other cultural and linguistic aspects. State-sponsored cultural processes like festivals, others kinds of rituals are also accommodated by the term 'Nepalization.' The term includes the linguistic aspect; especially the state enforced Nepali language and its impact on the other linguistic communities. Prior to the renaming of the Gorkha language (*Khas Kura*) into 'Nepali' language in the 1930s, the process was referred to it as 'Gorkhaization'. The twin process of Hinduization and Nepalization got accelerated after the Nepali state incorporated all the people speaking different languages, practicing different religions, culture and tradition into one political, social and cultural system.

How the process of Hinduization and Gorkhaization, which was termed as Nepalization after unification in 1769, has been accelerated in Nepal is the main concern of this chapter. In other words, the making of Hinduism as 'state religion' and Nepali as 'official language', and thereby marginalizing other linguistics and religious groups, is what this chapter aim to focus on. It examines the political scenario of Nepal before and after unification. The special concern in the chapter is to focus on the marginalized groups and their access to power in different political era. How the unification process took place, and what sorts of programs were continued, in the name of integration or unification, by the 'unified' Nepali state are the other focal points of this chapter. The chapter discusses the issues mentioned above in respect of five different periods.

2.1. PRE-UNIFICATION

Nepal's present international boundaries are of recent origin. In its present form, the boundaries were fixed after the Sugauli Treaty of 1816, which the government of Nepal and British East India Company had signed it. Prior to that, Nepal's territory was unstable and unclear. In fact, it covered the whole of the sub-Himalayan hill area; its boundary covered from the border of Bhutan in the east to Kangara in the west (Joshi and Rose 1966:3). Before 1769, only the Kathmandu valley with three Malla rulers was known as Nepal. At least 56 small princely states, which were outside the valley, were not referred to as Nepal. In fact, even after the unification until 1909, 'Nepal referred only to the Kathmandu valley and parts we now think of as Nepal was referred to various as "countries" (*desa*) all subject to the house of Gorkha' (Burghart 1984 cited in Gellner et al. 1997:5). Ranas were credited to have given a single name 'Nepal' to varied and complex names. It is said that the Ranas, for the first time, began to define the country (Nepal) 'as nation-state' (*Ibid*).

Kathmandu valley was a great lake prior to human settlement. It was known as Naghdaha (lake of snakes) and Naga tribes inhabited in its surroundings. They lived on fish, animals, and birds available in the lake and its surrounding areas. When the lake got dried up, it became a valley with fertile lands. Later, the Nagas along with *Gopalas* (cow-herders) and *Mahispalas* (the buffalo-herders) moved into this valley and made it their dwelling place. At that time, king or ruler of the valley was appointed through election (District Development Profile of Nepal.). 'A sage (*Muni*) called *Ne* appears on the scene as the protector (*pala*) of the land and the founder of the first ruling dynasty. Thus, the chronicles explain the origin of the name of the country *Ne-pala*, the land protected by *Ne*.' *Gopalavamsi* Guptas replaced *Ne* Dynasty and ruled for 491 years (Shah 1992:7).

Gopalvamsis dynasty was replaced by *Mahispalvamsi* regime (buffalo-herder dynasty) which lasted for a period of eleven years and seven months. Later, the Kirants of the Mangolian stock entered the valley and became the ruling dynasty by replacing the Gopalas and Mahispalas. The Kiratas who ruled for a period of 1,581 years and one month (cited in Shah 1992:7) were replaced by *Lichhavis* who entered Nepal around the middle of the fifth century B.C. from the republic of Vaisali in the present Northern Bihar of India. The Vaisali dynasty was overrun around 464 B.C. by Ajatsatru, the king of Mugadha and the first ruthless empire builder. The Lichhavis considered being inferior Kshatriya by the pure Kshatriyas of the plains. They constructed many Hindu and Buddhist temples. Four Narayan temples in Kathmandu valley were constructed during the Lichhavi period. Lichhavi Dynasty was based on some kinds of theory of divine right; justice and morality were associated with the religion of the time. The judges of civil and criminal courts were termed 'religious authority' (*Dharmadhikari*) at that time. There was a provision for a state minister for religious affairs or religious activities. Lichhavis are thus considered the first Hindu rulers of Nepal.

Before the Lichhavis, the indigenous peoples, who were originally non-Hindu and casteless community (Shah 1992:28), were subjected to Shaiva and Vaisnava influences. It is said that the men and women enjoyed equal status in performing religious and social duties in the early Lichhavi period. Mandeva's (a famous Lichhavi king of Kathmandu) mother Rajyavati's denial for performing *sati* (practice of burning oneself over the dead body of one's husband) after her husband king Dharmadeva's death and decision by her to be alive and support her younger son for ruling the state was seen as a pointer that there was no orthodox Hinduism at that time. However, some ambitious Lichhavi kings like Amsuvarma tried his best to impose occupation based caste system among the people (*Ibid*).

Non-Sanskrit names, in respect of a large number of places in the Lichhavi inscriptions, seem to suggest that the earliest settlers of Kathmandu were a non-Aryan people who used language other than Sanskrit. Shah mentions that the name of the three cities of Kathmandu valley was in Newari. The names were *Ye* for Kathmandu, *Yala* for Patan and *Khopva* for Bhaktapur (Shah 1992: 29). However, later Lichhavis made Sanskrit as the official and literary language of Nepal and extended it in the field of architecture and sculpture. These were a hallmark of the process of Hinduization and Nepalization by the Nepali rulers. On these counts, the Lichhavi period has been described as the golden age of the Nepali history by 'mainstream historians' and subaltern historians see it as 'a set-back to indigenous rights of people'.

Religiously, Shivaism was the prevailing religion. It owed its popularity to non-Aryan population although Vaisnavism and Buddhism were known and practiced as religion in the valley. The oldest religion of Kathmandu valley seems to be related to a non-Aryan who practiced a religion closely related to the *Pasupatas,* lord of animal, who later became identified as Shiva. Religious antagonism was not evident in the Lichhavi period. Father and son, and even the husband were free to worship any deities they chose according to their personal preferences. All the temples and monasteries of Shiva, Vaishnava and Buddhist sects made during Lichhavi period were subsidized by the rulers without discrimination (Shah 1992:29–31). All these evidences shows that there was 'religious harmony' within the society.

The Malla Dynasty replaced the Lichhavi Dynasty. The ancestry of the Malla rulers is unclear, but they are referred to in the Indian historical literatures. The early Buddhist texts mention Mallas' territory as adjoining the Lichhavis. Kusinagar and Pava known as Mallapuri were considered as the lands of Mallas in India. Ari Malla (1200–1216 A.D.), the son of Jayasi Malla was the first Malla king of the Kathmandu valley, but there is no evidence as to how—whether by conquest, election, or dynastic links—he acquired the throne. Earlier, the Malla rulers (1255–1383) spent their time fighting each other in the same dynasty; the main fight being between the house of Bhonta (the feudal lord of Banepa, the eastern city of Kathmandu) and house of Tripura (Shah 1992:46–47). When they became weaker by the internal struggle, they faced external invasions at the different time. The external attackers to the Malla Dynasty were Doya state (the state of Khas Malla kings), and the Muslim ruler of Bengal.

When Jayasthiti Malla came to the power, he restored order and stability, and managed a century-long anarchy of Kathmandu valley. He brought many Karnat priests from Mithila, and started social reforms by initiating many social rules and regulations (ISRSC 2004:4). Jayasthiti Malla started a long-term policy for consolidation of the Nepali society with the help of five Brahmins, who hailed from North and South India. The code of religious and social conduct did not lay stress on the four-fold traditional classification of *Varna*. Rather by analyzing the existing conditions of Nepal, the code classified people into 64 sub-castes, and introduced detailed rules in regard to their social activities and social behavior. Some writers consider the code as flexible and suitable to the given situation of Nepal. According to Shah, the non-Hindu Newar community of Kathmandu valley obeyed the code properly; it was because of the systems due regard and flexibility to local conditions (Shah 1992:57). The code is still valid and influential in the community with few modifications.

Although Jayasthiti Malla's reformist activities aimed at consolidating the Nepali society within the orthodox Hindu religious framework, he is considered 'liberal' in the matter of religion because of his belief in polytheism and especially his devotion to Shiva and Vishnu (Shah 1992:57). In the Malla period, it is said that the two religions—Buddhism and Hinduism—were developed harmoniously and simultaneously. Others said that there was a massacre of 770 Brahmans at a time during the Malla period. The mass murder, according to a popular legend, led to resistance by the Buddhists when Sankaracharya conducted Brahmanic revival movement. Except this incident, there was no hostile feeling seen between the two religions. It was probably because of the Hinduism, which itself has accepted Buddha as one of the ten incarnations of its god.

Because of limited information and reorganization of only the Kathmandu valley as Nepal, a comprehensive history of the other parts of the present Nepal until the medieval period is not known. The Dullu pillar and other inscriptions discovered by Prof. Tucci and Nath in 1955 are indications that there were two Khas Malla kingdoms in the Karnali region, the western part of Kathmandu valley. The territory of those two kingdoms ranged from western parts of Tibet to modern Jumla and Surkhet districts. Historians mention that there were *Baise* (twenty-two) states in the Karnali region in the far western Nepal, and *Chaubise* (twenty-four) states in region directly to the west and south of Kathmandu valley. Apart from that, numerous small local rulers in the eastern hills of *Kirat* tribal community was the exact scenario of ancient Nepal. The *Kirat* were there in tenuous fashion within the loose confederation. The Eastern parts of Nepal were under the Makawanpur, Chaudandi and Vijaypur kingdoms. Those three kingdoms were under the umbrella of the Sen Rulers of Palpa. Before the unification, Palpa was considered one of the powerful Chaubise states. At one time, the Chaudandi kingdom controlled the Vijaypur too. At that time, Chaudandi was the powerful and extensive kingdom and the Sen King was entitled 'Hindupati or overlord of the Hindus' (Shah 1992:68). Later, the Sen Dynasty of Palpa became flexible towards religious/ethnic sensitivity and accepted the autonomous Kirati units in the eastern hills. The Dynasty appointed a hill-based Kirati minister and devoluted the political power to the Kirati community.

There were two subdivisions in Kirati areas. One was *Majh* (middle) Kirat situated in the west of Arun River, and another was *Pallo* (further) Kirat located in-between the Arun River and the Sikkim border. Lots of sayings and predictions are there on the then division of the princely states. Every principality had their own historical, cultural, and ethnic values. Mentioning the values of those states, Joshi and Rose writes, 'The *Baise* states had all formed parts of the Malla kingdom of the 11th to 14th centuries, and the Chaubise states may initially had represented a loose affiliation of Hindu rulers in a region that was still predominantly non-Hindu in population' (Joshi and Rose 1966:4–5).

All the principalities were independent and sovereign for all practical purposes and had engaged in fighting each other rather than representing collective political entities and permanent alliances. The adversary state relation among these states paved the way for rise of the Gorkha house and ultimately for the formation of the present Nepal.

To summarize, prior to the unification, many principality states had their existences in the present territory of Nepal. As many as 46 kingdoms were in the western part. Makawanpur, Vijaypur and Chaudani kingdoms existed as provenance states under the Sen Dynasty of Palpa in the Southern and South-eastern part of modern

Nepal. Kathmandu, Patan, Bhatgaun and even sometimes Nuwakot and Banepa kingdoms were seen in the middle and surrounding areas of the Kathmandu valley. There is still debate about the *Baise* and Chaubise and other principality states and their territory under the medieval Nepal. Shah (1992), referring to Francis Bachanam Hamilton, considers Gorkha as one of the Chaubise states but Joshi and Rose (1966) contest this argument and write that Gorkha was never under the Chaubise states.

In terms of linguistic/social features of the then Nepal, at least three major racial strains are/were visible. These are: a) Indo-Aryans, who migrated to Nepal from plains or from the hill areas of India several hundred years ago in the wake of Muslim invasions of Northern India, b) the Mongolian origin, which inhabit the higher hill areas in the east and west including Kirat tribal communities like Rais and Limbus, and c) a numbers of tribal communities which may be remnants of indigenous communities whose habitation of Nepal predates the advent of Indo-Aryan and Mongolian elements. Among the three, the third one had gradually been driven back into the more isolated sections of *Tarai* jungles and the hot, malarial river valleys in the hill areas during the course of the Indo-Aryan and Mongolian incursions (Joshi and Rose 1966:10).

Although there are not enough literatures about religious affiliations of the above-mentioned groups, there are indications that they were practicing different religions like the Buddhism and Shamanism. Buddhism came to Nepal in its Mahayan form from Tibet and had tremendous influences in the Nepalese society up to the 7th century A.D. The Hindu Lichhavi rulers imposed the Hinduism on the various tribal groups of Nepal. There was also Indian impact that helped the growth of Hinduism in Nepal during the Lichhavi rule. Before the Hinduism got ascendancy in India, the old form of Hinduism and Buddhism continued to survive, but later on, a majority of Nepalese came back to the Hindu religion (Chauhan 1989:1). Rose and Scholz assume that during the Lichhavi period, a number of ethnic communities such as the Rais and Limbus in eastern Nepal, various Tibetan groups (Sherpa, Tamang etc.) in the north, the Magars and Gurungs in the central-western hills, and the Khas in the far west, established themselves in areas of what is now Nepal. Those communities, except Chaubise states, had tribal culture, and culturally and economically, they were more dependent on the Buddhist north rather than on India or Kathmandu valley (Rose and Scholz 1980:12). It is important to note that Buddhism was not only dominant among the Newars of Kathmandu valley but also in other Mongolian, and tribal and indigenous communities. Shah has a different view. He writes that the Kiratas, who are considered as ethnic groups with remarkable skill in archery and warfare also used to celebrate the well-known Hindu epic, the Mahabharata, and the Puranas (Shah 1992: 8). There is a saying that the Buddhism existed side by side the Vaishnavism and Shaivism. Such situation continued till the rule of Manadeva in Nepal. Manadeva seemed sympathetic to the both Buddhism and Hinduism, although he was a Hindu ruler. The Buddhist monastery, which is situated at Swayambhu, Kathmandu, is thought to have been built on Manadeva's order. It is said that the Vihar is named as Mana Vihar because it was constructed on Manadevas' initiation (Shah 1992:14).

Jayasthiti Malla of Kathmandu (1382–95), Ram Shah of Gorkha (1606–33) were the orthodox Hindus who before unification attempted to codify the structure of Nepali society—both Hindu and non-Hindu—within an orthodox Hindu framework. The first imposed the social code on the Newars of Kathmandu valley. For this task, he received guidance or advice from the Indian Brahmans. The latter did the same thing to the non-Hindu tribal community of Gorkha. Jayasthiti Malla divided the Newars of Kathmandu valley into 64 sub-groups and imposed on them the essential characteristics of *Jatis* (caste) applicable in the context of the Hindu caste system. These two incidents were considered as a setback to religious freedom so far enjoyed in Nepal. These incidents played critical roles in the ongoing 'Nepalization' and 'Hinduization' process among the Newars and other low-caste groups. The impact of the process was that the low-caste or non-Hindu communities gradually adopted the rituals and ideology of high-caste Hindus. Another notable thing of Jayasthiti Malla's reform was that it had given similar status to the Buddhist Newars and Hindus. Such a social code was retained throughout the Malla period, which helped Newars to be nearer to the Hindu religion (Joshi and Rose 1966:11–12).

2.2. POST-UNIFICATION

2.2.1. Shah Regime (1769–1846)

Dravya Shah, younger brother of the king of Lamjung (Lamjung is about 30 miles north-west of Gorkha), conquered Gorkha, in the middle of 1559. After assuming the position of the king of Gorkha Dravya Shah began conquering the neighboring states. Invocation of the Rajput heritage was the driving force behind it. However, he succeeded in conquering only two small states—Siranchock and Ajirgarh—during his rule (Gyawali 1992 (B.S.): 3, 31). Evidences show that the newly established Shah Dynasty, with the exception of Ram Shah, had made continuous plan to expand the state territory. Nara Bhupal Shah, descendent of the Ram Shah and father of Prithvi Narayan Shah, unsuccessfully tried to defeat the neighboring state of Nuwakot in 1737. His son Prithvi Narayan Shah ultimately conquered Nuwakot in the fall of 1744 (Gyawali 1992 (B.S.): 3, 83).

The credit of unification goes to Prithvi Narayan Shah, who brought about the 'central Himalayas' into a single state. Apart from his personal contribution, he used many strategies to make unification process easy. He strategically maintained marital relation with powerful Sen Dynasty of Palpa, and had *Miteri* relation (ritual friendship within the same gender) with other principalities. Because of such affection based on relation, religion, culture and traditions with Gorkha principality, several other neighboring principalities accepted Prithvi Narayan Shah's request to help him in his dream to make a unified and great Nepal. Some weak neighbors helped Shah by submitting their states into Gorkha states. There was an open declaration by the Gorkha regime that if a state accepted the offer to submit its sovereignty into the Gorkha regime, the rulers of the state could enjoy a broad degree of autonomous control over their 'subjects' on internal matters. Those local rulers and elites who surrendered to Gorkha continued to enjoy 'a fully autonomous status with a tenuous political authority' (Joshi and Rose 1966: 4-5).

In terms of strategies enforced by the Gorkha ruler to unify Nepal, there are many stories. The ruler used religion, relation etc. as weapons to unify other principality states. Before unification, most of the rulers were the Hindus in those small states. In the central parts of Nepal, there were some autonomous indigenous tribal areas under the Rajput-ruled principalities; however, it was under the domination of the high-caste Hindu elites. They started establishing socio-cultural relations among the neighboring kingdoms through marriage and Miteri relation as they belong to the same religion and culture. This helped to promote the concept of 'we feeling', and led to the psychological nearness. Ultimately, this nearness helped for 'integration into a unified nation-state system.' Ram Shah's 'first written legal code in the hill area' also brought the hill principalities closer to each other as the 'legal code evoked positive responses from other hill principalities.' The legal code was based upon the orthodox Hindu religion but 'suitably modified to accommodate the social and political traditions of the non-Hindu subject of the principality in the 17th century' (Rose and Scholz 1980:15). There is a proverb, 'if one doesn't find the justice, then, go to the Gorkha.' It is imagined that the proverb might come after Ram Shah's legal code applied to Gorkha.

Prithvi Narayan Shah could not capture Kathmandu valley easily. He was successful only after his third attempt because of powerful presence of Malla rulers and Newars who defied the 'unification' process. However, when he captured the valley, he ordered that the ears and noses of the people of Kirtipur (the gateway to Kathmandu valley), should be slashed, which weighted 18 dharnies (equivalent to 42 kg) when collected (Bhattachan 2000:140, cited in Pyakurel 2006:115). There is a debate as to whether Prithvi Narayan Shah's policy of a united Nepal was 'unification' or a 'conquest'. After all, he used not only diplomacy and consensus but also military force in the name of unification of the state. Not only the rulers but also the people of the other states, which declined the offer of the Gorkha states, faced lots of violence and brutality by Gorkha soldiers. The process was even termed 'based on the right of sword' (Hachhethu 2003:221), and 'the forcible annexation' (Yami and Bhattarai 2004:281).

Gorkha regime killed all the men and young boys of Khumbu-Kirat community of the eastern Nepal also, who had not accepted or surrendered to the proposal of the regime. Hudson's collected sources tell that the pregnant women, for fear of giving birth to male offspring, were compelled to get abortion, and the fetuses were also snatched by putting it into *Okhal* (the mortar in which rice is husked). Such brutal behavior of the Gorkha ruler compelled all other people either to surrender to the ruler of Gorkha or to leave their birthplace and enter to the Indian Territory (Dhungel 2006). Another example of such a brutality was seen in Jumla. Jumla was one of the powerful principalities before unification, which is situated in mid-western Nepal. When it denied surrendering to Gorkha ruler in 1794, the regime of Gorkha ordered its local authority to 'kill all rebels of above the age of 12 years.' The regime warned Jumli people by using very arrogant terms. The regime told that if anyone engages in rebellion or intrigue, the Jumli regime would degrade the 'culprit' into a lower caste even, if he were a Brahmin. However, if the 'guilty party' belongs to other castes, or else, enslave or behead him according to his caste. Chauhan termed it as 'abidance elicited through reign of terror' (Chauhan 1989:111). People of different region were considered not as the citizen but the 'subject' of unified Nepal by the regime. With the unification of the country, it was hoped that the people could do trade at the place of their liking, but the government imposed religion, caste, and social code on the people and wanted that the people should adhere to the regime and their traditional professions and their places. Royal order of 1846 banning Jumli to visit for trade (Chauhan 1989:112–13) was an example of such an imposition, which made people frustrated in the so-called unified Nepal and became the major cause of the marginalization of the region.

There are several sayings about Gorkha state and its rulers' flexibility or liberality towards the policy related to ethnic and tribal community. Bista presents Prithvi Narayan Shah as an egalitarian who regarded Brahmans, Khas and Magars simply as different ethnic groups with none of them superior or inferior to the others (Bista 1991:45). Sharma agrees with Bista's argument and writes that Prithvi Narayan Shah 'was able to rally a broad cross-section of Gorkhali society, including the Brahmans, the Khas, the Gurungs, the Magars and others to his cause.' His argument was that there was social harmony among the different caste groups, which led the migration of the people from other places to Gorkha. To justify the argument, he writes, 'even the Newar of Gorkha who originally went to settle there from Patan' (Sharma 1997:477). Whelpton writes that the two ethnic groups, Magar and Gurung were found among the ruling elite of Gorkha house (Whelpton 1997:43) when there was a practice of *Chha Thar Ghar* (six family linage) system to support the king for policymaking. Even, one can assume such a feeling when one reads the famous quotation by Prithvi Narayan Shah. The quotation says, 'Nepal is a garden of four Varnas and thirty-six Jatis or caste.' There are many evidences that prove such quotations. Prithvi Narayan Shah himself says, 'I (Prithvi Narayan Shah) am king of Magars' (Gurung 1997:501). Being the then king of Gorkha, Shah's expression should be considered as radical expression in the society. It is because the Magars were/are considered as a lower caste people by the society and high-caste-dominated society still behaves the Magars not as citizen but as subject.

Yogi and Acharya elaborated other argument to support the quotation. According to them, prior to unification, king of Gorkha used to hear the voice of people before the action. King's hearing would base on 'the local populace with its composition and function.' 'When the king had to choose the minister, he obtained a consensus of his court and subject' (Yogi and Acharya 1953:5–9). Shah rulers, in the name of hearing from 'local populace' before the action, used to ask the consensus of six elite families (Chha Thar Ghar). These families, belonging to different caste and ethnic groups were prominent in the social and political life of Gorkha (Joshi and Rose 1966:26). However, after having a look at Prithvi Narayan Shah's long-term policy of Hinduization and Gorkhaization, one is inclined to conclude that his quotation was more of a slogan to draw the different groups for the 'unification process.' Repeatedly after the above-mentioned quotations, there is another quotation said by Prithvi Narayan Shah, which had just an opposite meaning. The quotation says, 'Yo *Asali Hindustan ho* (this is the pure land of Hindus)' (Gurung 1997:501). This statement helped us be clear about his actual position on the religion. After this quotation, one can easily argue that his earlier mentioned statements were only the strategy for getting support from the non-Hindu and lower caste people. In addition, his real position reflects in his latter statement. To Gellner, his role was neither as a wisher 'of becoming a garden of every sort of people' nor 'really a nationalist,' but he was 'very far from being a multiculturalists celebrating cultural diversity for his own sake (Gellner 1997:25)

After he had successfully conquered the Kathmandu valley, he reduced the *Chha Thar Ghar*, his consultative body, into *Char Thar Ghar* (four family lineage) by excluding the two ethnic groups, Magar and Gurung. This exclusion also indicates his actual position on non-Hindus and lower caste people. The position was later converted into state policy. The policy was the process of Hinduization (concept of Asali Hindusthan) and Gorkhaization. The state tried to establish the Gorkhali peoples' hegemony over all the Gorkha defeated states. Prithvi Narayan Shah launched such a policy when he declared that the Nepal was an ideal garden for the flourishing of Hinduism along with its four Varna and 36 caste systems. For fulfillment of these objectives, the state began the process of granting new *Guthis* (the land donated to priests for performing daily Pooja to deities and for managing food, shelters and so on of the pilgrims during there is religious festivals) to the Brahmans. Most of the fertile lands were granted as Guthi. Such a practice was accelerated 'particularly in those areas where the Hinduism was nominal, i.e. towards the eastern region.' The settling of 28 Brahman families once at a time in July 1811 in the Hattigisa of Morang, a part of eastern Nepal (Chauhan 1989:89) was an example of such a policy initiated by the state.

Upon the emergence of Nepal as a nation state in 1768 under the leadership of Prithvi Narayan Shah, the participation of two high-caste Hindu groups—Brahmans who were considered as the intellectual elite and spiritual preceptors and Kshatriyas who were considered warrior caste—started ruling the state where 'participation in the political process became the virtually their exclusive prerogative' (Joshi and Rose 1966:23). The state enforced the ancient Hindu scriptural requirement where 'the ruler of the state should always be recruited from the Kshatriyas and that they should exercise their political function with the advice and consent of the Brahmans.' Brahmans were given the role of priests, lawgivers, astrologers, and diplomatic emissaries. Other governing and administrating posts were given to the Kshatriyas. Among the Kshatriyas, especially the members of four prominent families—the Shah, Pandes, Thapas and Basnyats, enjoyed such privileges. This system continued until the emergence of the Rana Family in 1846 (Joshi and Rose 1966:11–12). For making Brahmans as a respectable group, the then government referred after references of royal order wherein the people were urged 'to respect Brahmans and not to take the flesh of dead cattle.' The government further ordered that 'only the Brahman could perform religious ceremonies in the house of individuals and none else,' and 'Brahman would not be put to death throughout the kingdom howsoever heinous his crime might be.' Although there was exercise of the death penalty system, Brahmans were free from such a penalty; 'he could be degraded from his caste and imprisoned, but he could never be executed' (Chauhan 1989:93). There was also the caste discrimination in practice. For example, the government employed 65 postmen during the year of 1825-26 and each one was allotted rice land on *adhiya* tenure as a repayment for their service. However, the high-caste postmen were allotted lands measuring from 95 to 105 *Muris* (one Muri is equevalant to 45 kg. paddy and 50 kg. corn), and the low-caste who were doing same job were allotted only from 35 to 45 Muris (cited in Chauhan 1989:97) as emoluments for the same work.

In the later Shah Dynasty, the state policy became more rigid. The dynasty started recruiting the military and civil stalwarts only from one region of the country—the Gorkha, the name of 'the trusted' people. Gorkha was the dynasty's native land. Further, even from Gorkha, the dynasty chosen exclusively from the high-caste Brahmans and Kshatriyas families. On account of such an established practice of the Shah dynasty, Chauhan defined the term 'Gorkha' 'as those progeny of Brahmans and Kshatriyas who had migrated from southern plains and had come into contact with the Khas and Magars of this region, and who had accepted the Hindu religion, including diet and deity' (Chauhan, 1989:79). Chauhan mentioned seven imbibed characters as basic criteria to be considered as Gorkha people by the ruler. These were: a) they had contempt against the elite of other religions; b) they abhorred religion except Hinduism, c) they did not hold high opinion about the low castes, d) they had no respect for the vanquished, e) they did not regard trade, commerce and other business activities as respectable professions, f) they had no esteem for art, literature and architecture; and g) possession of land and military post was their prize holding. Examining the 'Gorkha' culture, Chauhan writes, 'in Gorkha there was no Gorkha in the sense that it was populated by the *Matwalis*' (Chauhan 1989: 79). The Khas Magars, who had not accepted Hindu religion and its dietry restrictions, were not known as a Gorkha by the criteria. For general information, there is a trend in Nepal to classify people into *Tagadhari* and Matwali group on the basis of wearing the scared thread. Those who wear the sacred thread are called Tagadharis and the others Matwali. Taking note of those seven characters, one can conclude that such a policy was introduced to ban other native and indigenous groups to be state elites to preserve the posts only for high-caste Hindus. There were Newars of Kathmandu valley, the Tamangs in surrounding area of Kathmandu with good knowledge as entrepreneurs, skillful in arts, architecture and trader, but they got fewer chances to be in state mechanism.

Literature is not available about Shah Dynasty's policy towards other religions like Christian and Muslim. An example of Gorkhas' policy towards other religion could be described from the fact that 'as soon as Gorkha conquered the Kathmandu valley in 1968-69, Catholic missionaries and their local converts were expelled by new ruler.' The regime even used derogative terms to address other religions. The term '*Ulto Dharma* (opposite religion)' was used to characterize Islam and Christianity by the regime (Goborieau 1972: 84–89). It can be considered as an example of the regime's attitude towards other religions.

2.2.2. Rana Regime (1846–1951)

Whether by 'consensus' or by 'the power of sword' the Shah Dynasty unified more than 56 principality states in a single garland. However, the dynasty was not able to maintain its aim of a unified and prosperous Nepal. Soon after the demise of Prithvi Narayan Shah, the dynasty started losing its luster, power, and control over the administration of the country. The situation was 'the more the time passed, the Shah King became the more powerless.' The dynasty had enforced exclusive and prerogative political process with the influential participation of two high-caste social groups—Brahmans and Kshatriyas. It had become the ruling style of the regime. However, the 'intrigues and conspiracies' were not absent in the scene within the members of four prominent Kshatriya families—the Shahs (royal family), Pandeys, Thapas and Basnyats. Those families considered as 'the noble family' were seen entangled in the political game leading to 'blood and violence.' It is to be noted that 'none of the *Mukhtiyars* (equivalent to prime minister) or regent between 1769 to 1846 died a natural death; their lives were ended abruptly either by the assassin's bullet or sword or by their own hand' (Joshi and Rose 1966:23–25). The Shah Dynasty had become so incapable and insane that they virtually became pawns in the hands of a few rival groups, which had monopolized the army and bureaucracy (Chauhan 1989:118).

In the history of Nepal, the Rana hereditary system came to the power in 1846 as a result of 'intrigues, counter-intrigues and conspiracies' within the members of four prominent Kshatriya families. Janga Bahadur Kunwar, backed by the then younger queen Lakshmi Devi, organized a massacre and 'established virtually dictatorial control over the government' (Joshi and Rose 1966:29). The massacre is named as *Kot Parva* (Kot Massacre) and Janga Bahadur is considered as an initiator of the Rana regime. In the Kot Parva, most of the prominent Kshatriya elites were either assassinated or compelled to leave the country. According to Acharya, 30 were killed, 26 fled the country, and 26 other were banished from prominent four Kshatriya families. Again, one and half month later in October 13, 1946, at least 23 Basnyats prominent noble of Kshatriya caste, were killed by Janga Bahadur Rana. They were accused as organizer of the *Bhandarkhal* Parva or 'Basnyat conspiracy' (Acharya 2005:107, 115)

After establishing himself in power, Janga Bahadur combined in himself the roles of the chief of army, the prime minister and the

'Maharaja' (His Majesty) of Kaski and Lamjung, two small principalities of Nepal. Then, the third title 'Maharaja' made as inheritable title of Rana family. Within 10 years in power, the Ranas ruled the country by their hereditary premiership system. The system was termed as the 'Rana oligarchy' in the history of Nepal.

When Janga Bahadur came to the power, a seven-decade long rule of four Kshatriya nobles disintegrated. However, the change did not move towards inclusive and democratic system of government. Indeed, the Rana system had been more repressive towards the people. The regime sought to perpetuate backwardness and ignorance among the people by discouraging opening up of the education institutions. The system imposed orthodox and discretionary social rule. The regime not only tried to ban people from getting education but also banned travel abroad. Further, it controlled the people by intensifying communal disputes and rivalries through the social controls exercised by the royal priests. In the name of religion or *dharmashastra*, the priest were vested the authority to punish any attempt on the part of the people to modify social, ethnic, and caste inequalities. As a political system, it was observed:

> 'The Rana political system was an undisguised military despotism of the ruling faction within the Rana family over the king and the people of the country. The government functioned as and instrument of carry out the personal wishes and interests of the ruling Rana prime minister; its main domestic preoccupation was the exploitation of the country's resources in order to enhance the personal wealth of Rana ruler and his family. No distinction was made between the personal treasury of the Rana ruler and the treasury of the government; the Rana ruler as private income pocketed any government revenue in excess of administrative expenses. No budget of the government's expenditures and revenues were ever made public. As a system accountable neither to the king nor to the people, the Rana regime functioned as an autochthonous system, divorced from the needs of the people and even from the historical traditions of the country, and served only the

interests of a handful of Ranas and their ubiquitous non-Rana adherents (Joshi and Rose 1966:38–39).'

Rana regime, initially, promoted the process of 'Ranaization' or their hegemony over the society where, for assuming power and getting privilege, one must be from Rana family. For other people there was no opportunity; they were even banned from getting education. In army, which was the key to the survival of the system, generals and colonels were appointed from Rana families soon after their birth, and sometimes even before the birth. Ordinary people were restricted from wearing cloths, ornaments, making houses etc. For such a societal sanction, they used the orthodox Hinduism as a weapon. For middle and lower level's opportunities in military and bureaucratic post, Brahmans and the earlier explained noble family member were selected. The selection itself was the strategy to win the support of those families (Joshi and Rose 1966:40).

Rana regime introduced the first Muluki Ain (Civil Code) in 1854. It was not new in the strict sense, because it was practiced earlier as a 'legal code' during the period of Jayasthiti Malla (1382-95) from late 14th century in Kathmandu valley, and in the period of Ram Shah (1603-36) in Gorkha from first half of 17th century. What was new was that the regime put it in a nationwide legal framework. Before being declared as a law, it was practiced as a tradition. By promulgating it as a civil code, Rana regime compelled all the 'subject' to obey it. It was a part of their strategic policy to continue their regime for a long time. They were aware that they could control the people only by such religious code of conduct, which had already gained legitimacy as a tradition. The orthodox Hindus accepted it and even claimed it as a vital step for promoting the Hinduism as a national religion. The code had revised caste categories from the four Varna classical Vedic models into six categories. It had provisioned different punishment system on the basis of caste; to the higher caste, there was one punishment and another to the lower caste people in the same crime. In other words, the system did not break the continuation of discrimination between the people of higher and lower castes. Another characteristic of the code was that it tried to accommodate the ethnic identities into Hindu Varna system, which 'translated diversity into inequality.'

Comparing the Shah Dynasty and Rana oligarchy in Nepal, Chauhan termed Rana administration as 'less cruel and not that exploitative' (Chauhan 1989:119). However, no one is of the view that the system was not exploitative. The classification of Rana family into 'A', 'B' and 'C' classes on the basis of their purity of blood itself was a saleable example of the regime's exploitative nature. Later on, the classification was also made on the basis of caste of their mothers and kind of marriage (whether she was concubine or formally married). Such classification led the Ranas to divide themselves into three groups as noted above. The three groups started fighting each other for power and position. In fact, the struggle within the Rana family became the most important cause for disintegration of their 104 years of long rule.

The Hinduism was practiced in a very orthodox mode in this period. Traveling abroad was termed as a 'violation of religious and social tradition' by conservative Ranas. Even Janga Bahadur, the initiator of the Rana regime, was accused as a violator of the code. He was told that he had lost his caste by dining and socializing with Europeans when he visited Europe in 1950–51. After his return to Nepal, he visited important Hindu pilgrimage centers of India to be purified. Another intention of his visit of pilgrim centers might have been to shut the mouth of conservative people. Another example of the Rana's religious orthodoxy was that they were not even ready to reform the Hinduism and when some Nepalese started reforming movement of Hinduism in the name of Arya Samaj, they were socially disgraced, paraded through the streets, beaten and sentenced to jail.

Ranas were more concerned about the impact of education and exposure. They knew that education and exposure would have helped on people's freedom and awareness. On this context, they seriously observed the returnees of 'Gorkha' army and western education holders. One of the fears to Rana Regime from those people was that they might bring modern ideas of freedom into their villages and society. Therefore, the Ranas requested British authorities not to promote Gorkha recruits beyond the rank of sergeant and upon their return rigidly enforced on them the rules of caste purification (Joshi and Rose 1966:52). Although the other religions were allowed 'except for doing acts prohibited in the code, including the slaughtering of the cows', conversion of people from Hindu religion to others was prohibited. The permission to enjoy other religion was only for those who 'were already Muslims or Christians when they entered Nepal, and were born there from Muslim or Christian parents' (Gaborieau 1972:87).

Linguistically speaking, Rana regime continued the process of Nepalization of the Shah regime but also accelerated the process. For the first time in the history, Khas Kura or Gorkhali Bhasa was declared as the official Nepali language in 1930. Chandra Shamsher Rana was the prime minister. The regime in the process gave rise to the idea of a 'nation'. Prior to that, Nepal was referred only to the Kathmandu valley and rest of the parts were known by their own names. The job of Ranas during their period was in the pretext of the 'nationalist objectives' (Whelpton 1997:45). In aspect of other religions and languages, Ranas again followed the path of Shah regime. The late Dharmaditya Dharmacharya, a brilliant Buddhist scholar, was expelled from Kathmandu valley in the 1920s for the 'crime' of publishing and circulating Buddhist and other books in the Nepal Bhasa (Newari language). Buddhist monks Mahaprajna and Amritananda were imprisoned, and Tsering Narbu Lama was expelled in 1937. In 1925, another four monks, and in 1944, eight more monks were expelled from Kathmandu (Bajracharya and Khatŗy 2005:73-74). The state sponsored rampant migration of people from the west hill to east hill in this period. The main objective of such migration was to scatter Nepali speaking and Hindu people with a view to promote and expand their cultural hegemony to all the territory especially in the eastern hill where Rais and Limbus—the non-Hindu indigenous groups—inhabited.

In regard to the ethnic issue, both the Shah and Rana regime played the same role of suppressing the indigenous people. Earlier the regime wooed the indigenous people by distributing land as *Kipat* (land given to indigenous community for enjoying as common land of the community) to encourage them to support the unification process, but latter the regime abolished the Kipat system. Many indigenous groups including Bhote, Chepang, Danuwar, Gurung,

Tamang, Pahari, Majhi, Rai, Limbus Thakali had customary occupation of land. All except the Limbus got alienated by the land under the regime. In case of the Limbus, the land got alienated only after 1964. The regime faced several revolts like Gurung revolt against Ranas 1857 because of such policy (Joshi and Rose 1966:43).

2.2.3. Pseudo-Democratic Period (1951–60)

For examining the period of 1951–60 in the Nepali history, the term 'pseudo' is used because it was the period which had a character of both, democracy and autocracy. During the period, Nepal became free from 'isolation' from the world, and people's movement in 1951 brought out even constitutional and social changes. One of the significant changes was abolition of 104 years old Rana oligarchy. An interim government with the people's choice was constituted to change the existing system into a democratic system. Election of the Constituent Assembly was one of the promised things by the state. The king, who was caged without rights in the palace by the Ranas, was also freed with the support of people. After the freedom, the king promised to let the democratic system run the country. The 1951 interim government made some important decisions in favor of democracy and people. Later in 1959, the first general election was held; peoples' government got constituted and began to work. These were some sort of democratic exercises during the period. It however lasted for a period of only two years out of ten years. The king captured the power and ruled the country for the remaining eight years.

Earlier in 1951, the king appreciated people's sovereignty and declared that the monarch would be accommodated as a 'constitutional monarch' under the constitution. However, after two years of such a commitment, he denied to be under constitution and declared that the supreme rights were vested in the king. Another factor for using the term pseudo has been that in democracy, government has been always elected from the people, but in this case, elected government governed only 19 months (May 27, 1959 to December 15, 1960) out of total of ten years period.

The first elected government (May 27, 1959 to December 15, 1960) under the premiership of B. P. Koirala, who himself was reported to have 'antagonized orthodox Hindus and the conservatives' (Joshi and Rose 1966:308), resumed the goal of strengthening democracy and to make Nepal prosperous. He had set this goal when he held the post of home minister in the interim government in 1951. He started implementing the programs promised in the election manifesto. The main slogan of the party was to 'end the very roots of the traditional social and economic inequalities.' The highlights of the Nepali Congress (NC) manifesto included: abolition of the proprietor system, abolition of *Rajyas* (small principalities which enjoyed the semi-autonomy), a ceiling on landholding and redistribution of the excess landholdings, forests' nationalization, promotion of co-operative farming etc. Respect for religions and a guarantee of the right of any citizen to practice the religion of his/her choice and encouraging the development of regional and local languages were other important highlights of election manifesto of NC in 1958. The government started functioning on the basis of its commitment to the people in election. It designed and declared a 25 years plan to achieve socialism in Nepal. The aim of plan was to fulfill basic needs of people in the name of socialism. 'A cow for milk and some land for cultivation of grain for every family' was the target of the plan. To reach in the target, the government initiated the land reform program that gained much popular support. However, due to the intervention of the king, the elected government could not continue its popular and progressive programs. It is said that the king got jealousness over the program and policies of B. P. Koirala-led government. Ultimately, the king took action against the government. He dismissed the 19 months old government and imprisoned all the political leaders on December 15, 1960. This led to stop of the entire reformist program.

The king resumed the policy launched by the Shah Dynasty after 'unification' of Nepal. There was resumption of state policy for Nepalization. The king nominated government constituted a committee called Nepal National Education Planning Commission, 1955 which recommended the use of Nepali language in a manner that other languages gradually disappeared. This was expected to provide greater national strength and unity' (Whelpton 1997:49). This idea was accommodated in Panchayat system. The slogan under the Panchayat system was *ek bhasa, ek bhesh, ek desh* (one language, one dress, one country). It is to be noted that in 1959 the elected government of B.P. Koirala had given the status to other languages like Newari, Hindi and Maithili as national languages.

Unfortunately, the first democratically elected government of Nepali Congress, which was set up 'as the champion of the poor and indebted peasantry,' started facing the disturbances from Nuwakot and Gorkha districts. The nature of the disturbance took the form of looting, rape etc. That led the disorder and chaos in the society. Such activities coming from these two districts, had historical meanings. Nuwakot was the surrounding district of Kathmandu valley where the royalists and feudals were influential. Gorkha was the homeland of the Shah kings before the conquest of the Kathmandu valley. The populace in those districts comprised a wide variety of ethnic groups. Their primary political identification was 'loyalty to the Shah Dynasty' as a 'militant Gorkha nationalists.' It was assumed that the Gorkha Parisad, a political party that represented the 'feudal exploiters, cruel moneylenders, and profiteers,' backed such disturbances (Joshi and Rose 1966:357). It is said that orthodox Hindu advocates and royalists like Yogi Narahari Nath backed those disturbances. Another disturbance faced by the government was the semi-autonomous Bajhang principality, which was unhappy with the declaration of government to abolish Rajya Courts exercised by the few principalities. The declaration was credited to establish uniform court system in the country.

Although there were many constitutional and practical shortcomings in this period, some positive aspects of the period have also to be appreciated. These positive aspects were that the state, for the first time in the history, recognized the people as 'citizen' with civil and political rights. Another aspect was the concern shown by the state for the welfare of the people by securing all sorts of justices. The interim constitution dealt the social security and said, '...a social order in which social, economic, and political justice will infuse all the institutions of national life' (article 4 of the Interim Government of Nepal Act 1951). It also guaranteed the freedom of speech and freedom of expression, assembly, association, and movement throughout the country. Right to property and practice of any profession or business was also guaranteed.

Still another positive aspect of the period was the interim cabinet, which was constituted with the participation of popular force like Nepali Congress. Nepali congress is a major political party, which played a vital role to abolish the Rana oligarchy and to establish the democratic system in the country. Its primary objective of that period was to make constitution through the election of constituent assembly, although it never happened. The interim cabinet abolished many feudal practices 'at the initiative of the Nepali Congress' such as monetary exactions in the forms of mandatory gifts and presents, forced labor to maintain public works which had been an integral part of Rana political system. Birta (rent-free land), the traditional base of the Rana economic power was abolished. The monopoly of Ranas in the high position of the army was brought to end by the government. Further, those positions were made accessible to other caste/ethnic communities. All government schools were directed to open the gate of the school for children of untouchable castes. Prior to that, only the 'male children of elite families' were permitted to go to the school and 'mainly Brahman boys were taught in the classical Sanskrit Pathsalas or school' (Hoftun *et al.* 1999:4). Again, for the first time in 1959, news was broadcast in languages other than the Nepali. The motive forced underlying such a decision was the promotion and appreciation of other languages (Gellner 1997:29). Hindi language was accepted for use in Parliament discussions in 1959.

Likewise, the ethnic activism was first noticed with the dawn of democracy in 1951. NGOs and other organizations like *Pichhadieka Barga Sangathan* (the backward class organization) including Gurung Kalyan Sangh, Tharu Kalyankari Sabha, Kirat League and *Dalit* Sangh were established during this period. The Tarai Congress, the first regional party in Nepal, was established in 1951. The first parliamentary election was held in 1959. Such developments brought out the hill ethnic and Tarai community to the mainstream parliamentary process from complete exclusion. The first general election gave the excluded groups the chance for exposure. The share of the hill ethnic and Tarai community in the first elected government was 26.3 percent and 15.5 percent and in the parliament 15.6 percent and 22.0 percent, respectively

(DREFDEN 1992:7 cited in Hachhethu 2003:233). Although there was kshatriya-Brahman-Newar domination, such a space for the marginalized groups was the good beginning. All these new developments had its roots in the 1950's revolution organized by the Nepali Congress. Such a attempt to bring excluded groups into the main stream became success because it was the Nepali Congress (which mobilised) 'mostly ex-service man from ethnic minorities' as the Mukti Sena (Liberation Army) insurgents in the 1951 revolution. After the participation in the revolution, the excluded themselves became assertives to search space for them.

2.2.4. Panchayat Regime (1960–90)

This period could be seen as a resumption of early Shah Dynasty. Shah family ruled over the people as an 'absolute monarch'. The only difference during the period was that the king started his rule by deploying a system called 'Panchayat'. It was a party-less system which was termed as 'suitable system to soil' by the king Mahendra. The system was innovated by the king after the dismissal of the elected prime minister and the democratic system. The king charged the elected government as 'incapable of maintaining law and order.' Other charges he made were that the government 'produced a disturbed and vitiated atmosphere by pursuing impractical measures, and encouraged anti-national elements etc.'

Panchayati slogan—*ek bhasa, ek bhesh, ek desh* (one language, one dress, and one country) was a perfect example for examining policies and programs of the Panchayat period in respect of the plural identity of the country. The regime continued the Hinduization process as it enjoyed all the power in the name of god's incarnation. The king continued the process because he knew that only in the name of religion he could continue his hegemony over the society. Imposing such a religious feeling, the regime tried to legitimize the throne. The weapon of the king seemed somehow possible, because the then society was more traditional to believe the god and so on due to lack of education and awareness. For the first time in the history, Nepal was constitutionally recognized as a Hindu state by the king made Panchayati constitution, 1962. It was written in accordance with the king's Interest Panchayat resumed

Nepalization process also. For maintaining the hegemony of Nepali language in society, the regime stopped the news broadcasting service in Newari and Hindi from Radio Nepal in 1964. The program was started by the first elected government in 1951 (Gellner 1997:29)

The state accelerated both the process of Hinduization and Nepalization through internal migration. In the name of cultural assimilation, and to avoid the demand for autonomy raised by Tarai people since 1950, the regime supported the migration of hilly Nepali speaking people (who were culturally Hindus) to the Tarai, which is/was considered the homeland of tribal and Indian origin people. Such a program showed that the regime was keen to change Nepal's plural character into the 'homogenous, monolithic unitary state ignoring the reality of diversified and pluralistic character of the Nepali society.' The people lost their 'fundamental rights to speak and to organize against its ideology and value system' in the Panchayat system where all the opposition activism including ethnic and other cultural issues were banned. (Hachhethu 2003:225).

As Prithvi Narayan Shah did earlier, king Mahendra followed his ancestral role for wooing the support of indigenous community to the regime though Hinduization and Napalization process were their primary motto. The differences among the role played by two kings were that the strategy of Prithvi Narayan Shah was based on community but King Mahendra tried on individual basis. He took some elites individually from the indigenous and minority community and vested power in them. The elites got privileges and power in the name of ethnic and regional representation. For such opportunity, the elite had to support the Panchayat and surrender activism based on his/her community. Bedananda Jha, president of the Tarai Congress was appointed a minister after he dissolved his party in 1963. In the name of accommodation to diverse groups, some middle and higher class elites from indigenous communities were given state power and facility by the king, but the groups, as such, remained excluded. Panchayat policies towards other religions and ethnicity can be illustrated through some examples. To make Hinduism influential into other community and to achieve its primary goal of Nepalization, Panchayat officially declared Buddhism as a branch of Hinduism (Reiper and Hoftun 1992:154-63). Gopal Gurung's book, the first blueprint for ethnic resentment was banned by the regime for 'its allegedly communal overtones and for inciting mutual hatred between different cultural groups' (Sharma 1997:487). Likewise, Limbu's traditional customary rights over the land, which was called Kipat system was abolished by the Panchayat regime. It is sais that, because of the abolition of this customary right, the Limbus now faces severe problems. In fact, 71 percent among them live below the poverty line.

National symbols and National anthem are other examples which exposed the their regime's desire. In respect of a set of national symbols—the crown, scepter, royal crest, royal standard, coat-of-arms, cow, national flag, pheasant, rhododendron, and the red blob-invented by the Panchayat system, seven out of ten were related to 'monarchy and Hinduism' (Gurung 1997:505). The National Anthem of the country was written by using only the buttering words to the monarchy.

Although the Panchayat constitution made provision for the freedom of profess and practice of one's own religion, it was only *de jure* provision. The actual practice was an autocratic because it had neither 'accepted the westernized concepts of liberty, freedom and equality' (Chauhan 1971:199) nor sovereignty was vested in the people. The system was that 'the King was everything (executive, legislative and judiciary)'. The constitution itself was made by king without people's participation and it could be amended, rewrote, or removed if he alone was convinced. Analyzing the situation, one can conclude that it was the rule, which was regulated largely by the 'hukum' (order) of the king rather then the constitutional norms and values. It means all the constitutional provisions and traditionally accepted norms and values had no place before the will of king. Nobody was allowed to preach Islam and Christianity and destroy the dharma practiced by the Hindu people though the procision for religious Freedom was mentioned in the constitution. If anybody attempted to convert people, he could be imprisoned upto the period of three years. On that ground, 'non-Hindus were imprisoned many times for their anti-Hindu views' (Bajracharya and Khatry 2005:73-74). It was not because that such activities were unconstitutional or illegal but because it was against the king's real motto—Nepalisation and Hinduisation. All the Constitutions and laws of the Panchayat system seemed as shield of the regime to accelerate the Hindu religion at the cost of other religions in the country.

Although King Birendra was considered a more democratic king than others, he also followed his father's path in the process of Nepalisation and Hinduization. He tried to reform the Panchayat system after the referendum in 1980 but was not willing to change his father's policies. Indicating his belief in "ethical code," Birendra once said, "the king can not change the value system" of Hinduism. He further said, "the monarch and his subjects have been governed by Dharma, a system drawn from Hindu religion" (*Newsweek*, September 10, 1973 cited in Shah 1990:9). This statement is pointed to the fact that he was also in favor of the orthodox Hinduism to legitimize his rule. No fundamental change had occurred on ethnic, gender, regional and religious issues during his two decades long rule in Nepal.

2.2.5. Democratic System (1990–2002)

After 30 years of imposed autocratic Panchayat system, Nepal again entered in the democratic system. It was possible after the success of 1990s' people's movement. With the restoration of democratic system in 1990, ethnic, lingual, and cultural issues have once again surfaced in the public sphere as a debate. This was obvious because the dominant issue in the pre-1990 was to restore the 'multiparty democracy' rather than the caste, ethnic, religious, linguistic and gender question. Everyone knows that the liberal kinds of social character cannot be imagined in any kinds of autocratic system. Such feature is possible only in democracy. Democratic system could accommodate the identity issues only by making state mechanism inclusive. But on the other hand, 'all types of non-democratic regime—whatever names and forms—by nature were exclusionary as they generally prohibited and discourage people's participation' (Hachhethu 2003: 228). Keeping the fact in mind, all the then opposition political parties including all caste/ethnic, lingual and religious groups reached in a consensus for ending the autocratic Panchayat and establishing the democracy in the country, and joined hand to launch a successful peaceful movement against the system in 1990.

After the end of the Panchayat, different groups started to raise their own slogan and demand on the state. When new constitution making process began, the issues of language, religion and ethnic conflict came to the public attention. During the six months' transitional period those agendas were very much influential than that of power game. In the debate on secularism vs. Hinduism, not only the minority religious groups—Buddhists, Muslims and Christians—but also the Hindu fundamentalists became visible in public life and started to articulate their ideology. Although all the indigenous groups including the civil society were in favor of secular state, the constitution came out with the status quo provision of its earlier version of 1962 as the 'Hindu kingdom'. Several rallies and even demonstration were organized for making a secular status of Nepali state. The largest one with 150,000 protestors was held in Kathmandu. Gellner mentioned that such largest protest 'ever held in Kathmandu' (cited in Gellner 1997:178). Their demand to declare Nepal as secular state was sidelined because of the neutral position of two main political parties viz. NC and CPN (UML), and 'the influential intervention' of king backed by in-service and ex-service army officers, Hindu fundamentalist groups of Nepal and India (Pyakurel 2005:6; Pyakurel 2006:110). It is said that king Birendra had a desire to remain Nepal as a Hindu state. It was proved when the king recommended the then cabinet minister Achut Raj Regmi went to the hunger strike until the death for not changing the religious status of Nepal.

Although the phrase 'Hindu kingdom' remained unchanged, the constitution of the kingdom of Nepal 1990 accepted Nepal's 'multi-ethnic, multilingual' character. It recognized orphans, women, the aged, the disabled and incapacitated persons as well as socially and economically backward groups and communities as marginalized groups, were deserved special treatment from the state in education, health, employment, and social security. The constitution says, 'the social objective of the state shall be to establish and develop, on the foundation of justice and morality, a healthy social life, by eliminating all types of economic and social inequalities and by establishing harmony amongst the various castes, tribes, religions, languages, races and communities' (Directive principles and policies of the state, the constitution of the kingdom of Nepal, 1990). In the state policy, the constitution provisioned that 'the state shall, while maintaining the cultural diversity of the country, pursue a policy of strengthening the national unity by promoting healthy and cordial social relations amongst the various religions, castes, tribes, communities and linguistic groups, and by helping in the promotion of their languages, literatures, scripts, arts and cultures' (Directive principles and policies of the state, the constitution of the kingdom of Nepal, 1990). Freedom of press, organization and expression, which the constitution guaranteed were also better provisions provided to the people. It helped them to organize and to raise their common voices against the state. Many caste/ethnic and religious organizations sprang up in this era. The government identified 59 castes/ethnic groups and announced some affirmative programs for them. On the language issue, although Nepali was declared as an official language, all languages spoken as mother tongues in Nepal were also declared as 'national languages'. In addition, government committed itself to provide education in languages of mother tongue till primary level following the recommendation of the Rashtriya Sanskritik Samiti, 1992.

In 1992, the government formed a committee called Rashtriya Sanskritik Samiti to formulate programs for a national cultural policy. The committee recommended the formation of a national coordination committee. Recognizing the multilingual character of the state, Nepal for the first time started news broadcasting in eight minority languages. These were Rai, Gurung, Magar, Limbu, Bhojpuri, Awadhi, Tharu, and Tamang. Earlier news was being broadcasted only in three languages—Hindi, Newari and Maithili. The government offered thousands of scholarship for schoolgoing girl and boys from deprived and unprivileged groups. For promotion of girl enrolment in school the government began 'two liters oil program'; according to which a family would get two-liters oil per month if a girl was admitted in primary school. There was 'free textbook program' for girls whereas boys were to buy school textbooks. Other affirmative action programs like scholarship for higher education for backward community students, reservation in scholarship and in admission in educational institutes, quota for foreign employment were also provided during the period. Provisions for compulsory women's candidacy (at least 3 percent candidates must be women for being registered as a party in election commission) in lower and upper houses and 20 per cent in local level government were made. The formation of National Women Commission, National Dalit Commission were other positive aspects.

Although a lot was done by several democratically elected governments in Nepal from 1990-2002, the governments also showed some shortcomings, especially in regard to enforcing the spirit of the constitution that is abolition of all kinds of gender, religion, region, caste and ethnicity related disparities and discriminations. Among the glaring shortcomings was the continuation of the status of the Hindu state rather than secular one. Inclusion of Sanskrit as compulsory part in lower-secondary and secondary level curriculum, as well as the decision of broadcasting news in the Sanskrit from Radio Nepal are, according to the ethnic elites, other negative aspects of the democratic government. Sanskrit is termed as 'a dead language' by ethnic elites in Nepal. The NC and UML have been accused of giving space to Brahmanism through making Sanskrit compulsory in secondary school and introducing newscast in Sanskrit in 1995. Both the decisions are criticized as ploy 'to create government jobs for unemployed Brahman boys' (Malla 1992 cited in Gellner 1997:178; Gellner 1997:9)

The Supreme Court's verdict of 1 June 1999 against the use of local language as official language along with Nepali language has been criticized as a continuation of Nepalization process in the recent democratic period. The court invalidated the announcement of Kathmandu Metropolitan City, Dhanusa District Development Committee and Rajbiraj Municipality to use their respective dominant language as additional official language. Most of the people under these three local bodies speak their own language (*Nepal Bhasa* in Kathmandu, and Maithili in Dhanusa district and Rajbiraj Municipality) rather than the Nepali language. The court's decision has been criticized as 'a clear case of linguistic discriminatory' by the state. Apart from that, inability to get equal development of all the region by allocating adequate budget and deploying sufficient manpower, lack of attention to prevent caste-based discrimination in society especially in public spheres such as public tap, temple etc. are other grievances that have been raised against the democratic government.

As all know, Nepal's democratic system again went into 'coma' on October 4, 2002, when the king 'unconstitutionally' dismissed the elected government. During the period of October 4, 2002 to April 24, 2006, a question that was being raised by various sections was whether there was any working constitution in Nepal. It was a genuine query because the country was being ruled then neither by previous constitution nor there had been amended constitution. In the pretext of 'removing difficulties' in the system, the king misused Article 127 of the constitution, and took over the state power. During the period, the political parties were sidelined, people's rights provided in the constitution was made inoperative by the king. The action taken by the king was criticized 'as misinterpretation of the spirit of constitution.' Such situation ended in April 24, 2006 after the king was compelled to restore the parliament and give up the power. For the change, millions of Nepali people came to the street, protested against the four years long 'regressive and repressive action' of the king. During that democratic movement, some 21 people lost their lives, hundreds injured, and thousands of people were imprisoned and tortured.

Actually the February 1, 2005 coup was fourth intervention by the monarchy in the Nepali democracy; first was by king Tribhuwan in 1952, second by king Mahendra in 1960 and third by king Gyanendra in October 4, 2002. Because of the monarchy's such interventions into democracy, people from diverse area of interest joined hand and fought for return of democracy repeatedly in the country. Alongside this process, civil society, and academician began articulating the model of inclusive democracy for the heterogeneous country like Nepal. According to them, only such democracy could solve the identity issues arising out of disparities existing in the society. The agenda of inclusion has become the main agenda of the parliamentary political parties today. In April 2005, the seven parliamentary parties' alliance (SPA) reached an agreement called common agreements and commitments. The agreement focused on the progressive and democratic restructuring of the state structure to lay a solid foundation for social, political and economic inclusion. The parties have realized their mistakes and have resolved that such thing would not happen again. In November 26, 2005, the SPA and the Maoist reached 12-points understanding to end the king's rule and to restructure the Nepali state. The SPA, with the backing of the Maoist, called a four-days general strike as a protest against the king's autocratic regime in April. The strike went until the king agreed to reinstate the parliament, and to hand over the power to the people. The reinstated parliament unanimously resolved to go to the Constituent Assembly (CA) to make new constitution and declared Nepal as a secular state. Today, people have hope that the decision to go to the CA will not only bring the peace in Nepal but also transform Nepal into an inclusive country. Keeping that in mind, the political forces, civil society, and other society activists have been working together to restructure the state for more inclusive democracy.

3 ORIGIN, GROWTH AND SPREAD OF THE MAOIST MOVEMENT IN NEPAL

BACKGROUND

This chapter examines the origin and development of Maoist Movement in Nepal. The hypothesis of the research is that the Maoist Movement has capitalized on the agenda of socially, culturally and economically marginalized people of Nepal especially women, the Dalits and ethnic groups. To substantiate the hypothesis this chapter looks into the history of formation of Communist Party, with radical agenda, its shift to the 'revisionist' position and eventually marginalization of some of the sections of Nepali masses because of its own inner party conflict. There are almost a dozen of communist parties in Nepal. Each of them accuse the other to be 'revisionist', 'liquidationist' etc. The chapter examines the various ups and downs faced by the Maoist following the armed revolt in 1996. Apart from that, the chapter examines the Maoist movement in Nepal with reference of four basic criteria of a social Movement. These are ideology, environment, organization, and strategy.

3.1. COMMUNIST HISTORY IN NEPAL

Unlike the history of other parties, the history of the communist parties in Nepal is quite recent. Nepal was isolated from rest of the world during 104 years of Rana's oligarchy. The Nepalese people came to know about the rest of the world only after the Nepalese military joined the First World War. Of course, some Nepalese were becoming aware of politics even before that and had also participated in the Indian independence movement. The Nepalese who started political movement in Nepal, were in India either for their education or in exile in 1940s. Although a nascent communist movement had emerged in 1947 during the Biratnagar Jute and Cloth Mill strike, the Communist Party of Nepal (CPN) as a force of the democratic struggle in Nepal, came into existence only in 1949. In 1950, the communist party, which denounced the Delhi Compromise between the Nepali Congress (NC), king Tribhuwan and Ranas, was having just a fledgling entity. Earlier, the party was not very clear about its role during the democratic movement in 1951, which is termed as a 'revolution' in Nepalese history. The party termed the revolution however not to be a total revolution. NC was the leading party, which took weapons to overthrow the Rana regime in the movement. The movement ended when the king and Ranas signed an agreement before the then Indian Prime Minister Jawaharlal Nehru. The accord also called 'Delhi Compromise', paved the way not only to the end of Rana oligarchy but also Paved the war to form interim government in Nepal. The agreement was termed as 'betrayal' by the CPN.

The CPN which got annoyed with the NC after the latter join the interim government started tying up with other small anti-NC parties and made a United Front in July 1951. Apart from that, the party tried to prove its credentials by adopting an anti-Indian stance by declaring the NC as 'Nehru government's toy.' Later, CPN was banned till April 1956 after it claimed responsibility for January 1952 revolt.

The first convention of the CPN was held in secret in January 1954. It elected Manamohan Adhikari as a general secretary. Adhikari was already holding the post after replacing Puspalal in 1951. Although, the First Congress advocated republican state by replacing the monarchy, the party shifted its stand and accepted the king as the country's head in 1955. Since there has been never ending leadership struggle within the party. Keshar Jung Raimajhi replaced Manamohan Adhikari during Adhikari's visit to China. In 1959 general election, the party took part the election and won four seats out of the 109 seats in the lower house.

The leadership struggle of CPN had shifted into ideological struggle and led to the division of the party into two factions in 1960. These were the pro-Peking and pro-Moscow factions. The faction saw in the existence when Keshar Jung Raimajhi, the then general secretary of CPN, welcomed the dissolution of parliament by the king Mahendra. However, the king's action was termed by other politburo members including Puspa Lal Shrestha and

Manamohan Adhikari as 'military terror'. Three distinct thoughts—Raimajhi thought to work with the king, Puspa Lal thought to work with NC to restore the parliamentary democracy and Mohan Bikram Singh thought to hold an election to a constituent assembly—were seen in the party in the Durbhanga Plenum in 1961. Among them, the first one was adopted as a party line by CPN. In April 1962, Raimajhi was expelled from the party on the charge of supporting the autocratic king. He was replaced by Tulsi Lal Amatya at the party's Third Convention in Banaras. Another party was formed under the leadership of Puspa Lal in May 1968 by Gorakhpur meeting. In September 1974, Mohan Bikram Singh and Nirmal Lama took lead to organize the Fourth Conference at Banaras, which paved the way to constitute another communist party named CPN Fourth Convention. The Fourth Convention, led by Mohan Bikram Singh as general secretary, was very clear on the question of armed revolution. It proposed to follow the path of armed conflict in 1979. However, the party gave up the idea after the announcement of the national referendum in the same year. It is said that the proposal adopted by the CPN Fourth Convention in 1979 is the very course that the Maoist has taken from 1996.

The CPN organized a Nationwide District Secretary's Conference in 1979, which forced Nirmal Lama to leave the post of general secretary. The conference charged Lama as supporter of the referendum declared by the king. This struggle of the leaders ultimately led another split in 1983 in the leadership of Nirmal Lama and Mohan Bikram Singh. The first led the same CPN Fourth Conference and the latter founded CPN (Masal). CPN (Masal) had been seen as one of the founder members of the Revolutionary Internationalist Movement (RIM) in March 1984 in London. The aim of the RIM was to engage in a worldwide grouping of the revolutionary parties committed to the scientific principles of Marxism-Leninism-Mao Tse-tung thought.

It was during the period when Lama and Singh were busy fighting for the post and blame each other as ideology shifter or, revisionists that another faction of the youth communist leaders started armed revolt in Jhapa district in Nepal in 1971. Jhapa lies just across the border Mechi River. The revolt was the first uprising in Nepal with the ideological and physical support of Communist Party of India (Marxist and Leninist) (Hachhethu 2002:70). By this revolt, some eight 'class enemies' were wiped out in the name of the 'campaign to eliminate class enemies'. There is a claim that the Jhapa uprising was the gateway for the process of forming CPN UML which became the largest Communist Party of Nepal after 1990.

On the other, the party breaking trend had been seen as a continuous process. In fifth Congress in 1985, Masal, once more broke up into CPN (Masal) and CPN (Mashal). The latter was formed under the leadership of Mohan Baidhya. Mashal became the crucial organization for launching the 'people's war' when Puspa Kamal Dahal alley Prachanda took over the post of general secretary from Baidhya. To summarize, the CPN (Fourth Congress) was divided into three factions—the Fourth Congress, Masal and Mashal during its 11 years journey since 1974. Among these three, the first one joined the United Left Front (ULF, an alliance of seven left factions' under the co-ordination of Sahana Pradhan) on the eve of 1990s mass movement. The front launched the 1990s movement after joining hand with NC. However, the other two formed the Samyukta Rastriya Janaandolan (United National People's Movement, UNPM) under the leadership of Baburam Bhattarai. The UNPM was not satisfied with the achievement gained by the 1990s movement and asked people to continue the movement after the NC and ULF called it off. The main demand of UNPM was the people's sovereignty and to hold the election of constituent assembly to write constitution.

On March 1991, Masal again got split into two factions on the issue of whether the party would take part of 1991 elections or not. The factions after the split were 'Masal' led by Baburam Bhattarai and 'Mashal' led by Mohan Bikram Singh. The first faction decided to participate in the 1991 elections in order to use the opportunity to 'expose the monarchy and the parliamentary system' (Pristhabhumi, March 21 1991 cited in Thapa (ed.) 2003:21) and the second faction decided to stay underground. For contesting the first general elections under the 1990s constitution, five radical forces—Forth Conference, Mashal led by Prachanda, a small faction of Masal led by Baburam,

Sarbahara Sramik Sangathan and NCP (Janamukhi)—came together, formed a new underground party by name CPN (Unity Centre) and decided to contest the election. They took part in the election by forming another party named United People's Front, Nepal (UPFN). The declared objectives of UPFN were to 'expose the inadequacy of the parliamentary system'. It got nine seats out of 205 in the House of Representatives in 1991 election and became third largest party in the parliament. After submitting 14-points demands to the prime minister Koirala in 1992, the Unity Centre joined hand with the Masal and two other smaller parties to launch a series of protests against the first elected Koirala government. Among the protests, the protests of April 6, 1992 turned violent in which more then a dozen people were killed in the police firing.

Ramming through Prachanda's political line with a Marxist-Leninist-Maoist ideology, the CPN (Unity Centre) at its Unity Congress in December 1991 passed 'a resolution to initiate a "people's war" to bring about a new democratic revolution' in Nepal (Thapa 2003:43). The decision became the cause of another split of the party into Prachanda faction and Nirmal Lama faction. It was divided in May 1994 where Lama left the party CPN (Unity Centre), and formed another party by the same name. Others blamed that the action taken by Lama was only because of his distrust in armed uprising. After the split, Prachanda-led Unity Centre went underground to prepare for its next phase of struggle. At the same time, the division in the mother party, the Unity Centre, effected to UPFN, which was formed to contest the election; UPFN also cracked into Baburam Bhattarai group and Niranjan Govinda Baidhya group. Both the groups went to the Election Commission for recognition. However, only the latter got formal recognition from the commission. This decision of the commission became a pretext for the first group to boycott the mid-term election in 1994. Ultimately, the group gave up the parliamentary electoral politics and started preparation for the armed revolt.

Having gone through ups and downs in its organization through splits and unities, CPN (Unity Centre) organized its 'Third Plenum' in March 1995. At the plenum, the party was renamed into the CPN (Maoist). It also came up with a major decision for raising the arms against the state. The decision said, 'for the true liberation of the people, all efforts must be concentrated for the development of a 'people's war' that would usher in the new people's democratic form of government' (Thapa and Sijapati 2003:45). The party also gave up its policy of taking part in parliamentary elections. In September of the same year (1995), the party adopted the 'Plan for the Historic Initiation of the 'people's war' and passed seven theoretical premises (Thapa and Sijapati 2003:45–47). Following this, the party started a series of public meetings or campaigns including the famous *Sija* campaign[1], which the party termed as 'final politico-ideological preparation.' In October 1995, a clash between the *Sija* campaigners (the Maoist) and the cadres of mainstream political parties specially the NC and RPP activists was reported. It was a campaign in which the local people also participated. In November 1995, the clash led to the police suppression of the participants of the campaign. The security force launched 'Operation Romeo'. Random arrest, torture, rape and extra-judicial killings became the normal things. This 'brutal' suppression was the turning point of the Maoist to speed up to establish rapport with the people by expressing its sympathy or concern for them. The 'Operation Romeo' became the vehicle to unite the villagers and the Maoist into a common agenda 'to escape and protect the life from the state repression'.

In January 1996, the underground party decided February 13, 1996 as the date for starting the People's War. In February 3, 1996, the open political wing of the party led by Baburam Bhattarai had presented its 40-points memorandum to the government. It warned the government that the UPFN would begin an armed struggle against the state unless appropriate measures towards fulfilling the demands were initiated by February 17. Citing the governments' indifference

[1] Sija is the shortcut term of Sisne and Jaljale. These are two different villages of the eastern parts of Rolpa District, where the party organized the political campaign and carried out some social works to mobilize party members to propagate the ideology of Marxism-Leninism-Maoism. Rolpa belongs to mid-western parts of Nepal.

to UPFN demands, the party cadres including Baburam Bhattarai went underground and launched attack on February 13, 1996 in four different places in four districts in the name of 'People's War'. The first four targets of the Maoist were Agriculture Development Bank in Gorkha District and three different police posts in Rolpa, Rukum and Sindhuli District.

Various scholars have considered the demands presented to the government and the issue of the denial of the recognition of the party by the Election Commission as critical causes for the eruption of people's war (Karki and Seddon 2003:17) . In fact, having a look at the strategic preparation of people's war, one can say that those causes are only a feint. It is because the leaders strategically made two parties—an underground and another open—to prepare for the armed conflict. Both the parties aimed to expose the inadequacy of achievements of 1990's movement. The party, led by Baburam Bhattarai, entered into the electoral politics with the expressed objectives 'to expose the inadequacy of the parliamentary system.' Another justifiable evidence for such a position was that the UPFN started attack on the government institutions even before the February 17 deadline. It seems that the attack was guided by the underground party's decision of January 1996 rather than the UPFN's given deadline. Another aspect is that the UPFN had presented similar 38-points demands to the UML government in December 1994. The then Deuba government claimed that the Maoist had begun its attacks before the government could formulate its response on the demands.

However, people had a doubt that if the Election Commission had favored Bhattarai group by recognizing his faction as party, the UPFN faction would not join the war. Even Prachanda expressed doubt about Baburam's 'jump' from pure intellectual ideology into the underground and rebellion war (*Janadesh* 2006:19). Prachanda's such 'benefit of doubt' over the communist leaders is valid in Nepalese politics because rarely the communist leaders came back and continued with their ideological stand if they once entered into the electoral politics. Most of the Communist leaders left their ideology and shifted to right once they went to take part in the elections in Nepal. Keshar Jung Raimajhi, Radha Krishna Mainali and Gore Bahadur Khapangee are those who from radical left changed to conservative royalists after engagement within the electoral politics. Another example is of CPN (UML). Most of the leaders of the party were 'Jhapa upspring' background (a replication of the Naxalite Movement of India), but after having adopted the path of socialism through competitive parliamentary democracy, they have forgotten their ideology as well as ultimate goal viz. socialism and classless society. Now they seem to be more liberal than other liberal democrats like NC are.

3.2. SOME ELEMENTS OF THE MAOIST MOVEMENT

For Saha, as mentioned earlier, revolts, rebellions, reforms, and revolutions are various forms of movements. The Maoist Movement, following Shah, can be conceptualized as a revolution which means it is 'a form of politics characterized by the extensive use of violent or other illegal means in competition for control of government power and authority' (Wolfenstien cited in Singh 2005:9). Referring to environment, ideology, organization, and strategy as four dimensions, Mohanty tries to provide a framework for study of the revolutionary movement (Mohanty 1977:10). Most studies on social movements speak out at least four components—ideology, strategy, organization, and objectives—as essential components of a movement (Louis 2002:31). Attempt has been made here to discuss these aspects in the context of the Maoist Movement in Nepal.

Ideology: The general meaning of the term 'ideology' is that it is a system of ideas concerning a phenomenon, especially the social life. Ideology not only provides the motivating force but also defines the aims and objectives of the movement. The Maoist claim that they are guided by Marxist and Leninist theories and that they apply whatever Mao applied in China. Accusing all other communists as revisionists and liquidationists, they claim that they are the only real followers of Marxism-Leninism-Maoism. The Maoist of Nepal quote Mao and say, 'Mao enriched qualitatively the theoretical treasure of Marxism-

Leninism by successfully fulfilling the necessity of class struggle in the imperialist era.' For Prachanda, contribution of Mao in relation to People's War should be understood in the context of the necessity of developing class struggle in the history (Prachanda 1993:182).

The Maoist take the position of Marx and Angels that the violent revolution has a universal character in the class society. They believe in Lenin's clarity on systematically developed theoretical concepts regarding necessity of armed struggle in the course of implementing it in the Russian revolution. Based on the theoretical assertions of Marxism-Leninism on violent revolution and the experience acquired from their practical applications, Mao developed the comprehensive theory of 'people's war' in the course of accomplishing new democratic revolution in China. They claim that the theory of 'people's war' developed by Mao represents the apex of Marxism-Leninist military science and will be applied universally in all kinds of countries according to the situation. (Prachanda 1999:146)

Ideologically, they believe that the revolt is the only path for changing the society. They advocate that the 'people's war' will end all kinds of other war' (Prachanda 1999:185). Therefore, they tried to revolt against the Panchayat regime in 1990 when strong alliance of NC and ULF were trying to defeat the Panchayat through peaceful movement. Those, who believed in peaceful means to change the society, are, according to the Maoist leaders, foolish and irrationals. Responding to Sayami's argument about the achievement of 2006 people's movement in Nepal, Baburam Bhattarai, one of the top most leaders of the Maoist, tried to give credit of the achievement to the armed revolt launched by the Maoist. Sayami had stated that the 19-days of long peaceful movement achieved more than that of the ten years long war in which some 15,000 lives were lost (*Kantipur*, May 3, 2006). Likewise, Bernstein's thought 'capitalism transforms peacefully into socialism' was termed as a 'counter revolution tradition' by Prachanda. Bernstain had said, 'through the methods of voting, demonstration and pressure we can bring about reforms for which a violent revolution was necessary hundred years ago' (cited in Prachanda 2004:121). The goal of political struggle, according to Kautsky is 'to win the state power by changing parliament to the master of government through a majority in it' (*ibid*). For Prachanda parliament and parliamentarian democracy is nothing. He said, 'in relation to the parliamentary system and parliamentarism, there have been life and death struggles in the International Communist Movement since the birth of Marxism' (*Ibid*:120).

The Maoist of Nepal state that it has been ideologically following Marxism-Leninism-Maoism and its ultimate aim is to apply Mao's thought in Nepal. First, it try to mobilize the masses to follow Mao, according to whom the masses are the 'creators of history'. It took to arms following their belief in the Maoist thought. To Mao, 'people with no army have nothing of its own.' Following this saying of Mao, Prachanda describes the relationship of civil-military—weapon. Prachanda says, 'in whatever way they are equipped with weapons, trained and powerful in the beginning their fall is inevitable when they stand against the interest of the masses. Final victory is theirs that fight for defending the interest of broad masses however weak they seem militarily in the beginning' (Prachanda 1993:183)

Apart from such belief in people's army and war, Mao had also shown his belief in people's power rather than the weapons. He used to say 'weapons are an important factor in war, but not decisive factor; it is people, not things, that are decisive' (Prachanda 1993: 183–84). It seems that the Maoist in Nepal followed the double standard Mao on people and army, and tried to attract general people by raising 'situational local issues related slogans'. Although Communist ideology was against the 'identity issues', they tried to bring these issues at the forefront. These issues not only touched native and suppressed people but also the migrants, laborers, peasants, women, Dalits etc. They even tried to win support by creating hostility among the different groups in the society; the cadres of the Maoist used to say that after their rule prevails in the society, the migrant landlords will have to give up the lands they occupied. The Maoist sells such agenda to the native people most of whom belonge to the ethnic communities.

However, the Maoist has had no constant policy; after it gained high support of native and ethnic communities, it has now trying to get support from high caste and elite communities advocating the necessity of the social harmony in the society. According to its leaders, harmony is needed for achieving its ultimate goal of 'Communism through socialism.' The Maoist site a quotation of Lenin, and has started convincing the people to give up the antagonist kinds of demand, which the party provoked earlier. The quote is, 'we don't want only a thing that is forceful work. We don't want our hegemony in heaven through *danda* (stick)' (Prasad 2005: 17)

Environment: Environment is another important component of the movement. Every incident will be guided and influenced by the environment. In this part of the chapter, I examine the given socio-political and cultural situation, which has given space to the Maoist Movement in Nepal.

As mentioned in the second chapter, Nepal is a highly diversified society. Pluralism is its integral features. Nepal is spread over an area of 147,181 sq. kilometers. It has a population of about 23.5 million. The country is divided into three topographically zones. One is the mountainous region which is inhabited by people of Tibetan origin i.e. Bhote, Sherpa, Thakali etc. It covers 15 percent of Nepal's land and 0.7 percent of its population. There are 15 districts in it. The second is a hilly region, which covers approximately 68 per cent land of Nepal with 36 districts. Caste and ethnic settlements overlap in this region. 25.8 percent out of total 36.4 percent ethnic population of Nepal resides in this region only. Likewise, 40.3 percent out of total 57.5 percent caste population in Nepal is in this region. The third is Tarai region which is considered a traditional homeland of tribal people i.e. Tharu, Rajbansi, Dhimal etc. Apart from that, the people of Indian origin are also in Tarai. It covers 17 percent of the area of Nepal, and has 24 districts. As per the 2001 census, Nepal has 100 caste and ethnic groups and 90 languages and dialects. Based on caste, ethnic, regional, cultural and linguistic considerations, the Nepalese population is broadly classified into three major groupings: *Parbatiya* (hill people) and *Madhesi* (plain people); jati (caste groups) and janjati (ethnic/tribal groups); and high-caste and low-caste Hindus. Nepal has, therefore, long been considered as a pluralistic state although every regime has tried to impose one language, one religion and one culture.

Of the total of 100 caste/ethnic groups, the number of people comprising each of these groupings ranges from 3.6 million to a little less than 1,000. The largest group is the Kshatriya with 15.8 percent of the total population and the smallest Kusunda with only 164 people. The social composition of Nepalese population is made up of 57.5 percent caste group, 36.4 percent ethnic groups and 6.2 percent others (Pfaff-Czarnecla 1997; Gurung 2003:5). There is of course a debate over the status of the Newars. The issue is whether they are to be treated as marginalized group or not. The debate is because the socio-political-economic status of Newar as group is higher than the other groups of the society. The caste groups are characterized by a four-layer hierarchy, consisting of Brahman, Kshatriya, Baisya and Shudra. The people of Tarai, except those who migrated from the hills, are called Madhesi and consist of both caste and ethnic groups. Madhesi is an ethno-regional identity of the Tarai people (Yadav 2003). They constitute over 31 percent of the total population of Nepal. The Madhesi caste groups alone constitute about 19.5 percent of the total population. This of course includes the Dalits of Tarai. There are 59 officially defined ethnic groups in Nepal. They are the *Adibasi/ Janajati* people who are considered as the original/pioneer people of Nepal. Among 59 groups, 18 are in the mountains, 24 in hills, six in inner Tarai and 11 in Tarai. Among 36.4 percent of the total population of *Adibasi/*Janajati in Nepal, Magar with 7.14 percent population is the largest one in the hilly region and Tharu with 6.75 percent population in Tarai.

Out of 90 languages recorded in the 2001 Census, 12 have 1 percent speakers each. Nepali, which is recognized as the 'language of the nation' as well as the official language, is the language of a little less than half, 48.61 percent of the population have assumed the place of *lingua franca.* Although Nepal was constitutionally declared a 'Hindu Kingdom', the people belonged to various religions. As per the 2001 Census, 80.6 percent of the Nepali people practice Hinduism, 10.7 percent Buddhism, 4.2 percent Islam, 3.6 percent Kirat. Christian, Sikh, and Jain etc. constitute less than 1 percent (Gurung 2003).

In the prevailing situation, the hierarchies of relationships have been discriminated and deprived on basis of gender, caste/ethnicity, and region. The lower strata, particularly women, Dalits, Janajatis and Madhesi people were discriminated from having equal and equitable treatment and sharing of resources. Because of the policy of 'Nepalization' accelerated by the Nepali state for 238 years the hill high caste Brahman-Kshatriya and an ethnic group Newar has long been in privileged position. The following tables show the socio-political-economic position of the above-mentioned groups.

Table 1 tells the socio-economic position of Nepal's different social groups. The Newars, who are also in the list of the ethnic population in Nepal, have the highest Human Development Index (HDI). The Brahmans are ahead of Newars only in life expectancy and education related index. Kshatriyas are after the Newars and Brahmans in the all aspect of HDI. Although Janajatis are ahead of Madhesi in life expectancy and education related index, Madhesi's position is ahead of Janajati in HDI. Dalits score the lowest in every aspect of HDI.

Table 2 would reveal that all social groups in Nepal except the Brahmans, Kshatriyas and Newars have under representation in key institutions and positions. The share of Brahmans and Kshatriyas are exceedingly high excepting in the fields of commerce and industry. In commerce and industry, Newar and the Madhesis share dominated positions. The Brahmans and Kshatriyas occupy the third position. The position of Ethnic and Dalit remains the same as in earlier Tables.

According the Table 3, the position of the Brahmans remain high in all occupations of respect and prestige. Interestingly, an ethnic group known as Thakalis occupies the position next to the Brahmans. Among the ethnic groups, the hill ethnic groups are ahead of the Tarai ethnic groups. The Dalits position is as same as in respect of HDI and Integrated National Index of Governance (INIG). However, the Tarai Dalits are ahead of the Dalits in respect of the white-collor jobs of the lower level such as clerks, office assistants etc.

Table 1: **Human Development by Caste and Ethnicity, 1996**

		Dominant Groups			*Marginal Groups*			
		Brahman	*Kshatriya*	*Newar*	*Madhesi*	*Janajati*	*Dalit*	*Nepal*
1.	Life Expectancy	60.8	56.03	62.2	58.4	53.0	50.3	55.0
2.	Adult Literacy rate %	58.00	42.00	54.80	27.50	35.20	23.80	36.27
3.	Means years of schooling	4.4647	2.786	4.370	1.700	2.021	1.228	2.254
4.	Per capita income Nrs.	9921	7744	11953	6911	6607	4940	7673
5.	Life Expectancy Index	0.957	0.522	0.620	0.557	0.467	0.422	0.500
6.	Educational Attainment Index	0.490	0.342	0.462	0.221	0.280	0.186	0.295
7.	Income Index	0.237	0.181	0.289	0.160	0.152	0.110	0.179
8.	Human Development Index (RDI)	0.441	0.348	0.457	0.313	0.299	0.239	0.325
9.	Ratio to HDI Nepal = 100	135.87	107.31	140.73	96.28	92.21	73.62	100.00

Source: NESAC. 1998. *Nepal: Human Development Report 1998*. Kathmandu: Nepal South Asia Centre.

Table 2: **Integrated National Index of Governance (INIG), 1999**

S.N.		*Dominant Groups*		*Marginalized Groups*				
		Brahman/ Kshatriya	*Newar*	*Madhesi*	*Janajati*	Dalit	*Other*	*Total*
1.	Court	77.0	13.6	7.6	1.7	0	0	235
2.	Constitutional Bodies	56.0	24.0	12.0	2.8	0	0	25
3.	Cabinet	62.5	9.4	15.6	12.5	0	0	32
4.	Parliament	60.0	7.6	17.4	13.6	1.5	0	265
5.	Public Administration	77.6	17.6	3.7	1.2	0	0	245
6.	Party Leadership	58.8	10.9	15.8	15.2	0	0	165
7.	Leadership: local elected bodies	55.5	15.7	16.2	12.0	0	0	191
8.	Leadership: Commerce and Industry	16.7	47.6	35.7	0	0	0	42
9.	Leadership: Educational arena	77.3	11.3	7.2	2.1	1	1	97
10.	Leadership: cultural arena	69.1	17.9	0	4.9	0	0	123
11.	Science/technology	58.1	29.0	9.7	3.2	0	0	62
12.	Civil society leadership	75.9	14.8	7.4	1.9	0	0	54
	Total	66.5	15.2	11.2	7.1	0.3	1	
	Population %	31.6	5.6	30.9	22.2	8.7	1	
	Difference with population %	+34.9	+9.6	−19.7	−15.1	−8.4	−1	

Source: Neupane, Govinda. 2000, *Nepalko Jatiya Prasana* (Question of Caste/Ethnicity in Nepal). Kathmandu: Centre for Development Studies.

Table 3: **Share of Caste/Ethnic Groups in Prestigious Occupations**

Caste/Ethnicity	*Legislative, senior officials, managers and professionals*	*Technical and assistant professionals*	*Clerks or office assistances*
Brahmans of Hill area	9.09	4.83	4.13
Dalits of Hill area	0.45	0.31	0.55
Dalits of Tarai area	0.30	0.26	1.06
Ethnic people of Mountain and Hill area	2.72	1.51	1.94
Ethnic people (*Thakali*) of mountain and Hill area	8.24	3.21	1.88
Ethnic people (Newar)	6.29	3.70	3.80
Ethnic people belongs to Tarai region	1.30	0.78	1.84

Source: Nepal Human Development Report 2004, Kathmandu: UNDP.

Table 4 gives two kinds of information. The first part examines the representation of different communities in the House of Representative (HOR). The data show absence of increase in the composition of representation from ethnic and other communities during the three elections. However, the representation Kshatriyas have been increased, Brahmans has maintained constant hegemony. In fact, the Brahman had three times more representation than its size of population. Interestingly, though the state and the political parties raised voices favoring the representation of the 'marginalized' groups, the presence of these groups (hill ethnic groups, Tarai communities and others) in the three recent parliaments have seen substantive decrease.

To show the representation of the different groups in the party at the central level is another aspect of Table 4. It is interesting to note that all major parties have somehow similar representation from higher caste groups (Brahmans and Kshatriyas). UML, which

Table 4: **Caste/Ethnic Composition of HOR and Party Central Committees**

	*House of Representatives**			*Parties' Central Committee (** & ***)*					
Caste/ethnicity *Total number*	*1991* *205*	*1994* *205*	*1999* *205*	*NC*** *29*	*UML*** *46*	*RPP*** *41*	*JM**** *38*	*NSP**** *29*	*NWPP**** *9*
Brahman	37.6	42.0	37.6	62.1	65.2	19.5	44.73	–	22.22
Kshatriyas	19.1	19.5	20.5	10.3	10.9	31.70	7.84	–	11.11
Newar	06.8	06.3	06.8	3.4	13.0	4.9	10.52	–	66.66
Hill ethnic groups	15.2	12.2	14.7	13.8	6.5	26.8	21.05	–	–
Tarai Communities	21.0	20.0	19.5	10.3	4.3	17.1	5.26	100	–
Others	2.9	2.0	2.5	–	–	–	10.52	–	–
Total	100	100	100	100	100	100	100	100	100

*Sources:** IIDS. 2000. *The Fourth parliamentary Election*. Kathmandu: Institute for Integrated Development Studies. ** *Nepal Human Development Report 2004*, Kathmandu: UNDP p. 190.*** Lok Raj Baral, Krishna P. Khanal and Krishna Hachhethu. 2002. 'Responsiveness of Nepali Political System'. (Unpublished Report).

Table 5: **Land Holding Position of Caste/Ethnic and Religious Groups**

S.N.	*Caste/Ethnicity*	*Landless*	*Semi-landless (below 0.2 hectare*	*Farmers with the land in-between 0.21 to 1 hectare*	*Small farmers (1.01-2.00 hectares)*	*Lower middle farmer (2.01-4.44 hectare)*	*Middle farmers (4.01-10 hectare)*	*Big farmers (over 10 hectares)*	*Total family*
1.	Nepal	24.44	6.98	27.59	20.15	13.42	6.25	1.17	4174374
2.	Ethnic community								
	Santhal, Jhangad, Kisan, Munda etc	58.46	4.91	10.44	7.07	9.5	8.76	0.87	16910
	Gurung	26.85	6.36	30.53	21.5	11.1	3.25	0.41	110574
	Tharu	22.83	6.36	17.93	15.65	19.25	15.18	2.79	235500
	Rai	20.04	4.89	24.97	24.24	17.69	7.4	0.76	125297
	Tamang	16.69	6.93	31.29	26.73	14.18	3.85	0.32	239755
	Limbu	15.83	4.57	27.06	25.0	18.67	7.95	0.91	67916
	Magar	14.41	5.88	33.33	26.53	14.71	4.51	0.63	296313
3.	Caste group								
	Tarai *Dalits*	43.98	9.89	26.19	11.3	6.01	2.29	0.34	231880
	Hill *Dalits*	15.32	15.24	44.55	17.25	6.14	1.27	0.24	308796
4.	Religious group								
	Muslim, Churaute	40.37	6.29	19.54	13.18	11.19	7.4	1.94	148036

Source: Central Bureau of Statistics 2002 Ka cited in *Nepal Human Development Report 2004,* Kathmandu: UNDP p. 194.

has been trying to show its status as a party of proletariats and 'marginalized', has the highest representation from Brahman. In fact, the ethnic and Tarai representation is higher in NC than in UML. In Rashtriya Prajatantra Party (RPP), the representation of the marginalized groups seems better. However, the persons kept by RPP in the name of the representation from different communities are more elites than the Brahmans, Kshatriyas and Newars. Most of the elites from different groups, who were allies of the king joined RPP when Nepal turned into democracy in 1990. It is said that neither are the RPP elites progressive nor they do they represent the 'marginalized' groups.

Another interesting event in the Table 4 is that the representation of two parties—the NSP and the NWPP—seems more homogeneous than the other four parties seems. Both the parties, according to their documents, have been formed to raise the voice of the 'marginalized' groups. The question is that if its own party has not addressed the diversity by accommodating all the groups in the party on the basis of their proportion of population, how can a leader raise such a question at different forum? In the issue of inclusion and representation, the position of Jana Morcha (JM) seems a bit progressive although the representation from the Tarai group is poor in the party.

For a country, where the economy is primarily based on agriculture, land is the main form of the property of the people. Property determines the economic status of the people. If one goes through the Table 5, one finds that the Dalits in Tarai and the Muslims overall suffer from the lack of access to land. The economic position of the major ethnic groups like Magars, Tamangs, Tharus, Gurungs, Rais, Limbus etc. is somewhat better. Exceptions are the Santhals, Jhangads, Kisans, and Mundas. Six out of ten people from Santhal, Jhangad, Kisan, Munda groups are landless. The position of Dalits in the hill is again somewhat better than the Dalits from the Tarai. Tharus, who belong mostly to Tarai region are better placed in terms of land holding.

Table 6: **Educational Status of the Caste/Ethnic and Regional Groups**

Caste/Ethnicity	*Literate %*	*SLC and equivalent %*	*Intermediate or equivalent %*	*Graduate or above %*
Nepal	53.74	100	100	100
Hill people				
Thakali	72.42	0.13	0.12	0.10
Newar	72.18	11.87	13.27	13.51
Limbu	59.64	1.40	1.01	0.68
Rai	58.77	2.30	1.72	1.25
Magar	57.70	4.58	3.08	2.16
Tamang	42.00	2.07	1.13	0.75
Tarai				
Upper caste	73.92	4.11	5.63	6.95
Tharu	46.54	3.52	2.75	1.69
Dalits	21.06	0.63	0.46	0.31
Hill				
Brahmans	75.64	29.91	34.85	41.48
Kshatriya, Thakuri, Sanyashi	60.90	21.99	20.17	18.25
Dalits	41.93	1.32	0.86	0.51

Source: Central Bureau of Statistics 2002 Ka cited in *Nepal Human Development Report 2004,* Kathmandu: UNDP p. 193.

Table 6 shows the educational status of the different groups in Nepal. The data show that the educational status of the hill groups is better than that of the Tarai. Between hill and the Tarai upper caste people, notable margin has seen there. About 2 percent is the difference between two upper caste communities in the literacy rate, but in the higher education, the defference went upto seven times. In respect of the Dalit groups, the literacy rate of the Tarai Dalits is only half of the literacy rate than the hill Dalits. The educational status of Thakali and Newar (both are considered as ethnic community) is higher than the Kshatriyas and Thakuris. Among the hill people, the position of the Tamang group, one of the major ethnic groups in Nepal, is the poorest.

Table 7: **Gender Participation in Economic and Political Activities**

Sector	*Details*	*Male %*	*Female %*
Economic level (job sector	Agriculture and forest	52	48
	Fuel and water supply	78	22
	Public adm.	88	12
	Education	74	26
	Health	71	29
	Other community, social and private work	85	15
Political level	National level (MP)	94.2	5.8
	District level	93.3	6.7
	Village level	92.3	7.7
	Ward level	80	20

Source: Central Bureau of Statistics 2002 Ka cited in *Nepal Human Development Report 2004,* Kathmandu: UNDP pp. 192-193.

Women are the other marginalized group in Nepal. As participation is considered as a major indicator of the empowerment, Table 7 shows the low participation of the women in every sphere of economic and political reality in comparison to men. Women are more by 0.26 percent than men in Nepal. However, they are on the margin (nowhere) in the economic and political level. They are significantly visible only in the agriculture and forest sector. In other spheres, men have four to 16 times more participation than the women. It is interesting to note that the participation of women is the poorest at national level politics, where all policies are being finalized.

The next section of the chapter analyzes the constitution and election manifestos of major political parties. This has been done to see how the constitution and the major political parties have addressed the socio-cultural and regional diversity in Nepal. Apart from that, the study also examines the Maoists' policies and programs, as it has been instrumental in attracting the marginalized groups.

The 1990 Constitution: The constitution is a supreme legal framework, which provides the main guidelines for the government. The constitution is not an abstract/shapeless document. It represents a document, which reflects the interest of the major political actors in the country.

After being discontented by the policy and program of the autocratic Panchayat regime, people from every walk of life took part in the 1990s' mass movement with the hope of emancipation, good governance and development. There was wide-ranged participation in the movement. Dalits, ethnic groups, women, religious groups, regional communities, linguistic groups, civil societies, all were participated in the movement in a big way. With the success of the movement, the participants tried to get their share from the democratic government. They expected their agenda to be addressed in the 1990 constitution. The question is whether the constitution provided for space raised by the stakeholders of the 1990s' movement or not. Table 8 shows the responses of the state towards the varied groups through the constitution of the kingdom of Nepal in 1990.

Table 8: **Constitutional Provision for the Different Communities in 1990 Constitution**

S.N.	*Issue*	*Constitutional provision*
1.	Nation/state	1. Nation constitutes of people irrespective of religion, race, caste or tribe 2. Strengthens national unity and harmony amongst various religious, castes, tribes, language, race and communities 3. Multiethnic, multilingual, democratic, independent, indivisible, sovereign Hindu and Constitutional Monarchical Kingdom
2.	All marginalized groups (ethnicity/gender/caste/class)	1. All citizens are equal before the law 2. No discrimination on grounds of religion, race, sex, caste, tribe or ideological conviction or any of these 3. Eliminate all types of economic and social inequalities

(*Table 8 Contd.*)

S.N.	*Issue*	*Constitutional provision*
		4. Maintain cultural diversity preserving and promoting language, script and culture of the different community 5. Pursue a policy, which will help promote the interests of the economically and socially backward groups and communities by making special provisions with regard to their education, health and employment.
3.	Religion	1. Officially Hindu kingdom 2. Freedom to profess and practice own religion as handed down to him from ancient times having due regard to traditional practices 3. Prohibition to convert person from one religion to another 4. Right to maintain independent existence of every religious group, and for this purpose right to manage and protect its religious places and trusts.
4.	Language	1. Nepali in the Devnagari script is the national as well as the official language of Nepal 2. All the languages spoken as mother tongue in the various parts of Nepal are the national languages of Nepal 3. Right to operate schools in its own mother tongue upto the primary level
5.	Civil Society	1. Freedom to form unions and associations 2. Freedom to assemble peacefully and without arms 3. Freedom to opinion and express 4. Freedom to move throughout the kingdom and reside in any part thereof 5. Freedom to practice any profession or to carry on any occupation, industry or trade

Source: The constitution of the kingdom of Nepal (1990), Kathmandu: His majesty government, ministry of law, justice and parliamentary affairs, law books management board computed by the author.

As already discussed, although the 1990 constitution aimed to be a democratic constitution by making provision for freedom and equality, caste/ethnic, religious, regional (Tarai and remote area) and linguistic groups were not happy by the 1990 constitution. It was because the constitution declared only Nepali Language as official language and unitary structure of the state. Apart from that, on the issue of religion, the constitution remained same as the previous constitution of 1962. Not withstanding that all groups tried to join the democratic process by getting memberships of different political parties and other institutions. New forums like parties, identity-related organizations and NGOs were formed not only to enjoy democratic rights but also to contribute to the country and people. After installation of democracy, about six dozens new political parties emerged. Along with parties, many frontier organizations of the parties came into the scene. Within a year of democratic system, some 15,000 NGOs were registered. Most of these were either Dalit or ethnicity, or gender, or language, or religion-based. All the NGOs started advocating their agenda to the people.

On the other, media came to enjoy freedom and autonomy after the installation of democracy. Electronic media, especially the Radio Nepal started broadcasting available news freely. Print media also got democratized during the period. Many FM radios, private television channels, and print media got permissions from the government to serve the country. Such increased media activities led to people's consciousness. People themselves started raising their agenda in the local and state level forums. The agenda, raised in different forms reached to the people through media. People through the media, got to know of the exploitative policy of the state with regard to the particular community, the hidden interest underlying every policy and program of the state. In summary, the 1990s constitution directly made the people annoyed, but because the democratic provisions in the constitution, people from all walks of life were benefited indirectly.

The Election Manifestos of Parties: Political parties are inevitable aspects of the democratic system. There is a strong tie between the parties and the people. The parties represent the people by getting their votes, and rule the country. The governments are formed by the political parties; gaining majority support is the main democratic norms to govern the country. Having realized this fact, those who had taken part in democratic movement to bring emancipatory democracy, tried to compel the main political parties to address their agenda at the policy as well as implementation level. Their demand was to implement agenda provided in the constitution and to accommodate new policy if that was not covered by the constitution.

In democracy each and every political party goes to the people with its policy and program and after being elected, they have obligation to go through the 'blue print' called election manifesto. This section explores the election manifestos of the parties in regard to two aspects. The first is to examine how the parties addressed the issues of people that arose in the 1990s mass movement. The second is to analyze whether the parties confine themselves on the policy and program they declared earlier or not. Table 9 examines the election manifestos of six major political parties in the last three general elections of Nepal. The analysis has primarily been done keeping in context of the aspect of caste/ethnicity, region, and language. These are:

Table 9: **Election Manifestos of the Parties in the Elections 1991, 1994 and 1999 (on Caste/Ethnicity and Regional Groups)**

Party	*Issues*	*Provisions*
NC	Ethnicity/ language	**In 1991** Preservation and promotion of different languages, cultures and traditions existing in the country; elimination of regional and community disparity in development **Added in 1994** Use of mother tongues in education and communication; establishment of institute relating to culture of different communities

(Table 9 Contd.)

Party	*Issues*	*Provisions*
		Added in 1999 Set up culture centers to promote songs, dance and cultures of different communities; set up an independent council of janajati; protect and promote knowledge, skill, art and culture of indigenous groups; empowerment of indigenous groups in education and health program
	Region	**In 1991** Equal opportunity for job in police, army and civil services without discrimination; distribution of citizenship certificate
	Caste/Dalit	**Added in 1994** Special provisions in education and law to marginalized groups; scholarship for Dalit students **Added in 1999** Representation of Dalits and backward communities in party, parliament and others; set up an independent council for Dalits; utilization of Dalits' skill and knowledge
UML	Ethnicity/ language	**In 1991** Secular state; abolish constitutional/legal provisions of discrimination on caste/ethnicity, language, religion, and culture; make constitutional provision for the representation of backward janajati to National Assembly; autonomy to local elected body for the promotion of caste/ethnic, language, religion and culture; primary education by mother tongue **Added in 1999:** Set up academy for ethnic, language, religion and cultural development
	Region	**In 1991** End region-based discrimination in recruitment in army

(Table 9 Contd.)

Party	*Issues*	*Provisions*
	Caste/Dalit	**Added in 1994** Abolition of untouchability; reservation for backward communities and areas in education, health and civil services
NSP	Ethnicity/ language	**In 1991** Freedom of religion; primary education on mother tongue **Added in 1994** Reservation of 30 percent seats to hill ethnic people in government and semi-government jobs
	Region	**In 1991** Reservation of 50 percent seats to tarai people in government and semi-government jobs; set up a separate battalion of army for Tarai people; making voter list of 1980 referendum as cut off year for distribution of citizenship; recognize Hindi as second national language; federal government
	Caste/Dalit	**In 1991** Free education and scholarship to Dalits
RPP	Ethnicity/ language	**In 1991** Protection and promotion of language, culture, tradition and religion of Janjati; promote interest of janajati on social, economic and political spheres; representation of janajati in governance **Added in 1994** Introduce language course of different mother tongues up to secondary school; special provision to include in education and job; representation in leadership at social, economic and political spheres; restructure National Assembly as a representative body of janajati, Dalit and Madhesi

(Table 9 Contd.)

Party	*Issues*	*Provisions*
		Added in 1999 Follow UN provisions related to indigenous concerned; include in National Planning Commission; equal respect to languages of all nationalities like that of national language; respect to right of education in mother tongue; public holiday for festival of all communities
	Region	**In 1991** Respect for causes/demands of tarai people; equal opportunity to tarai people in military, police and civil services; end of citizenship problem **Added in 1999** Representation in Public Service Commission; respect Madhesi sentiment in local leadership in both parties and in elected bodies
	Caste/Dalits	**In 1991** Priority to overall development of Dalits and backward communities **Added in 1999** Strict implementation of Muluki Ain; protection and promotion of traditional skill and profession of Dalits; representation in party
UPF	Ethnicity/ language	**In 1991** Secular state; equal status to all languages; right to use mother tongue in education, court and legislature; reservation for Dalits and ethnic groups in National Assembly **Added in 1994** Ethnic autonomy **Added in 1999** End of domination on caste, linguistic, religious group; make National Assembly as Ethnic House

(Table 9 Contd.)

Party	*Issues*	*Provisions*
	Caste/Dalits	**In 1991** End of untouchability; reservation for Dalits and backward communities in education, health and employment
NWPP	Ethnicity/ language	**In 1991** Freedom of religion and protection of tradition of religious tolerance **Added in 1999** Protection and promotion of language, literature and culture of different communities
	Region	**In 1991** Resolve citizenship problem

Source: Krishna Hachhethu 2003: Election Manifestos (1991, 1994, 1999) of NC, UML, RPP, UPF, NWPP and NSP.

Table 9 shows that there are much overlapping issues incorporated in the election manifestos of the different political parties. The freedom that came with parliamentary democracy in 1990 led to the formation of organizations, organization of peaceful protests to raise their voices and demands. Using such freedom, Dalits, women, and the ethnic communities expressed their grievances by forming different forums. Slowly, the elected governments tried to address their agenda such as the broadcast of news over the national radio in regional languages and the establishment of the National Committee for Development of Nationalities (NCDN), setting up of women as well as National Dalit Commission etc. Inability to declare Nepal as secular state and lack of effort to the affirmative programs of the government to empower the marginalized communities were the main causes, which led to the frustration of the ethnic/caste and religious communities. The Maoist 'capitalized' on this and got positive responses from the suppressed and marginalized people of Nepal.

The Policy and Program of the Maoist Party: The Maoist party (the then CPN Unity Center) began mobilizing oppressed ethnic communities in its struggle since 1991 when it adopted the twin agenda of secular state and linguistic/ethnic equality. Ever since, it has taken various initiatives on their issues. The significant ones were the formation of All Nepal Nationalities Association (1994), adoption of Ethnic Policy (1995), ethnic right to self-determination (1997), establishment of Ethnic Department at the central level and formation of 11 ethnic/regional fronts (1998), Ethnic and Regional Coordinating Committee (May 2001) and United Revolutionary People's Council (September 2001). In the meantime, the Maoist not only tried to capitalize the sentiments of the suppressed group by raising the radical slogans but also began its implementation by declaring autonomous zone, frontier organizations etc. it launched the insurgency in February 1996 with a Charter of 40-points demands. Of these demands, seven were related to nationalism, 13 to political, 13 to economic, and 7 to socio-cultural issues. Among seven socio-cultural issues, five (ethnic autonomy, devolution, secular state, ending ethnic oppression, and equality of languages) were in consonance with the ethnic agenda.

The Maoist, for the first time, declared the first district *Janasarkar* (people's government) in Rukum district and appointed Purna Bahadur Gharti, a member of 'marginalized' caste group, as convener of the Janasarkar in December 20, 2000. By June 2001, the Maoist had declared district Janasarkars in three districts—Salyan, Jagarkot and Rukum. It adjusted the political boundary of 24 hill districts into 21 districts, which is not properly on the basis of official political map of Nepal. It tried to merge two and more districts in a district Janasarkar (Sharma 2002:12, Seddon 2002:16). It declared 21 districts level Janasarkars in November 2001. These were: Rukum, Rolpa, Salyan, Jajarkot, Dailekh, Achham, Bajura, Jumla, Kalikot, Dolakha, Dhading, Gorkha, Tanahun, Parbat, Palpa, Lamjung, Sankhuwasabha, Remechap, Sindhuli, Sindhupalchowk, Gulmi, Nuwakot, Rasuwa, and Terhathum. The caste/ethnic compositions of those areas are given in Table 10.

Table 10: **Caste/Ethnic Composition in the 24 Districts with the Maoist Influence**

District	*Ethnic*	*Dalit*	*Newar*	*Total*
Nepal	34.6	8.7	5.6	
Rolpa	43.78	16.77	0	60.55
Rukum	23.15	6.16	0	29.31
Salyan	4.89	2.83	0.69	8.41
Jajarkot	8.69	24.9	0	33.59
Kalikot	0	2.35	0	2.35
Dolakha	28.73	7.22	7.75	43.7
Ramechhap	37.69	11.72	14.09	63.5
Sindhuli	41.37	20.55	6.49	68.41
Sindhupalchowk	43.93	6.08	11.09	61.1
Gorkha	36.83	10.48	8.11	55.42
Achham	0	29.36	0	29.36
Dhading	40	9.28	9.58	58.86
Tanahun	39.25	12.68	7.98	59.91
Dailekh	9.87	22.5	0.5	32.87
Parbat	15.81	20.57	2.49	38.87
Palpa	53.56	10.35	3.61	67.52
Lamjung	38.04	14.7	3.8	56.54
Sankhuwasabha	58	4.4	5.6	68
Terhathum	39.5	4.19	2.76	46.45
Gulmi	22.4	18.4	1.84	42.64
Jumla	0	13	0	13
Bajura	0	19.9	0	19.9
Rasuwa	72.73	2.02	2.8	77.55
Nuwakot	46.5	2.78	7.6	56.88

Source: ISRSC, 2004, computed by the Author.

Table 10 shows the composition of population of the caste/ethnic and Dalit group where the Maoist has already declared 'people's government'. The population composition in these 24 hilly districts show that in 12 districts more than half of its population is from ethnic/caste communities. In six districts, their population form 33 to 50 percent and in remaining six districts their share is less than 33 percent. The Maoist declared two types of autonomous areas based on caste/ethnicity and region. Out of 24 districts, where the Maoist government has been formed, 18 districts have 33 to 68 percent ethnic/Dalit population. Having a look of such scenario, one can conclude that the Maoist has gained appreciative support from the ethnic/Dalit population.

Between 1998 and 2000, the Maoist formed about a dozen ethnic/regional front organizations. These fronts were formed on the basis of nationalities and religions. Among 11 front organizations, only two (Madhesh and Karnali) are based on region. The rest are formed on the basis of the different nationalities. The Maoist nominated all the heads of the front from the same identity. It is said that the Maoist has applied the policy to lure the 'marginalized' groups. The name of front organizations with their heads, are given in Table 11.

Table 11: **Caste/Ethnic and Region-based Frontier Organization of the Maoist and its Leadership**

No.	*Name of organizations*	*President*
1.	Magarat National Liberation Front	Suresh Aale Magar
2.	Tamang National Liberation Front	Ganga Bahadur Tamang
3.	Tamuwan National Liberation Front	Mohan Tamu
4.	Limbuwan National Liberation Front	Bhakta Raj Kandangwa
5.	Nepal Dalit Liberation Front	Thaman Pariyar
6.	Tharuwan National Liberation Front	Ram Charan Choudhary
7.	Madheshi National Liberation Front	Jaya Krishna Goit
8.	Karnali Regional Liberation Front	Khadak Bahadur Bishowkarma
9.	Thami Liberation Front	Chun Bahadur Thami
10.	Majhi National Liberation Front	Tul Bahadur Majhi
11.	Newa Khala	Dilip Maharjan

Source: Sharma, 2002, Sharma, 2001 and *Janadesh* Year 15, Vol. (13) 2006.

Apart from the 11 fronts, the Maoist declared nine regional autonomous governments and its leaders were deployed as head of the government in January and February 2004. The strategy to win the sentiment of the 'marginalized' groups has been repeated again here. Of nine regions, six are named and formed on the basis of ethnicity and the three are on the basis of region. The details of the Maoist declared regional autonomous governments are shown in Table 12:

Table 12: **The CPN (Maoist) Regional Autonomous Government**

	Name of autonomous regions	*Areas*	*Head*
1.	Kirat Autonomous Region	Hill areas of Mechi, Koshi and Sagarmatha zones	Gopal Khambu
2.	Tambsaling Autonomous Region	Hill areas of Bagmati Narayani and Janakpur zones except Kathmandu valley	Hit Bahadur Tamang
3.	Newar Autonomous Region	Kathmandu valley	Yet to be announced
4.	Tamuwan Autonomous Region	Hill areas between Kali Gandaki to Budhi Gandaki	Dev Gurung
5.	Magarat Autonomous Region	Hill areas from west of Kali Gandaki to Dhulagiri, Rapti and Lumbini zones	Santosh Buddha Magar
6.	Tharuwan Autonomous Region	Western Tarai areas from Rapti to Mahakali zones	Ram Charan Choudhary
7.	Madhesh Autonomous Region	Tarai of Awadhi, Bhojpuri and Maithili-speaking areas	Matrika Yadav
8.	Bheri-Karnali Autonomous Region	Hill areas of Bheri and Karnali zones	Khadga Bahadur Bishowkarma
9.	Seti-Mahakali Autonomous Region	Hill areas of Seti and Mahakali zones	Lekh Raj Bhatta

Source: Computed by Sharma, 2002, Sharma, 2003 and *Janadesh* special issue 2006.

In short, the Maoist tried to capitalize on the sentiment of the 'marginalized' communities by making provisions and forming frontiers of nationalities. They tried to provide space for a higher proportion of Janajati representation. For example, of the then 55 members' central committee in 2002, 21 are from Janajati (Sharma 2002:26); of the 37 members of the United Revolutionary People's Council 17 are from Janajati and two from Dalit. Again, of 23 district 'Peoples' Government' chairperson 15 are from Janajati, seven from high caste, and one from Dalit (Gurung 2005). The Maoist party has still problem of inclusion at the top level; all the threefold Maoist organizations (the party, the UPF and the PLA) are headed by hill Brahmans. Out of seven members of the party standing committee of the Maoist, only two were from ethnic community

Organization: Nepal's Maoist has attempted to emulate the classic Chinese communist structure of 'three magic weapons': party, army, and united front. It has followed the Chinese threefold system, within which it has generally emphasized the development of the party over the army and both of these over the united front. For Mao Tse-tung, party, peoples' army and united front are the three weapons for a people's revolution. This has been 'embraced' by the Nepalese Maoist. The objective principle of these three weapons is also different. The party has to involve in spreading the party's ideology as well as formulating policies related to the 'people's war'; the army has to engage for attacking 'enemies' and defending the areas under its control, and the united front have a responsibility to consolidate friendly forces with the view to creating the prerequisites for the proposed 'people's government[9] (Sharma 2003:362).

The party, whose overall control remains firmly with the 'party headquarters', which in practice means Prachanda, has overall responsibility for all activities related to the 'people's war' and for the development of policy. The standing committee, politburo, central committee, divisional commands, regional bureaus, sub-regional bureaus, district, area, and cell committees are the hierarchical layers of the party. Seven to ten members must be in standing committee of the Maoist. At least 27 members including some alternative members must be in the politburo. In the central committee, the number of members is flexible. In 1996, there were nearly 100 members in the central committee. At the second national conference in February 2001, the number was only 55 members. Neither the standing committee nor the politburo exists in the Maoists' organization today. These, according to the Maoist, will be formed in the forthcoming general convention of the party. There are various central wings under the party headquarter, and also a central advisory body. The advisory body consists of nine to 11 members, who are elected/nominated from the heads of their frontier organizations. It has five regional bureaus under central committee, various sub-regional bureaus and in some places, even special sub-regional bureaus under the regional bureaus.

The People's Liberation Army (PLA), which is under the full control of the 'party headquarters', is responsible for both offensive operations against the 'enemy side' and defensive arrangements. It is said that the Maoist developed and organized the 'people's army' only after the Kilo Sierra 2 operation of the government on May 1998-April 1999 (*Nepal Samachar Patra*, December 17, 2000). In August 1998, the Maoists' fourth expanded central committee meeting (plenum) adopted the slogan of building 'base areas' and building up military strength in order to challenge government repression. Prachanda retains the top positions of the PLA as a supreme commander; total authority regarding the mobilization of the 'people's army is vested' in the commander. There are regional, sub-regional and district level military wings under the central military commission. The organizational structure of PLA is division, brigade, battalion, company, platoon, squad and then militias. There are even poorly armed fighters who have not received full guerrilla training. It is reported that there are areas such as Kathmandu, where 'special taskforces' have been established. Its strength is hard to estimate. Each and every army unit is under the dual control of the military commander and the political commander.

Analysts suggest that the Maoist has only a few thousand hardcore fighters. According to Gen. Ashok K. Mehta (Mehta, 2005:94) of India and Sadip Bahadur Shah, a military expert and retired RNA lieutenant-general, the Maoist has 4,000 armed guerrillas, 5,000 militia who have received guerrilla training and 20,000 armed militia (*Samay*, December 30, 2004). Militia members (a poorly armed and do not wear uniforms) are not generally expected to carry out the guerrilla duties as mainstream fighters. However, they can be called upon as reinforcements. According to the International Crisis Group (ICG) report of October 27, 2005, the Maoist claims to have more than 10,000 armed guerrillas in their nine brigades. In fact, at the RNA press conference, Colonel Victory

S. J. B. Rana had made a somewhat similar estimate; some 9,500 guerrillas and 25,000 militia (*The Kathmandu Post*, May 21, 2005). The number is either underestimated or exaggerated. For the Maoist, the number is their strength; hence they tend to give exaggerate their strength. The ICG report October 2005, termed the number claim by both the RNA and the Maoist as 'higher estimates'. It says:

> Of course, the Maoist and the RNA both have reasons to give higher estimates. The Maoist obviously wants to create the impression that they have a mass support base and a considerable fighting force. The RNA is faced with the problem that earlier state estimates of a small Maoist guerrilla cadre simply do not tally with their depiction of the current situation (*ICG Report*, October 27, 2005:9)

The concept of the 'united front' was central to Mao's thinking in China. Its principle objective is to 'unite with all forces that can be united with in order to fight a common struggle against the enemy and the unity is to win revolution, and to the construction' (Kwok-Sing Li (tr. Mary Lok) 1995: 451). The quotation seems a simple idea but it is too difficult in application. From the time of the anti-Japanese struggle, Mao formulated and continually emphasized the 'unity-struggle-autonomy' policy: 'develop the progressive force, win over the in-between force, and combat the obstinate force' (*Ibid*:452). From the beginning of the 1990s, the Nepali Maoist planned to create a particular type of united front, which will not only be a broad coalition of organizations assisting in the revolutionary struggle but also build bridges with mainstream parties. Later, the United Front has come to predominate in Nepali Maoist discourse.

Before 2000, there was a 16-members 'united people's front'. This was dissolved in February 2000 when the party concluded that it could not play the role of the grand united front that had been envisaged for it. Alternatively, it formed a similar type organization in the form of 'united people's committee'. The committee exists in parallel with the central and local government bodies. The central body of the 'united front' is the United Revolutionary People's Council, Nepal was declared in September 2001 during the first ceasefire. There were 37 members in United Revolutionery People's Council (URPC). Its role was to mobilize 'various left, progressive, patriotic and democratic forces'. The front partially reflects the 'people's democratic front' of the early People's Republic of China. The front was headed by Baburam Bhattarai; Krishna Bahadur Mahara worked as assistant convener and Dev Gurung as secretary (*Press statement of URPC*, November 26, 2001). Now, there are 'regional', 'district', and 'village' level people's governments under the URPC. Between 1998 and 2000, there were about a dozen ethnic and regional fronts formed by the Maoist with the aim of creating a grand united front. On the other hand, there were at least 22 front organizations working under the Maoist party (Mehta 2005:96–97). Before the declaration of a state of emergency in November 2001, the front organizations of the Maoist had carried out open or semi-underground activities. However, after the state of emergency in Nepal, all of them went underground. The most influential among these has been the All-Nepal National Free Students Union (Revolutionary) led by Lekhnath Neupane. Other active organizations include the Nepal Trade Union Federation (Revolutionary) led by Salikram Jamarkattel, the All-Nepal Women's Association (Revolutionary) led by Jayapuri Gharti, the All-Nepal Janajati Federation led by Suresh Aale Magar, the All-Nepal Teacher's Organisation (Revolutionary) led by Gunaraj Lohani, the Nepal National Intellectuals Organisation and the All-Nepal People's Cultural Union led by Mani Thapa, and the All-Nepal Peasants Association led by Shivaraj Gautam. The leadership of the Nepal National Intellectuals Organization has not been published yet. With the main tasks of advancing Maoist aims through industrial action and to mobilize a support base by organizing laborers in various sectors of the formal economy, Nepal Trade Union Federation (Revolutionary) brought together some dozen small unions. These have been the All-Nepal Carpet Workers Union, All-Nepal Transport Workers Union, All-Nepal Hotel and Restaurant Workers Union, All-Nepal Construction Workers Union, All-Nepal Meter Tempo Workers Union, All-Nepal Press Workers Union, All-Nepal Thangka Art Workers Union, All-Nepal Painters Union, Nepal Shop Workers Union, Nepal Progressive Newspaper Vendors Union and Himalayan Trekking Workers Union.

To assess the popular support of a party is a difficult task. Hisila Yami (Parvati), a women leader of the Maoist claimed women membership in women mass organization of the Maoist around

600,000 (Parvati 2003: 271). Likewise, Shiva Raj Gautam, chairperson of All-Nepal Peasant Union (Revolutionary) has claimed some 1,950,000 members in his organization (*Kishan Sandesh* 2005:48). It has already mentioned that there are at least 22 front organizations and the all claim their membership in hundreds of thousands. It seems that the Maoist has distributed hundreds of thousands memberships through its front organization as well as the party.

If the party were take part in the election, it may have been possible to address the question. Again, if an organization were to work in transparent manner, the membership of an organization may have been taken as a reliable source to indicate its base among the people. However, both do not seem to be applicable in the context of the Maoist. On the one hand, they have not participated in the elections after declaration of the 'people's war', on the other, the party has equipped itself with arms and weapons, and has worked in an underground manner. In the given situation, it is difficult to analyze whether people took the membership of the Maoist party and its front organizations by people's own will or the Maoist rebels compelled people to take its membership.

The membership of NC and CPN (UML), the major parties in Nepal, were 250,000 and 450,000 respectively in the late 1995. However, in the recent three general elections of 1991, 1994 and 1999, the NC got only 2,752,445 (37.75 percent), 2,545,287 (33.38 percent), and 3,214,746 (36.15 percent); respectively the UML got 2,040,102 (27.98 percent), 2,352,601(30.85 percent) and 2,734,586 (30.74 percent) votes (Hachhethu 2002:75). It is to be noted that the Maoist had participated in 1991 election in which they had owns only nine out of 205 seats in the parliament. They had polled only 351,904 votes (4.83 percent vote) and were the third largest party in the parliament. In 1994, a faction of the UPFN led by Baburam Bhattarai boycotted the general election. It joined the 'people's war' in 1996. Another faction led by Niranjan Govinda Baidhya took part the 1994 and 1999 elections in which it polled only 100,285 (1.32 percent) and 74,669 (0.83 percent) votes respectively.

To examine the grassroot hold of the Maoist we have to wait till the elections result of the 'Constituent Assembly Election' which are in the process. According to the RNA estimate, 'beyond their armed cadres and 14,000 political workers, the Maoist may have some 100,000 supporters' (*The Kathmandu Post*, May 21, 2005). Examining the approximate strength of the Maoist in December 2004, Gen. Ashok K. Mehta categorically mentioned that there were 2,67,000 people's support to the Maoist. Among them 4,000 are armed guerrillas, 5,000 militias trained as guerillas, 20,000 are unarmed militias, 14,000 are political activists, 24,000 are supporters and 200,000 sympathizers (Mehta 2005:94). The assessment is similar to one predicted by Retired RNA Lieutenant-General Sadip Bahadur Shah (*Samay*, December 30 2004).

After analyzing the situation of threefold system of the organizational structure, the Maoist party can be drawn as follows:

Organizational Structure of the CPN (Maoist)

The Party	**The Army**	**The United Front**
Standing Committee	Headquarter	United People's Revolutionary Council, Nepal
|	|	|
Politburo	Divisions (3)	Ethnic and regional 'autonomous people's governments' (8)
|	|	|
Central Committee	Brigades (9)	United District People's Committees
|	|	|
Central Command (3)	Battalions (29)	United Area People's Committees
|	|	|
Regional bureaus	Companies	United Village People's Committees
|	|	|
Sub-regional bureaus	Platoons	United Ward People's Committees
|	|	
District committees	Squads [The 'people's militias' organized on a local basis are separate from other military units]	
|		
Area committees		
|		
Cell committees		

Source: Sharma 2003 in Deepak Thapa 2003:379 and Crisis Group Asia Report, October 27, 2005:40.

Strategy: As mentioned earlier, for Maoist, party, 'peoples' army', and united front are the three weapons for a people's revolution. Their 'single' objective is to capture power through 'people's war'. To attain that, the party tried to influence the people to join the war. In the process, it laid to rest the myth that Nepal is a peaceful country whose citizens are naturally averse to violence. The Maoist has consistently maintained that violence has been at the heart of the state power throughout Nepal's history. Prachanda argued against the popular notion of Nepalese being peace-loving and non-violent people. Such idea ascending to him is against the historical fact. To Prachanda, such 'historical fact' is a conspiracy to mentally disarm the people, and to protect their rule for their reactionary violence (Prachanda 1996:202). To him, Nepalese society has reached to its present style through the course of increasing struggle of the Nepalese people and deception, conspiracy and repression of the reactionaries. The struggles are local and nationwide including rural class conflict for nationalism, democracy, and livelihood. According to the Maoist, historical materialism has shown that the process of violent conflict among men is inseparably linked with the situation of division of labor, emergence of private property and development of social class division. Prachanda further says, 'we communist are clear on the scientific fact that it is necessary to raise the flag of just war in order to oppose the unjust war being conducted by the exploiting class and to end war forever amongst the human being.' (Prachanda 1997a: 205). The policy on armed struggle adopted by the CPN (M) in its third plenum in March 1995 made it even more explained.

> 'The reactionary propaganda that the Nepalese people are peace-loving and that they don't like violence is absolutely false. It is an incontrovertible fact that the Nepalese people have been waging violent struggle for their rights since...historical times. Till today whatever general reforms have been achieved by the Nepalese people, behind them there was the force of violent and illegal struggle of the people' (CPN (M), March 1995).

This point was reinforced by Prachanda in a separate essay. He wrote, 'people have not obtained even the least of gains without waging violent struggles. Today, the Nepalese society has arrived at such a point of crisis under the existing political system that there is no alternative on the part of the people other than to smash it' (Prachanda 1996:202). According to Prachanda, to become a genuine Marxist-Leninist revolutionary, one has to support the theory of 'people's war'. Elaborating the three stages of strategy he says, 'for the success of a revolution in the country like ours that lies in the semi-feudal and semi-colonial condition it is essential to pass through the three stages of the strategic defense, equilibrium and strategic offence with the strategy of seizing towns from the rural areas' (Prachanda 1999:146, 206). Initially they adopted Guerrilla war because it had a key role in the first stage. The Maoist itself compared the Guerrilla war to the Shah Dynasty's state expansion campaign. It was even compared to the world history and said, 'the guerilla warfare has been effective when pro-people forces carry on war against anti-people army with relatively more equipped with training and arms' (Prachanda 1997a:207). Prachanda has mentioned five key conditions for the success in Guerrilla war in Nepal. These are:

- A correct ideological and political line (Marxism-Leninism-Maoism) of the leadership.
- To be conducted for the masses and by the masses.
- Need for a continuous process of awakening and organizing more and more people through faster and better methods.
- Basic tactics must be followed. Under the tactic of 'hit and run', Prachanda referred some sub-tactics. These are: when enemy advances, we retreat, centralizing our forces to fight the enemy, decentralizing it to arouse the masses, finding out the weakest points of the enemy with adequate preparation and to attack by ensuring victory, carrying out dependable geographical and other surveys, always trying to keep enemy in surprise, maintaining regular alertness, mobility and secrecy etc.
- Building base area for mobilizing and regularizing the war. (*Ibid*:208-209)

In an other essay Prachanda mentioned six strategies and tactics of war. They are: (1) tactics of surprise attacks, (2) to attack weak enemy at first and stronger the later, (3) to take advantage of contradictions among the enemies, (4) to adopt a policy of intrigue, conspiracy and deception, (5) to apply the method of embargo against enemy, and (6) to adopt the technique of protracted war. According to the Maoist, these are developed from the experiences of the past wars like Gorkhalese war (Prachanda 1996:197-198) for 'unification'. Mao argues, 'Correctness and incorrectness of ideological and political line decides everything. If the line is correct everything will come in its way if it is wrong everything will be lost which one hand before'. Ananta ally Barsaman Pun, a division commander of Maoist army says that the concept of 'correctness of the political line decides everything'. Through that one is able 'to educate, organize, and make millions of masses agitate', on the basis of the ideology of the party is 'advancing ahead in the direction of acquiring universal character' (Ananta 2003:214-220). The following are ten tactical principles expressed in the Prachanda path:

1. Give priority to the work in village, but do not leave the work in cities too.
2. Give priority to the illegal struggle, but do not leave the legal struggle too.
3. Give priority to certain strategic areas, but do not leave other areas too.
4. Give priority to the work of war, but do not leave works of the mass movement too.
5. Give priority to clandestine work, but do not leave open works too.
6. Give priority to the rural class struggle, but do not leave countrywide struggle too.
7. Give priority to the guerrilla actions, but do not leave political exposition and propaganda work too.
8. Give priority to the work inside the country, but do not leave worldwide propaganda work too.
9. Give priority to the work of military organization, but do not leave work of building front organizations too.
10. Give priority to depending upon own organization and strength, but don't leave tactical unity and the question of taking help and support from international opinion too (Prachanda 2004:20).

The Maoists' another important strategy is to capitalize the sentiment of the suppressed groups of people like Dalit, women, ethnic/native group, regionally backward groups like Tarai people and Karnali area people, etc. which has been providing a vital role to strengthen the movement. The Maoist advocate the united front at the level of all oppressed nationalities and regions under the policy of 'unite and struggle' in the place of their enemy's policy of 'divide and rule'. Realizing the importance to address the sentiment of the entire suppressed group, the Maoist began to think the need of a concrete and practical program to struggle against national and regional oppression. It made special efforts to do 'serious studies on the nature of national and regional oppression of the people of different areas, their economic, political cultural and geographic background and to prepare a concrete plan for national autonomy and to build united front accordingly' (Prachanda 1997b:277-278). After the politburo meeting of January 1997, the Maoist agreed to integrate the demands of all the suppressed groups/minorities as integral part of their campaign and agreed to give the right of self-determination to the ethnic and regional groups. To 'lure' the ethnic community the Maoist established an ethnic department at the central level in 2000, which was headed by Dev Gurung.

3.3. ORIGIN, GROWTH AND SPREAD OF THE MAOIST MOVEMENT IN NEPAL

Origin: The Maoist first started its people's war from Gorkha, Sindhuli, Rolpa and Rukum districts. The first two districts are situated in central-western and central-eastern hill respectively and the last two are located in the mid-west of Nepal. In February 13, 1996, some hundred Maoist captured the office of the Small Farmers Development Program (SFDP) of Chyangli Village Development Committee (VDC) of Gorkha. The SFDP program launched under the government-owned Agriculture Development Bank is assisted by the Asian Development Bank since 1974. The Maoist seized Bank's cash, loan papers and land registration certificates deposited by peasants. A short speech exposing the mechanism of exploitation of poor peasants and need of capturing the government institution was made in front of the local people. After that, they dispersed.

In Sindhuli, it was the Sindhuligadhi police post, which was captured by the Maoist. This was followed by a long discourse on 'new democratic revolution' to the captured police and their families. They tied down the captured policemen, covered them with warm quilts and disappeared with substantial amount of high explosives and other utilities.

Another attack by the Maoist was on the Athbiskot-Rani police outpost in Rukum. There too they followed the same line as they in Sindhuli. These three attacks were quite smooth. The Maoist did not face any counter-attack by the state security. However, in Holeri police outpost of Rolpa there was firing from both sides, which went on almost for two hours. Ultimately, the Maoist ransacked the post, seized the store, and took all hold of the useful warfare materials. They made a short speech before leaving the post explaining objectives to policemen, their family members, and the curious villagers gathered at the site.

Apart from their actions, as per the Maoist report, a multinational company (Pepsi) situated in Kathmandu valley was attacked and a portion of the building was torched. A distillery 'owned by a comprador bourgeois' was blasted in Gorkha, and the house of a 'notorious feudal-usurer' in Kavre in the central-eastern Nepal was also raided on the same day. Along with that, they have distributed thousands of leaflets and posters; organized the 'March on' program, where the slogan raised by the party was 'the path of people's war to smash the reactionary state and establish a democratic state.' The 'March on' program launched in the major cities and headquarters of more than 60 districts in Nepal (*The Worker* 1996).

There are lots of statements and presumptions about the principle causes of the Maoists' attacks on different places. The Maoist in Nepal has been trying to show the cause which are based on 'class'. However, the cause 'class' is a traditional and a readymade show card to all, who believe in communism. According to the Maoist, they got support from poor people and hit the 'semi-feudal and semi-colonial' Nepali state. They used to say, 'we communists are clear on the scientific facts that it is necessary to raise the flag of just war in order to oppose the unjust war being conducted by the exploiting class and to end war forever amongst the human being. In the class society, it is impossible to make a forward leap without a revolutionary war' (Prachanda 1997a:205). However, in reality there are many causes, which led people to join the Maoist.

There are various factors to examine why the Rapti zone became initiating area of the Maoist movement. Of these factors, I have focused mainly on three: (1) the role of Mohan Bikram Singh, who spread the communist ideology in this area after going underground since 1957, (2) the brutal state repression on the Magar community while they were engaged in the struggle, and (3) the presence of the forest, which offers a natural opportunity for guerrilla operations.

No doubt, there is poverty in Rapti zone as well. However, poverty alone has not only been responsible for the people of Rapti to join the Maoist Movement. Tharus, one of the major ethnic groups in Tarai, and other Tarai communities are very poor in comparison to Magars in Rapti. Again, the situation of Tharus and other Tarai communities seem far worse than the Magars in the issue of the exploitation by large landlords. Baburam Bhattarai, the then convener of UPFN, accepted this fact and told that the Tharus have to work in a kind of feudal relationship. He wrote, 'the feudal relation in Tarai is very much strong.' To him, 'majority of the people are poor peasants and substantial production system is there is hilly region' (Bhattarai, 2005:3-7). However, why the Tarai is not influenced by the Maoists' activities? If the movement is class-based, one wonders as to why the movement is in the hill, where, according to the Maoist, the feudal relation is nominal.

Some districts of the mid-western region like Rolpa, Rukum and Pyuathan had been exposed to communist influence since 1957. Mohan Bikram Singh, one of senior and very influential communist leader started his communist carrier in this region. Singh sensitized people on the issue of their rights and freedom. Because of political consciousness and value for democracy and freedom, people of the region contributed a lot to the democratic struggle of Nepal. Thawang, a VDC of Rolpa district, cast only four votes in 1980s referendum in support of the Panchayat system. The VDC boycotted the elections and returned empty ballot box in the first Rastriya Panchayat elections in 1981. Barman Buda, one of the followers of Singh started leading the Magar people of the region. He was later imprisoned for five years on charge of having burnt the picture of the king and queen in the 1980s. He was freed after the mass movement of 1990s, became a member of the parliament from UPFN party. In this election, UPFN won both the seats in Rolpa, and the party was right behind the NC in Rukum district.

The antagonism between the UPFN cadre and ruling NC cadres in Rukum and Rolpa after the first local elections of 1992 played vital role in increasing the Maoist influence in Rolpa and Rukum. In 1991 elections, the UPFN came close to the NC. After the elections, NC started ruling the country with the absolute majority in the parliament and the UPFN was busy in the village in the people's awareness campaign. Along with the campaign, the UPFN began 'taking action against those they considered exploiters, usurers and cheats' in the villages. Those affected by the UPFN action were most of the NC cadres. The local influential NC leaders were from the background of previous ruling Panchayat system. It seemed that the initial struggle was the two-party struggle. Latter, the nature of the struggle went into the state versus community.

Being the cadres of ruling party, many of local leaders of NC used the state machinery against their opponents. Three special police operations—'Operation Romeo', 'Kilo Siera II' and 'search and kill'—had been launched in the region. In November 1995, the government deployed a squadron of 165 policemen with 50 special military trained policemen and launched 'Operation Romeo'. The impact of the operation had been after described in INSEC Human Rights Year Book 1995 reports as follows:

> The government initiated … suppressive operations to a degree of state terror. Especially the workers of the UPFN were brutally suppressed. Under the direct leadership of ruling party workers of the locality, police searched, tortured and arrested, without arrest warrants, in 11 villages of the district. Nearly 6,000 locals had left the villages due to the police operation. One hundred and thirty-two people were arrested without serving any warrants. Among the arrested including elderly 75 years of age. All the detained were

subjected to torture (INSEC 1996).

Police in a collusion with the local NC leaders started to file 'false accusations' against its opponents. The District Administration Office (DAO) treated these as 'matter of public order'. The accused were asked to furnish such of Rs. 28,000 as a deposit for bail. The sum was far from affordable to the villagers. There was also doubt among the accused about free and fair hearing of the case. In this situation 'the majority of the accused found that the only solution was to run away into the forest or to the city, or the plains, or even to India in the hope of passing time until their relatives managed to sort out the dispute' (Sales 2003:81). The Maoist, which was trying to win people's sentiment, started capitalizing on this problem. It sent its 'hooded guerillas' to kill the informers or 'class enemies'. For the Maoist, the class enemies were those who made a 'false accusation' on the people. Those who left the village were compelled to face accusation of supporting the Maoist and taking part in the attack on villages. Baburam Bhattarai, in an interview said that more than 10,000 rural youth, out of a population of 200,000 for the whole district of Rolpa, have been forced to flee their homes and take shelters in remote jungles. The situation was created by the government, which sent around 1,550-especially trained commando force from Kathmandu (*Himal* 14/5 May 2001:10).

Such operation of the government helped to increase the cadres of the Maoist and eroded the credibility of the government in rural area. The following passage points to the scenario of the village after that operation;

> The organization of the daily life in the village is paralyzed: peasants who leave the village risk being arrested by the police who suspect them of helping the guerillas. Thus tiling animals to pasture, departing for summer residences, going to the forest to collect berries and mushrooms, which form a not insubstantial part of the village diet, have become either impossible or extremely problematic. Schools are closed. Young men, those who have not joined the guerillas in the forest, have left to hide in the big cities or in India. It is said that the women plough and the old people keep silent (Sales 2003:81).

The villagers were harassed by both; at night by Maoist who had to be fed and during the day by policemen looking for suspects, which Sales terms 'an impossible living situation'. However, villagers, irrespective of their political inclinations preferred the Maoist rather than the police. It is so because of the behavior of police who treated the villagers not only as an 'evil' but also as a 'milk giving cow'. In contrast, the Maoist which was similar to the security force in behaving the villagers has changed its modus operandi and started social work, raised socio-cultural agenda and respected villagers as parents. Even while Maoist cadres asked for food, they used to ask cheap, simple, and easily available things like maize and salt from the villagers whereas the police's demand would not be less than chicken and alcohol. Another cause of the villagers' hostility towards security personnels was that they were often beaten without any further investigation if the police suspected them. An opinion poll conducted by the then *Himal Khabarpatrika* of March 2001 proved that the brutality of security force had been seen as one of the main cause of support for the Maoist. According to the poll, 30 percent of the respondents attributed the rise of the Maoist to highhandedness of the security force.

The third factor for the emergence of the Rapti zone as the Maoists' initiating area has been the zone's geographical location. More than half of the districts of Rukum and Rolpa are forested which gives 'natural opportunity' to the guerrillas to hide from state security forces and to launch the training and other sorts of campaign in the jungle. The dense forest and remoteness became easier to the Maoist to hide its cadres from the state security. It became fruitful for their movement, and for supplying their weapons from one part to another. In the case of Tarai where there is 'more influential feudal culture than in hill', the Maoist realized that 'the geography is negative there to start the insurgency' (Bhattarai 2005:3-7). Such a natural opportunity has been used not only by Nepalese Maoist but also by Naxalites of India (Benerjee 1980:33-34).

Apart from those three causes, the hung parliament and its impact to instability on the government played a vital role in making the Maoist Movement influential. Power game among the parliamentary parties gave chance to the Maoist to put forward their agenda against the parliamentary democracy. In the mid-term elections of 1994, no party got majority in the parliament and people faced five prime ministers within four years. Deuba headed a coalition government from September 11, 1995 to March 6, 1997; Chanda headed the government from March 12, 1997 to October 4, 1997. The people had to make a very negative perceptions towards these two governments. Both the governments were busy in horse-trading in the parliament. The MPs used the parliament as a platform to make money and got their bill reimbursed submitting all sorts of bills; Male MPs submitted the pregnancy related bills and got reimbursement for their expenditures from the state. The state fund was much misused during the time. The government decided to give 'Pajero and pension' facilities to the MPs, which were very much criticized by the people. Those agenda were picked up by the Maoist and raised in front of the general people.

Having a look at Nepal's performance of parliamentary democracy after 1995, one can argue that the Maoist Movement has its backing from the 'frustrated' mass of the society. In the communist history of Nepal, preparation of such an armed struggle was made in 1980s and 1990s also. In 1982–83 Ayodhya plenums, Mohan Bikram Singh presented a report on the basic of the preparation of armed struggle keeping in mind 'Baghe Odhar' experience. Prachanda told that he had started to think about the theoretical and practical parts of the armed conflict when he had started to lead the youth league in 1983. Some radical communists of Nepal under the leadership of contemporary Masal group rigorously tried to prepare and launch such armed revolt against the Panchayat regime on the eve of the 'mass movement of 1990'. In the preparation phase, Prachanda himself was involved in preparing the armed skill training to the cadres by collecting arms. According to him, he with two other prominent leaders Badal and Dev Gurung were involved in active collection of the weapons. The three were able to buy two guns from Ganesh Bdr. Gurung of Manang district in 1989. However, Prachanda and Badal were able to escape the police search only by a few margins. They were on the way to Gorkha from Tanahun district with a gun and some explosives provided by Lekhnath Bhatta to the party. With those three guns, the party started a skill training Tiranchowk of Gorkha district against the state in Sirubari to use arm. Some 16 people participated as trainees. (*Nepal* 2006). After the training, they attempted a revolt in support of the movement, which according to Prachanda could not success because of a 'lack of proper preparation on ideological, political, and organizational level' (*Janadesh* 2006:19).

Realizing the above-mentioned weaknesses to launch armed revolt, the Maoist started to gather the scattered 'revolutionaries' and ultimately got success by organizing the CPN (Unity Centre). The 'unity general convention' of the CPN (Unity Centre) in 1991 has given the mandate to the 'Peoples' War'. After the convention, four types of preparations—ideological-political, organizational, technical and revolt—carried forward by the party for waging the 'People's War'. It tried to use both the underground and open way 'to strengthen rural class struggle' through underground party led by Prachanda. It tried to train people by continuing people's movements, mass meetings, and 'Nepal *bandh*' on issues such as 'nationality, people's democracy, and people's livelihood.' These were done through Baburam Bhattarai-led UPFN which was involved in open politics.

In its review on the great success of the struggles, the leaders of CPN Maoist intentionally and repeatedly put the term 'class' in the forefront. However, Prachanda once accepted the socio-cultural agenda they raised as influential cause. He told that the Maoist got people's support because of the 'right decision to address the problems based on caste/ethnicity, region, and gender' (*Janadesh* 2006:18). Even today, the Maoist has been strategically bringing the concept of the 'Joint front' to address the socio-cultural issues. However, it termed the concept as 'the experience of specific nature' (*Janadesh* 2006:19).

Growth and Expansion: The Maoist started the 'People's War' with only 200 cadres in 1996 (Philipson: 2002:19). Until September 1999, the Maoist was busy in 'struggle, propaganda and mobility'. Within that strategy, the Maoist launched some token/small attacks in its area with a view to draw the national and international attention. It ambushed two policemen in Tak VDC of Rukum on May 6,

1996. This is considered as its first attack. On January 4, 1997, the Bethan police post of Ramechap was captured by the Maoist rebellions. Three Maoist guerrillas lost their lives in this encounter. These guerrilla attacks were waged for propagandas. Till May/ June of 1997, it was assumed that the Maoist preserved and showed its effective influences only in 83 Village Development Committees (VDCs) of four neighboring districts of Rolpa, Rukum, Salyan and Jajarkot. The assumption was based on the Maoists' agenda of boycotting the 1997s local election. The boycott worked only in those 83 VDCs.

The Maoist declared the 'people's army' or 'Central Military Commission' under the leadership of Prachanda only on February 13, 1998. On the eve of the second year's anniversary of Bethan attack on January 3, 1999, the Maoist attacked the Bhattedanda police post of Lalitpur district and seized all the weapons. Lalitpur is in the Kathmandu valley and the attacked post was considered 'the nose of the Kathmandu valley'. In between the 'successful' attack of Bethan and Bhattedanda, a number of small and symbolic attacks like the attack on police patrol in Kalikatar of Tanahun district, Khahare in Dhading district, *Korbachong Nimri* of Rolpa district, Sourpani of Gorkha district, Jhimpe tower of Salyan district, Phalate of Kavre district, Nirmal Basti of Parsa district, Laliya of Dhanusa district were carried out. In all, the Maoist killed five policemen and got some weapons and money from those attacks. Apart from that, they captured local office of Nepal Bank and looted Rs. 20 lakh only from Khahare. The diversified and simultaneous attack, which covered at least four zones out of 14 total zones of Nepal, worked as propaganda. These attacks led to scare among the people as well as awareness about the Maoist.

After the Maoist disturbed 83 VDCs' local elections in Rapti zone in 1997, the government started thinking the program to 'sweep out' the Maoist from the villages. In May 1998 to May 1999, the government launched the Kilo Sierra II Operation in 18 Maoist-affected districts. This led to the killing of at least 500 people within a year (Sharma 2003:372). The Maoist attacked Mahatgaun police-base in Rukum on September 22, 1999, killed seven policemen and abducted Thule Rai, the Deputy Superintendent of Police (DSP). It is said that the Mahatgaun attack was that from which the Maoists' shifted from offensive war to defensive one. At the same night, the Maoist demonstrated its presence and strength in 25 different districts by carrying out simultaneous attacks. When the Ghartigaun police base camp was captured in February, the government started centralizing the police forces by removing the police posts in villages. In April, other two police camps were captured; one was the Tak *Ilaka* (area) police office in Rukum and the Harmi police post in Gorkha. In-between July and August 2000, three police posts—Panchkatia Ilaka police office in Jajarkot, Dhawadi Ilaka in Nawalparashi and Mahawari Ilaka office in Jhapa—were captured. Till May 2001, the Maoist related deaths saw in 52 districts out of total 75 in Nepal. (*Himal*, May 2001:5).

In September 2000, the Maoist for the first time attacked the district headquarter Dunai of Rolpa district and not only captured all the police posts but also looted the money from Dunai Bank. After two days of the Dunai attack, Bhorletar Ilaka police office in Lamjung district was captured. In November 2000, the Maoist captured the Doramba police post in Ramechap. In December of the same year, the Maoist declared its first 'District people's government' in Rukum district. By its second national conference in February 2001, the party passed 'Prachanda Path' as a party's guiding principle. The principle assumed 'a kind of revolution that would be a fusion of the Chinese model of protracted People's War (to expand from villages to towns) and the Russian model of general armed insurrection' (Sharma 2003:375). The conference carried out a slogan 'let us consolidate and expand our base areas and move forward towards a people's government in the centre.'

In April 2001, the Maoist attacked three security bases (Rukumkot of Rukum, Naumule of Dailekh and Mainapokhari of Dolakha) and destroyed. Again, in May, the Maoist repeated the same incident in Okhaldhunga where Khanibhanjyang Ilaka police office was captured and destroyed. On June 1, 2001, there was Royal Massacre in Narayanhiti Royal palace of which the Maoist declared 'the official end of the traditional monarchy from Nepal'.

When the royal massacre happened in Nepal, both the 'people's war' and the intra and inter-party antagonism in the parliament were going on side by side. The first struggle was confined in villages and the last was in Capital for the post and power. Apart from that, the struggle between the two factions of NC was increased. The opposition parties disrupted the parliament for more than eight weeks. Taking note of the weaknesses of the state and parliamentarian parties, the Maoist accelerated its activities in the countryside. It increased the attacks on May 2001. The Maoist abducted some six policemen after its attack on Holeri police post in July. The government led by G. P. Koirala tried to deploy the army to free the abducted 69 policemen from the Maoist but failed to do so owing to the king's 'non-co-operation'.

The 'non-co-operation' increased of the antagonism between the king and the then government on the issue of the deployment of the army. Koirala resigned from the post of Prime Minister on July 19, 2001. The situation went very tense. The struggle shifted from bi-polar to tri-polar after king showed 'non-co-operation' to the democratically elected government. The parties of the triangular struggle were the Maoist, the parliamentary parties, and the king with the army.

After the resignation of G. P. Koirala, Deuba, the new leader of NC parliamentary party, became the prime minister on July 23, 2001. By the time of Deuba's appointment, the truce was announced by the government. The Maoist too reciprocated the truce. It was on force until November 21, 2001. In between, there were two rounds talks between the government and the Maoist. One was on August 30 in Kathmandu and another on September 14 in Bardiya. However, after the Maoist attacked two district headquarters—Dang and Syangja—on November 23, 2001, the truce was suspended and the country again entered in the violent activities. It is said that the truce was used by the Maoist to raise fund as well as people's support by asking donations, addressing mass meetings, and extending the memberships. On the day before calling off the truce, the Maoist announced 41 members United People's Revolutionary Council, Nepal under the leadership of Baburam Bhattarai (*Janadesh* 2006:6).

After calling off the truce, the Maoist repeatedly attacked three district headquarters. These were the district headquarters of Dang,

Syangja and Solukhumbu. By November 26, the government declared the state of emergency in the country. Within nine months of emergency, there were formidable encounters between the Maoist and security forces. Three district headquarters—Achham, Arghakhanchi, Jumla, along with Saphebagar airport of Achham, Gam base camp of Rolpa, Bhiman Ilaka police office of Sindhuli were attacked and destroyed by the Maoist during the period. Thousands of people got displaced from their houses, villages, and districts. Table 13 shows the killing scenario between February 13, 1996 and December 27, 2005.

Table 13: **Killing by the State and the Maoist**

Period	*Killing*			*Per day killing ratio*
	By the security forces	*By the Maoist*	*Total*	
Killing upto November 27, 2005	8,283	4,582	12,865	3.65
Killing before emergency (13/2/1996 – 25/11/2001)	992	811	1,803	–
Killing during the emergency (26/11/2001–31/8/2002)	3,849	1,952	5,801	2.43
Killing before king's takeover (13/2/1996–3/10/2002)	3,849	1,952	5,801	2.43
Killing after king's takeover (4/10/2002–27 November 2005)	4,438	2,630	7,086	6.28

Source: INSEC report 2005.

The table shows that between the suspension of the ceasefire and declaration of the state of emergency in November 2001, the brutal killings became rampant from both the sides. The killings during emergency period (November 26, 2001–August 21, 2002) was almost doubled in comparison of the numbers of the total killings during five years of the Maoist movement. The number of killings reached 3,538 during the emergency, where there were only 1,803 killings till November 25.

Torture, extortion, violation of human rights and destructive activities saw enormous increase. According to government figures, 1,321 VDC buildings were completely destroyed in the first year of the state of emergency (November 2001-November 2002). The region-wise breakdown of the damage of the VDC buildings were; 316 (82.5 percent) out of 383 in the far western region; 165 (28.7 percent) out of 575 in the mid-western region; 221 (25.5 percent) out of 865 in the western region; 334 (27.8 percent) out of 1,199 in the central region and 285 (31.9 percent) of 893 in the eastern region. Until early 2003, some 440 post offices were destroyed. Another effect of the Maoist Movement is the displacement of the people from the conflict area. As per Human Rights Yearbook 2005 published by INSEC, as large as 38,191 people were displaced by the conflict upto end of 2004. The report further stated that more than 22,000 people had been displaced from their homes only from the mid-western region by the end of 2003 where IDP project of the Norwegian Refugee Council estimates the number over 200,000 as displaced people (INSEC 2005:ix).

On the other hand, the conspiracy against the democracy had started in the parliament process itself. On May 22, 2002, the king, 'on the recommendation of prime minister', dissolved the parliament. The parliament was dissolved because of the debate in NC over the issue of the extension of the state of emergency. Deuba proposed the extension of the emergency in the parliament on which the party (NC). By the time of the dissolution of the parliament, the government declared the new poll date and reinforced the state of emergency in the country. The next step against the democratization process was the postponement of the elections of local bodies, which had to be held by July 2002. However, by the time the elected representatives were replaced by bureaucrats in the local body. Later, King Gyanendra interrupted the democratic process by dismissing the then Deuba government on October 4, 2002. The king charged Deuba of incompetence in not holding elections. This incident accelerated a three-party struggle between the Maoist, the monarchy backed by the security forces and the political parties. The daily killings reached from 2.43 before the king's takeover to 6.26. Dissolving parliament and doing away with local representatives resulted in a political vacuum at all levels. The situation became convenience to the Maoist to expand their bases at local level. Arbitrary arrests, an increasing number of disappearances, violent activities, random searches all of which had a negative impact on the local communities. They were constrained to stay under the Maoists' rule.

After dismissing the elected Prime Minister Deuba and taking over the power, the king appointed two successive governments, the first under Prime Minster Lokendra Bahadur Chand (October 2002) and the second under Surya Bahadur Thapa (June 2003). However, both the governments were sacked by the king on May 30, 2003 and May 7, 2004 respectively. The king charged of the government of incompetence to get the support from major political parties. The first government announced truce on January 29, 2003. The Maoist reciprocated with the ceasefire. It was the second ceasefire declared by the Maoist and the government. They held three rounds of formal talks—the first was on April 24 in Kathmandu, the second on May 9 in Kathmandu, and the third on August 11 in Hapure, Dang. The last talk was held while Surya Bahadur Thapa was the prime minister. The second truce came to end after the Maoist unilaterally called it off on August 26, 2003. On the eve of January 26, 2003, the Maoist killed the Inspector General of Armed Police Force (IGP of APF), Krishna Mohan Shrestha and his wife, while the couple was having a morning walk in Kathmandu.

As already mentioned, the killings got increased after the declaration of the state of emergency on November 26, 2001. The figure of death saw noticeable increase after the takeover of power by the king on October 4, 2002. The increment continued after the break of the second truce. The figure is as follows:

Table 14: **Killing by the State and the Maoist (after Assumption of the Power by the King)**

Period	*Killing*			*Per day killing ratio*
	By the state	*By the Maoist*	*Total*	
Total Killing until November 27, 2005	8,283	4,582	12,865	–
Killing after king's takeover (4/10/2002–27/11/2005)	4,438	2,630	7,086	6.24
Killing after the take over and before the second truce (04/10/2004–29/01/2003)	688	337	1,025	8.91
Killing after the break up of second truce (28/08/2003-27/11/2005)	3,626	2,211	5,837	7.22

Source: INSEC report 2005.

At the end of the second ceasefire on August 2003, the violent conflict got further worsened and human rights abuse increased. The per day killings had touched the ratio of 8.91. Prior to the second truce, the ratio was 7.22 and it was 2.43 before the king's takeover. On March 2004, Bhojpur and Beni, the headquarters of Bhojpur and Myagdi districts were attacked along with other small attacks by the Maoist.

The security forces were accused of torture, rape, murder, and arbitrary arrests—but were under impunity. Political opponents were the Maoists' main targets who abducted teachers and students and brought them to indoctrination camps. The state was not able to ensure the safety and security of its citizens. By the beginning of 2004, members of the political parties, civil society and student organizations joined in the streets protest against the 'autocratic' king and demanded for the restoration of democracy. These demonstrations led King Gyanendra to the reappointment of Sher Bahadur Deuba as Prime Minister in June 2004.

Deuba tried to make 'all party' government, but was able to get only the support of UML from the than Five Parties Alliances which was protesting against the king. UML left the street and the alliance, and joined the Deuba government. Other major political parties, including the mainstream Nepali Congress Party refused joining the government citing the government as another conspiracy and the continuity of the king's regressive action. Their argument was that the government was formed to continue and to strength his autocratic regime. Deuba formed a 'multy-party' government with the help of his own party Nepali Congress (D), the UML, and some small parties in the parliament. However, those parties which were in the street, formed the Four Parties Alliance (FPA) continued their protest and for restoration of democracy.

Deuba government was given the task of negotiation with the parties and the Maoist to settle the existing conflict. Deuba set mid-January 2005 as a deadline for the Maoist for the truce and negotiation. However, the Maoist declined Deuba's offer raising a question on the status of government.

On February 1, 2005, King Gyanendra finally dismissed the Deuba government by a proclamation. It was king's second dismissal of Deuba from the post of the prime minister. In the proclamation, the king declared that he would assume power for three years. He installed a Council of Ministers under his chair. All the ministers appointed by the king were the supporters of the previous Panchayat system. He suspended all democratic rights and 'installed military rule' in the country. Immediately after this announcement, the army occupied the streets of Kathmandu; political leaders were put under house arrest or detention; telephone and Internet communications were disconnected for several days and the international airport was shut down. Fundamental rights such as freedom of speech and assembly were abrogated under the proclaimed state of emergency. However, the king defended himself by saying he was forced to take this step to defend multiparty democracy.

The king's move on February 1, 2005, led to a new battle with the king, parliamentary parties and civil society in cities while there had already been another battle in the villages with the rebellions. Within 11 months of king's direct rule (from February 1, 2005 to November 27, 2005), about 6,112 political activists and human rights defenders were arrested. At least 1,000 journalists and media personnels became jobless because of the restriction on broadcasting news from all of the 47 FM radio stations. Thousands of political activists and human rights defenders were re-arrested by security forces and a total of 40 persons were restricted from leaving Kathmandu valley (INSEC 2005).

On the other hand, king's February coup effected to the Maoist Movements also. The RNA which had been loyal to king was deployed not only to suppress the political party's activities in the cities but also to control the Maoist activities in the countryside. It was the first time when RNA was properly mobilized against the Maoist Movement. Therefore, both the RNA and the Maoist had fought each other which led to more than 1,370 killings during the period. During the year of 2005, there were several Maoists' attacks. These attacks took place in Bandipur of Sirah district, Mirchaiya of Sarlahi district, Narke of Kavre district, Pandhare of Bhojpur district, Khanda of Argakhanchi district and Pili of Kalikot district. There was four month unilateral ceasefire declared by the Maoist but the king's government did not reciprocate. The people faced two long general strikes—the first being three days long in February, and second 11 days long in April. Both the strikes were called by the Maoist.

Interestingly, Nepal found certain positive outcomes by the king's coup to restore peace and democracy in the country. Main of which are:

1. The regime's repressive actions against all political forces helped to realize the parliamentary parties the fact that it is important to be united to fight for democracy and for their existence as well in May 8, 2005. This reduced the antagonism within the parties and formed Seven Parties Alliance (SPA). Prior to that, the main parliamentary parties were divided; four parties were on the street to protest against the king's October 4, 2002 move and two other were in the royal government. However, followed by the February 1st move Deuba and UML realized the king's intension i.e. the divide and rule policy. The coup not only made the political parties to unite against the autocracy but they also agreed

on a pro-democracy agenda based on common understandings.

2. The Maoist had reached to the commitment to the peaceful democratic means during the king's active rule. The Maoist, by its party plenum on August 2005 in Rolpa, decided to opt 'competitive democracy' by giving up the 'people's war'. The Maoist, which was having a tacit understanding with the king to defame democratic forces, left the alliance with the king and decided the momentous decision to join multiparty competition after getting to know about the king's intension. It was the landmark decision by the Maoist which helped the SPA to rethink over the intension of the Nepali Maoist. The SPA, after several meetings in June 2005, reciprocated the Maoist accepting the election of the CA as only way to bring the Maoist into the mainstream. The SPA reciprocated the Maoist commitment by accepting the elections of the CA, which was one of the three main demands of the Maoist. The two events became main elements to get the SPA and the Maoist closer which later on had contributed to the agreement regarding the twelve-points understanding to fight for establishing 'full-fledged democracy' in the country.
3. It directly and indirectly helped people to be aware about democracy and democratic system. People came to know about the importance of freedom and democracy when the king seized all the means of communication like telephone, news and the movement of the people. Prior to the king's direct rule, many people mainly the elites had shown their reluctance over the political parties and their modus operandi.
4. The king's strategic weapons like the charge of corruption became setback to the king himself. Some groups of people were arguing against the democratic parties and its leaderships with the charge of corruption, nepotism etc. When they found notorious, corrupt and culprit persons in the king's cabinet and advisory boards, the people changed their mindset on political parties and its leaders and started supporting the parties and democratic movement as well.

> In April, the earlier mentioned Four Parties Alliance (FPA) became the Seven Parties Alliance (SPA) when the Deuba headed Nepali Congress (democratic), the UML and the United Left Front joined the FPA. With this began the nation-wide protest against 'the king's autocratic regime'.

On November 23, 2005, the SPA signed a twelve-points agreement with the Maoist. The main point of the agreement was to put forth common front with a view to end the king's autocracy. The SPA declared four days general strike from April 6, 2006 to April 9, 2006 against the regime. However, the general strike converted into 19-days indefinite Mass Movement-II. The movement on which 21 protestors lost their life, hundreds became disabling, thousands injured compelled the king to address the SPA's agenda of the restoration of the parliament.

There were two main bases of the Mass Movement-II. The first was the popular discontent caused by the repeated failures of the king's direct rule. The second was the hope that the twelve-points agreement between the mainstream parties and the Maoist would bring peace and democracy in the country. An ICG report of May 10, 2006 states the then development of Nepal as follows:

> 'King Gyanendra's capitulation on 24 April 2006 in the face of a mass movement marked a victory for democracy in Nepal and, with a ceasefire between the new government and the Maoist now in place, the start of a serious peace process. Forced to acknowledge the 'spirit of the people's movement', Gyanendra accepted popular sovereignty, reinstated parliament and invited the mainstream seven-party alliance to implement its roadmap—including election of a constituent assembly to rewrite the constitution in line with the parties' five-month-old agreement with the Maoist.' (*ICG report*, May 10, 2006).

Talking of the Maoist Movement, the causes of its growth seem more or less same as mentioned earlier about the causes of the origin of the Maoist Movement in Nepal. Brutal action of the security forces towards the villagers, geographically favorable hilly area for the guerrilla warfare, and poor performance of the government has been the important causes for the rampant growth of the Maoist

Movement. Apart from that, the 'capitalization' of ethnic/Dalit sentiment by the Maoist party by deciding the ethnic/regional governments seems another important cause. To install the marginalized population in the position of power, the Maoist declared autonomous regions and made provision for the representation of ethnic, Dalit and minorities in proportion to their size of population in the autonomous body.

The split of CPN-UML into CPN-UML and CPN-ML in 1995, the sweep out of ML from the 1999s' general elections, and the palace massacre 2001 are other major factors, which helped for escalating the Maoist Movement. Mahakali treaty between the Government of India and the Government of Nepal led to split of the UML. According to the then ML faction, the treaty was discriminatory. With the division of the party, radical elements within UML joined the ML. However, after the ML was swept out in the 1999 elections, tne cadres with radical orientation started shifting to the Maoist party. When the UML and ML got merged, most of the ML cadres refused to go back to the UML and joined the Maoist party.

In the midst, the Royal Massacre happened in July 2001 became another opportunity to the Maoist in capitalizing people's anti-monarchy feelings. The Maoist was the first political force to declare the end of traditional monarchy by the massacre, and appealed the people to move forward for the republican state. Prior to that, the Maoist leaders spoke out that they were having a 'tacit understanding' with the king (*Kantipur* June 6, 2001; *Nepal Samachar Patra*, June 15, 2001, Singh 2003). The decision and appeal of the Maoist to move forward the republican state became landmark to draw attention of those youth and others who were having reservation over the report related to the massacre issued by the investigation committee. By then it had realized that the people lost their faith over the new king, Gyanendra, the Maoist started raising the republican issue as a 'cardinal demand' leaving its 'tacit understanding' with the monarchy.

Another cause of its rapid growth was that it not only raised the people-oriented slogan but also started implementing those slogans into practice. It deployed its leaders to the *Janasarkar* and started to give justice through the 'people's court'. It established school and co-operatives. It offered loans to the poor and needy charging lower interest than the government banks. This was welcomed by the general people and the women in particular. It banned gambling and alcohol drinking. It tried to control child marriage and polygamy as it considered these as 'social evils'.

The political situation of Nepal has changed recently by the April uprising 2006. Prior to the movement, there were triangular clashes between the king's autocratic regime, the parliamentary parties and the Maoist. The SPA and the Maoist came closer by the 12-points understanding, and made the municipal elections declared by the king's regime in February 2006 a failure. Again, the SPA and the Maoist conducted a long dialog in India and formally agreed to strengthen their coalition and announced a second memorandum of understanding in March 19, 2006. The second memorandum, according to parties, was essential to give another strong message to those who took the 12-points understanding slightly. They came to a consensus to launch separate and common protest to defeat the king's regime and to establish democratic system. The Maoist withdrew a 20-days economic and transport blockade after the request of SPA and the civil society which was declared in all district headquarters, including Kathmandu from March 14, 2006. It was because the blockade affected the life of the people in general. The SPA reciprocated the withdrawal of the 20-days blockade announcing a four day general strike from April 6, 2006. The proposed four-days general strike diverted into April Uprising and continued for 19 days until the king announced to give up power and reinstate the dissolved House of the Representatives on April 24, 2006. Millions of people from every walk of life ignored the 'shoot-at-sight order of the king during 18-hour curfew' enforced by the security forces and came to the streets.

During the 19-days general strike, there were three proclamations by the king. Among them were, traditional address on the occasion of Nepali New Year on April 14, 2006, and other two were made due to pressure of the people. The king, in his New Year address called upon all political parties to join in a dialogue in order to assume responsibility and contribute towards activating the multiparty democracy. He tried to teach political parties about democracy and said, 'we believe that there is no alternative to multiparty democracy in the 21st century and the verdict of the ballot alone is legitimate.' His intention of the proclamation was to lure political parties in the name of reactivating all representative bodies through so-called elections and to end the ongoing general strike. The political parties ignored the proclamation, continued protesting because every party had known what the king's intention was. In real, the king was not eager strengthen the democracy but to continue his autocratic regime.

The king's other proclamation came out after seven days of his April 14 speech. The speech came out in the 16th day of the general strike announced by the SPA on April 21, 2006. The declared intention of the speech was to hand over the sovereignty to the people by proclamation. The announcement stated, 'we, through this proclamation, affirm that the executive power of the kingdom of Nepal, which was in our safekeeping, shall, from this day, be returned to the people'. However, the SPA immediately rejected the announcement terming the proclamation 'a betrayal' to diffuse the momentum of the mass movement, and intensified the peaceful protest. The rejection of the king's offer was because the king called upon the SPA to join the government for implementing his agenda. Another fact of the denial of the call by the SPA was that the king expressed high regard for the duty consciousness, valor and discipline of the security forces which suppressed the peace protest and no reference was made on the importance to people's uprising.

When the SPA accelerated the massive protest denying the king's second offer, the king was compelled to accept all the SPA demands those were the reinstate of the House of Representatives which was dissolved on May 22, 2002, and let the SPA run the country according to their roadmap. The SPA accepted the third offer by the king when he recognized people's movement and extended his heartfelt condolences to all those who lost their lives in the people's movement and wished the injured speedy recovery. Earlier, he had been refusing to endorse the people's contribution in the Mass Movement-II.

The first meeting of the reinstated house was held at 1 P.M. on Friday, April 28, 2006 which endorsed a commitment resolution for the Assembly. The House declared the House as 'supreme', decided to put the king under normal laws placing him in par with normal citizens provisioning to collect tax, declared Nepal as secular state and changed the name of Royal Nepal Army into Nepal Army. Council of Ministers were empowered to appoint Chief of the Army Staff. It announced to bring the army under the parliament. Apart from that, the House of Representatives' proclamation provided the authority to the House to decide on royal succession.

On May 25, 2006, the Government of Nepal and CPN (M) signed a Ceasefire Code of Conduct respecting the popular mandate expressed through the historic people's movement for total democracy, progress and peace. Both the parties agreed to sign this code of conduct to transform the ceasefire into permanent peace and resolve the problems through negotiations. They both showed their commitment once again towards democratic values including the concept of competitive multiparty democracy, civic liberties, fundamental rights, human rights, press freedom and rule of law through the signature.

The SPA and Maoist hold three 'summit meeting' along with numbers of informal talks at the Prime Minister's residence. It was the first summit meeting on June 16, 2006 which made an eight-points agreement with the objective of implementing their earlier commitments effectively and honestly. They agreed to draft an interim constitution and to form an interim government along with the Maoist and hold the Constituent Assembly elections. Other points agreed upon were to dissolve the reinstated House of Representatives after making alternative arrangement and dissolving the 'People's Governments' of the Maoist across the country. Further, they both expressed commitment to multiparty system, human rights, press freedom, civic liberties, and rule of law; and decided to request the UN to help in the management and monitoring of arms and armies of both sides during CA elections through eight-points.

The third round summit meeting between the SPA government and the Maoist finally produced a historic deal paving the way for formal entry of the Maoist into political mainstream in November 8, 2006. Following the deal, the government and the Maoist signed a Comprehensive Peace Agreement (CPA) on November 22, 2006 declaring 'an end to the armed conflict ongoing in the country since 1995 by giving permanency to the ongoing cease-fire between the Government and the Maoist'. Another output after the deal was the sign in a tripartite agreement of arms and armies management between the government, the Maoist and the UN which held in November 28, 2006. These agreements include agreement on all issues such as fate of the monarchy, arms management, interim constitution, interim legislature, interim government and electoral system for CA. They decided to determine the fate of monarchy by the first meeting of the CA, to put the properties of late King Birendra under a trust and to nationalize the ancestral property of King Gyanendra. The king will be powerless till the CA determines the fate of monarchy.

Following these agreements, the Maoist army would be sent to cantonments very soon. Seven big cantonments and 21 smaller camps will be set up. According to the deal, the arms of the 'people's army' will be separated and put under single lock system; its key given to Maoist and the cantonments will be monitored by the United Nations through Closed Circuit Televisions (CCTVs) and siren alarm, which will be set off if there is any unauthorized tampering of the lock. The UN will start verifying arms and monitor it soon. Government would reciprocate by putting similar quantity of arms of Nepali Army (NA) under single lock system.

Replacing the House of Representatives an interim legislature will be formed and it will endorse the interim constitution. The interim legislature will consist 330 members with 75 seats for Nepali Congress, 73 seats for United Marxist and Leninist (UML), 73 seats for the Maoist and remaining 48 seats for civil society, professional organizations and various small party organizations. Of the mixed electoral system for 425 members of the CA—205 will be elected directly on the basis of existing electoral constituencies, 204 members will be nominated by various parties on the basis of their proportional strength of direct elections and balance 16 members to be nominated by the prime minister.

Today, everyone is optimistic on the resolution of ten years long armed conflict of Nepal. The hope was there in Nepal when Prachanda, through an extensive interview, disclosed a momentous decision which took by his party plenum on August 2005 in Rolpa (*The Hindu*, February 9, 10, 2006). The optimism is obvious because the SPA and the Maoist have reached the several agreements to resolve the conflict. Another interesting and hopeful thing is that every discussion between the government and the rebellion has been holding in the official residence of the prime minister without any national or international mediators which is unique in the world. Prachanda, an underground supremo of the Maoist rebellion, had broken his underground life at the residence of the prime minister, and has been seen there without feeling insecure which is another strength of the Nepali peace process. However, the process is not free from conspiracy, power game and vested interest of SPA, the Maoist and other national or international power centers. Therefore, the process has been moving a bit slow and the timeframe decided in several agreements could not be followed. All the same, people are hopeful of the success of the peace process because they have no other way except to wait how the situation will move on.

4 SUMMARY AND CONCLUSION

The political situation in Nepal has been in turmoil for a long time. Even 55 years after the end of the Rana hereditary prime ministerial system in 1951, the situation has not improved. Prior to the Rana regime, Nepal was isolated from the rest of the world. The 1951 movement brought some change in the political sphere but this could not continue. Just two years later, the king began to seize the political power repeatedly. In the transitional decade between 1951 and 1960, the king and the political parties fought each other for power. During these ten years neither was there the election of CA to make new constitution nor was there consensus among the then political forces to move forward. Political parties pressurized the king to declare the elections for parliament later in 1959, which paved the way for formation of the first elected government in the country. The king, however, dismissed the government after one and half years of its formation.

After two years of this coup d'état, the king proclaimed a constitution as well as a new political system viz. Panchayat. King Mahendra thought of the system as 'suitable to soil'. The main feature of the system was that the king was the source of the constitution and sovereignty. The system ended in 1990 when people launched a Mass Movement. The main demand of the movement was to restore the multiparty democracy in the country and to end the king's autocratic regime.

For the first half of the 1990s, Nepal tried to improve the political system. A new constitution was drafted and promulgated. This constitution was a negotiated document of the major political forces, the Nepali Congress, the United Left Front and the monarchy. General and local elections were held, which helped democracy to take root at the grassroots level. However, the 'pseudo' democracy did not perform well in the country. The decision of the then Prime Minister to go to the mid-term elections in 1994 led to political instability in Nepal. No party got majority, in the election which made the formation of coalition governments necessary. The coalition governments showed many shortcomings leading frustration and alienation among the people at large. By 1996 when the Maoist began its movement, the situation had become more fragile.

To understand the Maoist Movement in Nepal, first, we have to examine its ideology. The principle ideology of the Maoist, according to it, is Marxism-Leninism-Maoism. However, it was guided more by the ideology of Mao Tse-tung. For the Maoist, People's War is necessary to change society. It believe that the revolt is the only path for changing society and 'people with no army have nothing of their own.' Hence, it prefer 'people's war to end all kinds of other war.'

Though the communist history in Nepal could be traced to the decade of 1950, the ideological subscription to Maoism began after three decades of the inception of the communist movement. Some young communist leaders tried to apply the Maoist ideology in 1971 in the shape of Jhapa uprising. The uprising was a replication in the Naxalite movement of India. However, the Jhapa uprising of Nepal could not continue for long. It ended after wiping out 'eight class enemies' from Jhapa district. The youth participants of the Jhapa movement formed the CPN Marxist-Leninist (ML), which, later, played vital role in the formation of UML in 1990.

After the Jhapa movement, the Maoist ideology came to forefront in September 1974 during the fourth convention of CPN in Banaras, India. However, the convention resolved to follow the path of armed conflict in 1979. From CPN Fourth Congress (1974) to the CPN Maoist (1995), the ideology of Mao faced many ups and downs in its journey. The Fourth Convention saw three splits in 1983, 1985 and 1990. The main cause of the splits was the question: whether it was right time to take weapons against the state or not. Under the leadership of Prachanda, the party attempted to start a revolt in 1990 by collecting arms and providing the training to its cadres. The party could not continue the movement as the people still had a kind of faith in other political parties and their democratic agenda. However, the Maoist argued that the attempt failed because of its lack of preparation.

There is a question that could be posed why did the Maoist Movement got accelerated after the restoration of democracy in the country? The 1990 change was a political change brought through a compromise between the king, the NC and the ULF. The mass movement weakened the king but could not completely defeat the monarchy. While the movement was in momentum, the King Birendra invited the political leaders to the palace, had a discussion and tried to accommodate their demands. He was a tactful king who managed to dissipate the movement easily by working out a compromise with the opposition. The king was not eager to end Panchayat and re-establish the multiparty democracy. He was compelled to give up power to the people, which he enjoyed earlier.

On the other hand, when the democracy was restored, the people felt victorious and started dreaming for radical transformation of society. Prior to that, a common agenda of people from every walk of life was to establish democracy in the country. Democracy did bring some changes in society. The people enjoyed freedoms of speech, expression, movement and association as democratic rights. More schools, roads, and bridges were built and businesses were expanding. Though records have fluctuated, the GDP growth rate in 1995/96, when the Maoist began insurgency, was 5.4 percent, an encouraging figure for Nepal. However, such a change could not fulfill people's aspiration. The change could not touch the heart of the people, who were politically, socially and culturally marginalized for hundreds of years. The marginalized groups had actively participated in the 1990 movement with the hope that democracy would address their problems. In fact, neither the 1990's constitution nor the policies and programs of the elected government totally addressed fulfilled peoples aspirations.

Meanwhile, people began revealing shortcomings and limitations of democratic leaders, governments and parties through the newly found free and vibrant media. Leaders, government and political parties were involved in corruption and power struggle. When the first House of Representative (HOR) was dissolved by the then Prime Minister Girija Prasad Koirala for fresh mid-term election, inter- and intra-party struggle came to the forefront. The mid-term elections resulted in a hung parliament, which led to instability in the country. Nepal exercised minority and coalition forms of government during the period, which performed miserably. The governments and the parliament provided luxurious facilities such as the facility to buy Pazeros at highly subsidized rates. It also extended pension to the members of the Parliament. These decisions taken by the government and the parliament did not go well the people at large. Apart from that, the governments used every means to save their regime; they bribed MPs and even sent the MPs abroad to prevent them from the voting along with opposition.

On the other hand, other forces that had no faith in democracy were waiting for the chance to hit at the democratic system. The king as a traditional force and the Maoist as hardcore communist were these forces. For exposing the weaknesses of the democratic governments and the parliamentary political parties, the king and the Maoist reached into a 'tacit understanding'. Both the king and Maoist were happy when the performances of democratic governments were poor.

The state and the mainstream political parties also played a vital role towards the increase of the influence of the Maoist in Nepal. The then governments did mistake by using unnecessary force against the UPFN supporters (the later day Maoist) to contain local quarrels in the mid-western villages. Interparty local conflicts are common place during elections. Generally, such conflicts get resolved at local level after the elections. However, such hostility did not end but rather expanded after the election. Initially, the UPFN sympathizers and the NC supporters had fights in some VDCs of mid-western parts of Nepal while the first election campaign was going on in 1991. The NC supporters sought the support of the government to defeat their local competitors, the UPFN cadres. The NC government at the center ordered the local administration to resolve the local conflict. However, the administration followed the suggestion of the ruling NC cadres at the local level and started a series of retaliatory actions against the UPFN cadres through the local administration.

In the meantime, the UPFN began a campaign to publicize the excesses of the government against the people. They also raised issues related to social inequalities. Following the campaign, more confrontations took place between the NC and UPFN cadres. Ultimately, the government sent a special force to that area to resolve the problem. The force launched different 'operations' there. It was the area of Magars, who are known to have the qualities of 'naivety, courage, endurance, and loyalty to their leaders'. The security force misbehaved not only with UPFN but reportedly also with the general people. To escape atrocities of security forece, a large number of people were compelled either to join the rebellion or to flee to other places. The Maoist increased its activities in these areas to capitalize the situation in favor of its rebellion. The Maoist expressed its sympathy to those who were oppressed. The people were encouraged to take weapons and fight against the suppressive forces. The Maoist tried to convince the general people that the police behaved so atrociously because they had arms; if the people took up arms, the police would not be able to suppress them. Moreover, they could liberate themselves from all the oppression by the state and society.

Before the start of the Maoist armed revolt in 1996, the Communists in Nepal had attempted to take up arms twice before. The first, in Jhapa district in 1971 was the attempt to replicate the Indian Naxalite movement. The second was on the eve of 1990s Mass Movement. Both these attempts failed quickly. The failures were attributed to the exclusive focus on 'class' by Nepali Communists following the conventional script of Marxist ideology. The Maoist realized this and decided to give greater emphasis to local agendas of the people, which had come to the forefront after the reinstatement of democracy in 1990s. As mentioned earlier, prior to the Mass Movement of 1990, people from across the spectrum concentrated on only one agenda: the restoration of multiparty democracy. When the interim government was formed and the constitution-making process began, people came up with a myriad of their specific agendas, mostly related to social and cultural issues. During the constitution-drafting period, people belonging to different identity groups organized huge rallies and demonstrations to press their agendas.

Realizing the potential power of identity politics, the Maoist took up identity-related popular agenda. Ethnic communities mobilized themselves in 1991 around the twin agenda of secular state and linguistic/ethnic equality. The Maoist formed All Nepal

Nationalities Association in 1994 and adopted Ethnic Policy in 1995 to attract people from ethnic community towards the 'people's war'. To sell ethnic agenda to the people, the Maoist decided in 1997 to take up the cause of ethnic right to self-determination.

During the first two years, the 'people's war' seemed to be expanding relatively slowly. 'people's war' related incidents occurred in only six districts in 1996, and eight in 1997. It may be because of people's indifference towards the Maoists' political agenda, which the people had perceived as being not substantially different from those of other parties. However, when the Maoist started taking up the ethnic agenda in 1998, the support base of the Maoist expanded dramatically. In the year 1998, the Maoist influence spread to 26 districts. Further, the Maoist established Ethnic Department at the central level and formed 11 ethnic/regional fronts.

The Maoist declared its 21 District Janasarkars during December 2000 to June 2001. The interesting thing is that all 21 districts are situated in the hilly areas where the ethnic and Dalit population occupies the dominant position. Tamangs reside in the surrounding areas of Kathmandu. Newars are confined especially in Kathmandu valley. Gurungs are mainly in the western region. Magars are situated in the western and mid-western region, and Rais reside in the eastern region. Major Dalit habitation is found in mid and far western parts of Nepal.

Initially the Maoist Movement was confined to controlling anti-social activities such as anti-alcohol and anti-gambling campaign; its campaigned against polygamy, wife-beating culture etc. The Maoist raised the issues related to caste/ethnicity, gender, region, religion, and language. It demanded ethnic autonomy, regional autonomy, inclusion of all marginalized groups, freedom for the promotion of own language and religion, declaration of Nepal as secular state, etc. Because the Maoist took up these social agendas, this study has defined the Maoist Movement as a social movement. Considering these facts, one must say that the Maoist Movement is not based on class conflict. As mentioned earlier, most of the landlords reside in the Tarai, where feudalism is still prevalent and the gap between the rich and poor is higher than in the hills. However, the Maoist Movement has no strong base in the Tarai.

The Maoist is adept political strategist. Every major political force in Nepal has been used and entrapped by the strategy of the Maoist. The Maoist joined hand with the palace, UML, ML, RPP and even some leaders of NC in different stages. The conflict between the palace and the government came to the forefront in respect of the issue of the mobilization of the army in the Maoist affected areas. The case of the army mobilization led to the resignation of the prime minister Girija Prasad Koirala in 2001. It is said the king objected mobilization of the army against the Maoist because of the 'tacit understanding' between the king and the Maoist. Apart from that, the Maoist has had succeeded in increasing inter- and intra-party antagonism among almost all the major parties. The Maoist had killed and forced a large number of people to leave their home and community charging them of being 'feudal and government mole'. When it declared the 'people's war', the initial target of the Maoist was only the NC cadres. Other parties like UML and RPP supported the Maoist when it eliminated the NC cadres. These parties joined hand with the Maoist to win the elections and to defeat the NC. After 1999 the NC, which was the most affected party by the Maoist violence, was also divided into two factions in relation to the question of dealing with the Maoist. The situation was such that one faction of the same party or other parliamentary political forces sought the support of the Maoist to weaken another faction or party or government.

During the ten years of the Maoist Movement, the Maoist declared several truces. The first was on July 23, 2001, which continued for almost four months. During the truce, two rounds of talks were held between the government and the Maoist. The truce ended on November 23, 2001 when the Maoist attacked the headquarters of Dang, Syangja and Solukhumbu districts. The government declared a state of emergency on November 26, 2001. It is said that this period saw the Maoist engages more in terrorist than social reform activities. Because of a series of destructive activities, the Maoist was termed as terrorists and their activities as terrorist activities by the state and the international community. It is argued that the Maoist used the truce period to strengthen their organization and spread their influence. During the first truce, the

Maoist recruited a large number of youth in its PLA, collected lots of money by extortion and bought a lot of weapons.

Another truce started on January 29, 2003 and lasted till August 26, 2003. During the truce, three rounds of talks were held. Government and the Maoist both tabled their agenda for political and social change. However, the truce also broke after the royal nominee government rejected to endorse the main political demand of the Maoist—elections of the CA. Again, when the Maoist and SPA agreed on a 12-points understanding on November 2005, the Maoist declared unilateral ceasefire which continued only for four months after the government became reluctant over the truce.

During the 'people's war', many lives have been lost and huge amount of properties destroyed. However, the war brought positive and negative things together. The calculation is that the damage to infrastructure alone amounted to US$ 246 million. The amount was about 15 percent of Nepal's current annual budget. Apart from that, democratic process has been derailed. Elections of parliament and local level government could not be held. In the meantime, people became aware of their rights and other social issues. Those who were suppressed and marginalized for years got to know about the reasons of their marginalization. The Maoist mobilized villagers along with Dalits and Janajatis for the first time in Nepal. For such a change in society, the credit should be given to the Maoist. However, the acts like extortions from petty traders and contractors, and ruthless killing of innocent people suspected of being police informers are the activities that negate all the positive things the Maoist has brought about.

Now the concern is how to bring the Maoist into mainstream politics to strengthen the peace and democracy in the country, and how to end such a revolt forever. Today, Nepal has reached very near of the first concern. It is because the SPA and the CPN (M) signed CPA declaring an end to the armed conflict ongoing in the country since 1995 by giving permanency to the ongoing cease—fire between the government and the Maoist on November 22, 2006. In the background of this CPA, the government, the Maoist and the UN reached in a Tripartite Agreement on Monitoring the Arms and Armies in November 28, 2006. Now, there is no doubt to go to the election of CA for which the government has already allocated budget for the year, 2006-07 though the given dateline to declare the interim constitution and to form interim parliament could not follow.

Managing the agenda of exclusion raised in the street is another complex agenda, which need to be worked out. A possibility for the repetition of the war remains if the socio-cultural agenda raised in the street are not addressed properly. If people get frustrated from the new change, there would be a high possibility of such a repetition. For avoiding such situation, the state must work a lot. As mentioned earlier, the Maoist sold lot of radical social agendas to the people. Some of the agendas got implemented by its side during the war. The Maoist declared nine caste/ethnicity and region-based autonomous regions. Without considering the reality of a mixed settlement pattern in the country, such regions may not be viable. In reality, only 12 districts (Kshatriyas in seven, Gurung in two, and one each of Tamang, Tharu and Newar) out of 75 districts have absolute majority of particular caste/ethnic groups. How to satisfy the ethnic and other minority communities and how to maintain caste/ethnic harmony is the main challenge today.

Another challenge is how the Dalits and other oppressed and suppressed communities would be accommodated because they are not confined to a particular territory. The population of Dalits is about 12 percent of the total population of the country. Nevertheless, the representation of Dalits in economic, political and administrative sectors is almost nil. Until and unless the social agenda that have come out into street are addressed, there is no guarantee against another revolt. To assure the people to prevent another war, the many genuine social issues need to be addressed immediately.

ANNEXURE-I

40-Points Demand of the Maoists Submitted to the then Government in 1996

February 4, 1996

Right Honorable Prime Minister
Prime Minister's Office,
Singha Darbar, Kathmandu

Sub: Memorandum

Sir,

It has been six years since the autocratic monarchical partyless Panchayat system was ended by the 1990 People's Movement and a constitutional monarchical multiparty parliamentary system established. During this period state control has been exercised by a tripartite interim government, a single-party government of the Nepali Congress, a minority government of UML and a present Nepali Congress-RPP-Sadbhavana coalition. That, instead of making progress, The situation of the country and the people is going downhill is evident from the fact that Nepal has slid to being the second poorest country in the world; people living below the absolute poverty line has gone up to 71 per cent; the number of unemployed has reached more than 10 per cent while the number of people who are semi-employed or in disguised employment has crossed 60 per cent; the country is on the verge of bankruptcy due to rising foreign loans and deficit trade; economic and cultural encroachment within the country by foreign, and especially Indian, expansionists is increasing day by day; the gap between the rich and the poor and between towns and villages is growing wider. On the other hand, parliamentary parties that have formed the government by various means have shown that they are more interested in remaining in power with the blessings of foreign imperialist and expansionist masters than in the welfare of the country and the people. This is clear from their blindly adopting so-called privatization and liberalization to fulfill the interests of all imperialists and from the recent 'national consensus' reached in handing over the rights over Nepal's water resources to Indian expansionists. Since April 6, 1992, the United People's Front has been involved in various struggles to fulfill relevant demands related to nationalism, democracy and livelihood, either by itself or with others. But rather than fulfill those demands, the governments formed at different times have violently suppressed the agitators and taken the lives of hundreds; the most recent example of this is the armed police operation in Rolpa a few months back. In this context, we would like to once again present to the current coalition government demands related to nationalism, democracy and livelihood, which have been raised in the past and many of which have become relevant in the present context.

Our demands

Concerning nationality

1. All discriminatory treaties, including the 1950 Nepal-India Treaty, should be abrogated.
2. The so-called Integrated Mahakali Treaty concluded on January 29, 1996 should be repealed immediately, as it is designed to conceal the disastrous Tanakpur Treaty and allows Indian imperialist monopoly over Nepal's water resources.
3. The open border between Nepal and India should be regulated, controlled and systematized. All vehicles with Indian licence plates should be banned in Nepal.
4. The Gurkha/Gorkha Recruitment Centres should be closed. Nepali citizens should be provided dignified employment in the country.
5. Nepali workers should be given priority in different sectors. A 'work permit' system should be strictly implemented if foreign workers are required in the country.
6. The domination of foreign capital in Nepali industries, business and finance should be stopped.
7. An appropriate customs policy should be devised and implemented so that economic development helps the nation become self-reliant.

8. The invasion of imperialist and colonial culture should be banned. Vulgar Hindi films, videos and magazines should be immediately outlawed.
9. The invasion of colonial and imperial elements in the name of NGOs and INGOs should be stopped.

Concerning people's democracy

10. A new constitution should be drafted by representatives elected for the establishment of a people's democratic system.
11. All special privileges of the king and the royal family should be abolished.
12. The army, the police and the bureaucracy should be completely under people's control.
13. All repressive acts, including the Security Act, should be repealed.
14. Everyone arrested extra-judicially for political reasons or revenge in Rukum, Rolpa, Jajarkot, Gorkha, Kabhrc, Sindhupalchowk. Sindhuli, Dhanusa, Ramechap, and so on, should be immediately released. All false cases should be immediately withdrawn.
15. The operation of armed police, repression and state-sponsored terror should be immediately stopped.
16. The whereabouts of citizens who disappeared in police custody at different times, namely Dilip Chaudhary, Bhuwan Thapa Magar, Prabhakar Subedi and others, should be investigated and those responsible brought to justice. The families of victims should be duly compensated.
17. All those killed during the People's Movement should be declared martyrs. The families of the martyrs and those injured and deformed should be duly compensated, and the murderers brought to justice.
18. Nepal should be declared a secular nation.
19. Patriarchal exploitation and discrimination against women should be stopped. Daughters should be allowed access to paternal property.

20. All racial exploitation and suppression should be stopped. Where ethnic communities are in the majority, they should be allowed to form their own autonomous governments.
21. Discrimination against downtrodden and backward people should be stopped. The system of untouchability should be eliminated.
22. All languages and dialects should be given equal opportunities to prosper. The right to education in the mother tongue up to higher levels should be guaranteed.
23. The right to expression and freedom of press and publication should be guaranteed. The government mass media should be completely autonomous.
24. Academic and professional freedom of scholars, writers, artists and cultural workers should be guaranteed.
25. Regional discrimination between the Hills and the Tarai should be eliminated. Backward areas should be given regional autonomy. Rural and urban areas should be treated at par.
26. Local bodies should be empowered and appropriately equipped.

Concerning livelihood

27. Land should be belong to 'tenants'. Land under the control of the feudal system should be confiscated and distributed to the landless and the homeless.
28. The property of middlemen and comprador capitalists should be confiscated and nationalized. Capital lying unproductive should be invested to promote industrialization.
29. Employment should be guaranteed for all. Until such time as employment can be arranged, an unemployment allowance should be provided.
30. A minimum wage for workers in industries, agriculture and so on should be fixed and strictly implemented.
31. The homeless should be rehabilitated. No one should be 'relocated until alternative infrastructure is guaranteed.
32. Poor farmers should be exempt from loan repayments.

Loans taken by small farmers from the Agricultural Development Bank should be written off. Appropriate provisions should be made to provide loans for small farmers.

33. Fertilizer and seeds should be easily available and at cheap rates. Farmers should be provided with appropriate prices and markets for their produce.
34. People in flood and drought-affected areas should be provided with appropriate relief materials.
35. Free and scientific health services and education should be available to all. The commercialization of education should be stopped.
36. Inflation should be checked. Wages should be increased proportionate to inflation. Essential goods should be cheaply and easily available to everyone.
37. Drinking water, roads and electricity should be provided to all villagers.
38. Domestic and cottage industries should be protected and promoted.
39. Corruption, smuggling, black marketing, bribery, and the practices of middlemen and so on should be eliminated.
40. Orphans, the disabled, the elderly and children should be duly honored and protected.

We would like to request the present coalition government to immediately initiate steps to fulfill these demands which are inextricably linked with the Nepali nation and the life of the people. If there are no positive indications towards this from the government by February 17, 1996, we would like to inform you that we will be forced to adopt the path of armed struggle against the existing state power.

Thank you.

Dr Baburam Bhattarai
Chairman
Central Committee, United People's Front, Nepal

ANNEXURE-II

Nepal Prime Minister Sher Bahadur Deuba's Address to the Nation after Declaring the State of Emergency, November 28, 2001

In the aftermath of the wave of attacks carried out by ***Maoist insurgents*** *across Nepal on November 23, 2001, the government imposed a State of Emergency on November 26. Two days later, the then Prime Minister addressed the nation outlining the reasons for the imposition of emergency and the government's response to the Maoist attacks. The full text of the address is reproduced.*

Today our country is passing through a difficult situation. Terrorists by the name of Maoists have terrorized Nepalese life through killings, violence and bloodshed. Despite this, we invited them to the negotiating table for a peaceful resolution to our differences and country's problems so as to give an outlet to the problem. In fact the talks with the Maoists and the efforts for peaceful solution were not only the desire of the government but also of the entire nation.

However, the Maoist group has taken to the path of causing serious setbacks to the fabric of the national unity and security by means of violence, terrorism and killings. We showed utmost flexibility to bring the Maoist group that was expanding its activities through violence for the past six years into the mainstream of politics. But the Maoist terrorists totally ignored our honest efforts and people's wishes. At a time when our view that counter-violence cannot be an answer to violence has suffered a setback, the government has arrived at a decision of mobilizing all its security agencies to control such activities.

We patiently discussed their demands and requests with a hope that we could bring them into the mainstream of Nepali politics and society through talks based on mutual trust. And we made efforts to give space to the possibilities of peace and building of a violence-free civilized society. In course of facilitating and building a more congenial atmosphere for talks, we even fulfilled their many demands. Though they treated the Nepalese people and democracy as enemies, the government as a propagator of democratic culture did not behave with them as an enemy. Efforts were made to bring those who had lost their ways onto the right path.

Even after an understanding was reached to enter into talks by halting violence and murder and even after the talks got off the ground, the Maoists continued to engage in different criminal activities. They looted foodgrains from farmers and indulged in violence. They made assaults on religious ceremonies and faiths of people. They kept on attacking the institution of monarchy—the symbol of faith of Nepali people, the constitution, multiparty democracy and basic human rights. They made attempts to disturb social goodwill and weaken national unity and integrity.

We were optimistic of the possibility of hammering out a peaceful solution. But the group called the Maoists perpetrated violence and bloodbath unparallel in the history of peaceful Nepal. The country was optimistic of arriving at a certain conclusion through peace talks. Three rounds of talks were already held and we were in preparation for the fourth round of talks. But the Maoists unilaterally broke the dialogs and peace efforts all of a sudden. Consequently, the nation once again has bogged down in a vicious cycle of violence, killings and terrorism.

In an utter disregard to the government's efforts and people's goodwill, the Maoist terrorists carried out attacks on the innocent people, political party workers, civil servants etc. They even attempted to hurt the national integrity by assaulting the security personnel including police and army.

His Majesty's Government has decided to declare a State of Emergency in the country to prevent the worse situation in the country from being further deteriorated. Maintenance of peace and order by mobilizing security agencies has become our foremost duty and necessity. Though the declaration will cause some discomfort to the people, the inconvenience caused by declaration is minimal as compared to the one caused by terrorism widespread in the nation.

I am fully convinced that all Nepali people, political parties and the civic society is aware of the fact that a government accountable to the people won't take such a difficult decision if there was no unaffordable situation in the country.

I am also fully convinced that all political parties and every section of the civic society will extend their cooperation to the government in the present difficult situation. The government will be fully alert on civic liberty even if Emergency has been declared. Necessary legal provisions will be made so that the civic society is least affected. But there may be still some inconvenience during Emergency. In the present situation, all Nepali people should be united for the sake of public interest, monarchy, the present constitution, multiparty democracy and the welfare of Nepal and remain committed to root out terrorism.

I am of the belief that attention of the nation and the people will be focused on peace and order rather than on discomfort, which is only for short time. At this time of great challenge, which the country is passing through, the government is with the people because it is not separate entity aloof from the people. It is the foremost duty of the government to provide security to the life and property of the people.

I make an earnest appeal to all Nepalese brothers and sisters to focus our power and attention against terrorism so that we can shoulder the serious responsibility successfully. Encouraging terrorism under any pretext will be considered as a serious crime against the country, people and democracy.

All the persons, groups and institutions within and outside the country aiding and abetting terrorism through a supply of arms, money and information have to be brought under the purview of law and punished accordingly. I expect cooperation and guidance from all political parties, entire mass media and civic society in this national campaign.

His Majesty's Government will bring the terrorists before the people and to book. I want to assure the nation and the people that the security agencies of the government are capable of materializing the people's desires and resolve of putting the violence and terror to an end for good.

The government will move ahead by reaching an understanding with all political parties for social and economic reforms and development and for consolidating security arrangements. The cooperation of the civic society and the political parties in this endeavor is most crucial. I want to state here that all friendly countries and institutions having goodwill towards Nepal democracy in the country are with the Nepalese people and His Majesty's Government in combating terrorism.

ANNEXURE- III

Text Related to the Maoists Movement in the Common Minimum Program of the King Nominated Multiparty Government (*Nepali Congress (Democratic), Communist Party of Nepal-UML, Rashtriya Prajatantra Party and Nepal Sadbhabana Party)* disclosed during a press conference in the capital Kathmandu on June 30, 2004. (Printed section B only)

Section B. Resolution of the problems arising from the Maoists and restoration of peace.

1. Peace talks will be prioritized with maximum flexibility for the dignified political solution that is acceptable to all in the national politics on the basis of national consensus for restoration of sustainable peace in the country by resolving the Maoist problem that remains as a major problem of the country.
2. We will move ahead with a proposal of progression by studying alternatives presented by various sectors so far for the outlet and political solution to the Maoist problem and sustainable peace. A program of progressive political solution of consensus will be implemented after reaching a positive conclusion of the talks.
3. Programs of rehabilitation of the affected and displaced from the violent conflict and of the reconstruction of the physical infrastructure will be implemented with high priority.

ANNEXURE- IV

King Gyanendra's Speech, February 1, 2006

On February 1, 2006, on the occasion of the completion of one year of his rule, King Gyanendra addressed the nation. Presented below is the full text of his speech:

Beloved Countrymen,

It is now a year since the decision was taken to restore law and order and activate the multiparty democratic polity in the country in keeping with the nation's needs and the people's aspirations. Arresting a situation that was slipping into anarchy and reactivating a stalled democratic process has not been easy. Yet, given the commitment of our patriotic countrymen, all the Nepalese people have experienced the nation grow in confidence and the self-respect of the Nepalese people restored within a short span of one year, with the cloud of pessimism dissipating. We are confident that, remaining alert to the sensitivities of the self-respecting Nepalese people and our glorious ever independent history, we will be able to ensure for the nation peace, stability and prosperity within the next one year through mutual understanding and with patriotism as the focal point. We believe that a roadmap to sustainable peace and reenergising a meaningful democracy are two sides of the same coin. We are confident that a roadmap of consensus will forever end all possibilities of resurgence of violence and terrorism in our motherland, which will otherwise put at risk the universally acclaimed multiparty democracy and hurt the self-respect of Nepal and the Nepalese people. Guided by a national perspective that upholds our political, administrative and civic traditions, we are confident that by April 2007, all popularly elected bodies will be active in ensuring a bright future for the Nepalese people through a dedicated exercise in democracy so as to create a welfare society.

The nefarious designs to portray Nepal as a failed state a year back has now begun to unravel with acts of terrorism being limited to petty crimes. The elected government not only dissolved the popularly elected village, municipal and district bodies but also at the national level. The process of activating multiparty democracy and Constitutional Monarchy has now begun with the people exercising their franchise to reinstate these bodies for which the elected government had failed to conduct elections in spite of being given repeated opportunities. The people are determined to ensure the success of the municipal elections currently underway. In fact, the freedom to exercise one's vote through adult franchise forms the democratic basis for a honorable national consensus. Democracy flourishes only through the enfranchisement of the people and democrats are never losers when democracy is upheld. Therefore, the first and foremost preconditions for consolidating democracy are to gain the support of the people through the ballot and respect their mandate. In keeping with these universally accepted democratic principles, the process to reinstate all the elected bodies through free and fair elections has been initiated. We are confident of the active participation of all democrats who have faith in the people's democratic rights. Democratic norm dictates that, while upholding the people's rights, their confidence can be won only through participation in the democratic process.

Beloved countrymen,

With efforts to initiate a meaningful exercise in democracy in keeping with the accepted norms, measures are also underway to improve public service utilities for the benefit of the people. As the bureaucracy has been freed of political pressures and discipline instilled among them, criminal activities under political patronage is now under control. The ongoing fiscal and administrative reforms will be implemented in a more effective manner. Rule of law alone will ensure good governance. As long as corruption, which has proved to be a parasite to our society, is allowed to spread its tentacles, a system of governance as aspired by the people cannot be ensured. More effective measures will be adopted to realize the commitment to maintain fiscal discipline. The concept of Land Bank will be effectively implemented to make land available to the landless, agricultural tenants and freed bonded laborers. Internal and external investments will be mobilized to accelerate the pace of economic development, increase employment opportunities, improve transport infrastructure and attain self-sufficiency in the energy sector through optimum utilization of water resources. An effective integrated policy must be adopted to initiate development activities that have direct impact on the people. A conducive environment exists to utilize the opportunities created by information technology in the economic development of the country. Likewise, the role of the service sector is also increasing in importance. In this context, special programs will be introduced to create opportunities of self-employment within the country for talented youths. Measures will also be adopted to train those youths going abroad for employment so that their skills and abilities are duly recognised.

The Nepalese are well aware of the fact that character without any moral foundation, politics indifferent to national pride and a form of governance bereft of the people's confidence will neither benefit the nation nor the people. They also know that politics will not have the strength to inspire the people and overcome challenges if it is tainted. It is our belief that multiparty democracy cannot be made meaningful in the absence of significant popular participation in governance, effective decentralization of authority in the village, municipal, district, zonal and regional levels and maximum autonomy to elected local bodies in the formulation and implementation of development projects.

Democracy can be adopted into our way of life only if we are prepared to have faith in the people's abilities and the elected representatives. To achieve this, guidelines will be formulated in a transparent manner through collective wisdom and reflections based on experiences and aspirations. Appropriate measures will also be initiated to convincingly address, in the greater good of the nation, grievances regarding indigenous people as well as discrimination relating to regional and other issues. Contributing to efforts aimed at the general welfare of the people alone can ensure the collective well-being of the Nepalese. The nation can be freed from the clutches of poverty and made prosperous only through the collective participation of all. We are confident that all Nepalese, conscious of their national pride, will make significant contributions from their respective places towards the success of the pro-development strategies currently being implemented. While history will be the sole judge of an individual or a generation, it should be our endeavor to ensure that the present generation of Nepalese is given due credit.

Beloved Countrymen,

Nepal's foreign policy is now clear and stable. Our foreign policy and relations are solely guided by how best to serve and protect our national interest in a rapidly changing world. This has restored Nepal's prestige and credibility in the international arena. Nepal desires friendship with all and is always ready to cooperate for mutual benefit. Nepal has malice towards none and is ever alert in ensuring that her territory is not used against any friendly country. Nepal is ever ready to have mutually beneficial fruitful relations with both her neighbors. This policy remains unchanged. To act as a catalyst in enhancing economic ties between her two neighbors, Nepal is preparing to be the transit point between them. Nepal's role as a transit point will contribute to the welfare of Nepal, India, China and the region as a whole.

Nepal has unflinching faith in and is totally committed to the principles of human rights. It is in this spirit that our country has adopted the policy of institutionalizing the promotion and protection of human rights and rectifying its shortcomings. It is not easy for a country combating terrorism to strike a balance between the compulsions of national security and upholding the rights of the citizens—this is a reality faced by all democratic countries afflicted with the scourge of terrorism. But it is our strong belief that the people must be allowed to exercise their democratic rights in a peaceful manner, with due consideration to national security.

The Nepalese people desire for sustainable peace. This was clearly spelt out to us when we had direct contacts with our beloved people during our recent visits to various parts of the kingdom. The vigilant Nepalese have well understood the conspiracy to foment further acts of terrorism in the name of momentary cessation of violence. If those who have gone astray wish to rejoin the mainstream of peace and creativity, democracy and coordination, and if they wish to dedicate themselves in the service of the people through the ballot, abjuring their murderous acts against the nation and people, we make it clear that they will be given the security and opportunity necessary to shoulder the responsibilities of governance in their capacity as the people's representatives, having won the people's confidence through the universally accepted democratic exercise. The people can be won over only through peaceful political and constructive activities. Activities like disrupting peace, encouraging discord and creating hurdles on the road to rapprochement in the name of democracy will benefit none. Let us, therefore, unite, with patriotism as the focal point, in dedicating ourselves to the people's welfare and initiating a new chapter in the exercise in meaningful democracy. We wish to emphasise that all differences can be resolved within the framework of the Nepalese patriotic tradition in keeping with the Nepalese psyche, which has never had to put up with subjugation throughout history.

Beloved Countrymen,

We have always, single-mindedly and with determination, strived to fulfill our beloved people's aspirations in the greater interest of the motherland. We have no desire other than the Nepalese people's welfare and the responsibility towards Nepal's glorious history. While utilizing the indestructible synergy constantly spouting from the fountain head of patriotism, it will be in the interest of the nation to uphold, with utmost dedication, the glorious history of the kingdom of Nepal. The success of this alone will keep the nation secure and ensure a meaningful democracy for the people.

A clear decision was made for the country last year. Today, let us, once again, pledge to achieve this national goal. The Nepalese are determined to see a peaceful, prosperous and democratic Nepal in tune with the 21st century. The essence of Nepal's glorious history is the fact that the Nepalese people themselves determine Nepal's national agenda in the interest of the country and their own.

Patriotism is the only means of creating a democratic society. We, therefore, call upon all Nepalese to consign mutual recrimination to the bitter past and build a secure and prosperous future for the nation and people, while upholding democratic norms.

May Lord Pashupatinath bless us all! Jaya Nepal!

ANNEXURE- V

12-Points Understanding between parties and the Maoists on November 22, 2005

The long struggle between absolute monarchy and democracy in Nepal has now reached a very grave and new turn. Establishing peace by resolving the 10-years old armed conflict through a forward-looking political outlet has become the need of today. Therefore, implementing the concept of absolute democracy through a forward-looking restructuring of the state has become an inevitable need to solve the problems related to class, caste, gender, region etc. of all sectors including political, economic, social and cultural, bringing autocratic monarchy to an end and establishing absolute democracy. We make public that, against this existing backdrop and reference in the country, the following understanding has been reached between the SPA and the CPN (Maoist) through different methods of talks.

Points of Understanding

1. Today, democracy, peace, prosperity, social advancement and a free and sovereign Nepal is the chief wish of all Nepalese. We completely agree that autocratic monarchy is the main hurdle in (realizing) this. It is our clear view that without establishing absolute democracy by ending autocratic monarchy, there is no possibility of peace, progress and prosperity in the country. Therefore, an understanding has been reached to establish absolute democracy by ending autocratic monarchy, with all forces against the autocratic monarchy centralizing their assault against autocratic monarchy from their respective positions, thereby creating a nationwide storm of democratic protests.
2. The seven agitating parties are fully committed to the fact that only by establishing absolute democracy through the restoration of the parliament with the force of agitation, forming an all-party government with complete authority,

holding elections to a constituent assembly through dialog and understanding with the Maoists, can the existing conflict in the country be resolved and sovereignty and state power completely transferred to the people. It is the view and commitment of the CPN (Maoists) that the above-mentioned goal can be achieved by holding a national political conference of the agitating democratic forces, and through its decision, forming an interim government to hold Constituent Assembly elections. An understanding has been reached between the agitating seven parties and the CPN (Maoists) to continue dialog on this procedural work-list and find a common understanding. It has been agreed that the force of People's Movement is the only alternative to achieve this.

3. Today, the country has demanded the establishment of permanent peace along with a positive solution to the armed conflict. Therefore, we are committed to end autocratic monarchy and the existing armed conflict, and establishing permanent peace in the country through constituent assembly elections and forward-looking political outlet. The CPN (Maoists) expresses its commitment to move along the new peaceful political stream through this process. In this very context, an understanding has been reached to keep, during the holding of constituent assembly elections after ending autocratic monarchy, the armed Maoists force and the royal army under the supervision of the United Nations or any other reliable international supervision, to conclude the elections in a free and fair manner and accept the result of the elections. We expect reliable international mediation even during the dialog process.
4. Expressing clearly and making public institutional commitment to the democratic norms and values like the competitive multiparty system of governance, civil liberties, human rights, the concept of the rule of law, fundamental rights etc, the CPN (Maoists) has expressed commitment to move forward its activities accordingly.
5. The CPN (Maoists) has expressed its commitment to create

an environment allowing the political activists of other democratic parties displaced during the course of the armed conflict to return to their former localities and live there with dignity, return their home, land and property seized in an unjust manner and carry out their activities without let or hindrance.

6. Undertaking self-criticism and self-evaluation of past mistakes, the CPN (Maoists) has expressed commitment not to repeat such mistakes in future.
7. The seven political parties, undertaking self-evaluation, have expressed commitment not to repeat the mistakes of the past which were committed while in Parliament and in government.
8. In the context of moving the peace process forward, commitment has been expressed to fully respect the norms and values of human rights and press freedom and move ahead accordingly.
9. As the announcement of municipal polls pushed forward with the ill-motive of deluding the people and the international community and giving continuity to the autocratic and illegitimate rule of the king, and the talk of elections to parliament are a crafty ploy, we announce to actively boycott them and call upon the general public to make such elections a failure.
10. The people and their representative political parties are the real guardians of nationality. Therefore, we are firmly committed to protect the independence, sovereignty, geographical integrity of the country and national unity. Based on the principle of peaceful co-existence, it is our common obligation to maintain friendly relations with all countries of the world and good-neighbor relationship with neighboring countries, especially India and China. But we request the patriotic masses to be cautious against the false attempt by the king and (his) loyalists to prolong his autocratic and illegitimate rule and delude the patriotic people by projecting the illusory 'Mandale' nationalism and questioning the patriotism of the political parties, and appeal to the

international powers and the people to support, in every possible way, the democratic movement against autocratic monarchy in Nepal.

11. We call upon the civil society, professional organizations, various wings of parties, people of all communities and regions, press and intellectuals to actively participate in the peaceful movement launched on the basis of these understandings centered on democracy, peace, prosperity, forward-looking social change and the country's independence, sovereignty, and pride.
12. Regarding the inappropriate conducts that took place between the parties in the past, a common commitment has been expressed to investigate any objection raised by any party over such incidents, take action if found guilty, and to make the action public. An understanding has been reached to settle any problem emerging between the parties through peaceful dialog at the concerned level or at the leadership level.

ANNEXURE- VI

The Eight-points SPA-Maoists agreement Following Summit Talks between the Two Sides at the Prime Minister's Residence at Baluwatar on June 16, 2006

1. Effectively and honestly implement the 12-points understanding reached between the SPA and Maoists in November last year and the 25-points Ceasefire Code of Conduct signed between the SPA government and CPN (Maoists) on May 26, 2006.
2. Commitment to democratic norms and values including competitive multiparty system, civic liberties, fundamental rights, human rights, press freedom, and the concept of rule of law and carry out each other's activities in a peaceful manner.
3. Request the United Nations to help in the monitoring and management of the armies and arms of both government and Maoists sides for free and fair elections to the constituent assembly.
4. Guarantee the democratic rights achieved through the 1990 popular movement and the recent historic people's movement; draft an interim constitution based on the 12-points understanding and the Ceasefire Code of Conduct; form an interim government accordingly; announce the dates for Constituent Assembly elections; dissolve the House of Representatives through consensus after making alternative arrangement; dissolve the people's governments of CPN (Maoists).
5. Decide issues of national interests having long-term effects through consensus.
6. Guarantee the fundamental rights of the Nepali people to participate in the Constituent Assembly elections without any fear, influence, threat and violence. Invite international observation and monitoring during the elections

as per the need.

7. Bring about a forward-looking restructuring of the state so as to resolve the class-based, racial, regional and gender-based problems through Constituent Assembly elections. Transform the ceasefire between the Nepal Government and CPN (Maoists) into permanent peace by focusing on democracy, peace, prosperity, forward-looking change and the country's independence, sovereignty and pride, and express commitment to resolve the problem through talks.
8. The government and Maoists talks teams have been directed to accomplish all tasks related to above-mentioned points without any delay.

ANNEXURE-VII

King Gyanendra's Proclamation, April 24, 2006

Beloved Countrymen,

Convinced that the source of State Authority and Sovereignty of the Kingdom of Nepal is inherent in the people of Nepal and cognizant of the spirit of the ongoing People's Movement as well as to resolve the ongoing violent conflict and other problems facing the country according to the roadmap of the agitating Seven Parties Alliance, we, through this proclamation, reinstate the House of Representatives which was dissolved on May 22, 2002 on the advice of the then prime minister in accordance with the Constitution of the Kingdom of Nepal-1990. We call upon the SPA to bear the responsibility of taking the nation on the path of national unity and prosperity, while ensuring permanent peace and safeguarding multiparty democracy. We also summon the session of the reinstated House of Representatives at the Sansad Bhawan, Singha Durbar at 1 P.M. on Friday, April 28, 2006.

We are confident that this House will contribute to the overall welfare of Nepal and the Nepalese people.

We extend our heartfelt condolences to all those who have lost their lives in the People's Movement and wish the injured speedy recovery. We are confident that the nation will forge ahead towards sustainable peace, progress, full-fledged democracy and national unity.

May Lord Pashupatinath bless us all!

Jaya Nepal!

ANNEXURE- VIII

25-points Cease fire Code of Conduct Signed between the Government of Nepal and CPN (Maoists)

Preamble

Respecting the popular mandate expressed through the historic People's Movement for total democracy, progress and peace; Remaining committed towards the Universal Declaration of Human Rights-1948, and fundamental principles and values of international humanitarian law and human rights; Remaining committed to fulfill the 12-points agreement between the SPA and the Maoists; Remaining committed towards democratic values including the concept of competitive multiparty democracy, civic liberties, fundamental rights, human rights, press freedom and rule of law; Guaranteeing the fundamental rights of the Nepali people to participate in the process of constitution making through elections to the constituent assembly without any fear, threat and violence; Placing democracy, peace, prosperity, forward-looking social transformation and freedom, sovereignty and dignity of the nation in the center; and in order to transform the ceasefire between the Government of Nepal and the CPN (Maoists) into permanent peace and resolve the problems through negotiations, a code of conduct has been issued as follows as per the wishes of the Nepali people:

Guaranteeing fearless civilian life

1. Not to issue any statement or engage in any activities which could provoke each other.
2. Both the parties shall not mobilize, display or use their armed forces in a manner that could spread fear and terror amongst the people.
3. Not to attack or destroy each other's military or security installations, not to lay down mines or ambushes, not to recruit new people in one's military and not to spy against each other.

4. Both sides will extend mutual cooperation in order to maintain peace and security.
5. Discussion and understanding will be made as per need regarding the issue of management of arms and armed personnel. Creating an environment of trust among the people.
6. Both the parties will not participate in public meetings, conference or any other political activities in combat dresses or along with arms.
7. No hindrance will be made from either side for political activists and members of social organizations to move around the country and express their views, organize meetings or engage in their organizational works. They will not be subject to any mental or physical pressure. On basic services to the people and development activities.
8. During the period of ceasefire, activities like 'bandh' (general strike) and 'chakka jam' (transport strike) will not be organized, but peaceful demonstrations may be organized.
9. Essential services and facilities to the people will be allowed to operate without any disruption.
10. Not to create hurdles in undertaking regular development works peacefully and other works aimed at people's benefit.
11. Transportation of items like food, medicines, materials used in development works and daily utility items will not be obstructed or banned.
12. Both the parties will create an environment for the smooth functioning of schools, colleges and universities, hospitals, health centers and industrial institutions. Cooperation from media for peace talks.
13. Use civilized and dignified language while disseminating information about ceasefire, code of conduct and the peace process and other political activities.
14. Nobody should issue statements through media in a manner, which could hamper the talks and peace process. Not to collect donation and other financial assistance forcefully.
15. Donation or financial assistance in cash, kind or in the form of services will not be collected or mobilized against one's will. Release and rehabilitation.

16. Accusation, claims or cases filed by both the parties against various individuals will be withdrawn and the detainees will be released gradually.
17. Whereabouts of the people who have been disappeared will be publicized immediately.
18. To help in the rehabilitation of and extend cooperation to displaced people to return to their respective houses in a peaceful, comfortable and respectable manner.
19. Return the properties of the leaders of political parties, activists and civilians, which were seized, locked up or prohibited from being used during the period of the conflict, to concerned persons or their families. Problems arising while returning the properties will be resolved through mutual agreement. Facilitating the talks.
20. No hurdles will be created in the movement and activities of individuals involved in negotiations from both the parties monitoring.
21. On the basis of mutual agreement between the two parties, national and international monitoring teams will be asked to monitor the ceasefire. Miscellaneous.
22. Dispute, if any, in terms of interpretation of this code of conduct, will be resolved on the basis of agreement between the parties.
23. In accordance with the spirit of the preamble of this code, amendments could be made in the code of conduct through mutual agreement.
24. To enforce this code of conduct immediately after it is signed.
25. To make the code of conduct public immediately after it is signed.

Signed by:
Krishna Bahadur Mahara
On behalf of the CPN (Maoists)

Signed by:
Krishna Prasad Sitaula
On behalf of the govt. of Nepal

May 25, 2006

ANNEXURE-IX

Prime Minister Koirala's Letter to the UN Secretary-General

July 2, 2006

Dear Mr. Secretary-General,

I have the pleasure of informing you that the government of Nepal has taken a decisive step to consolidate achievement of the successful People's Movement that restored democracy and made the people of Nepal supreme and sovereign once and for all. This has set in motion Nepal's determination for real and lasting peace based on the national unity and reconciliation and move towards stability by strengthening and institutionalizing the democratic process in the country.

On June 16, 2006, the SPA and CPN (Maoists) concluded an eight-points agreement covering steps that are needed to create conducive environment to elect a constituent assembly to ensure permanent peace in the society. Earlier, on May 26, the government reached an agreement with the CPN (Maoists) on the 25-points Code of Conduct to be observed during the ceasefire between two sides.

In view of the firm commitment of the United Nations to promote sustainable peace and security, economic and social development and human rights around the world on the basis of fundamental principles of respect for sovereignty of nations, mutual cooperation and peaceful resolution of conflict, the Government of Nepal decides to request the United Nations for the following:

1. Continue monitoring of Human Rights through the Office of High Commissioner for Human Rights (OHCHR) in Nepal.
2. Assist to monitor the code of conduct during the ceasefire.
3. Assist in the monitoring of the combatants of the Maoists and decommissioning of their arms in order to ensure free and fair elections to the constituent assembly.

4. Monitor to assure that Nepali Army is inside barrack and is not being used for or against any side in order to ensure free and fair elections to the constituent assembly.
5. Observe the election process to the constituent assembly.

As we plan to hold the elections of the constituent assembly by end of current Nepali year (mid-April 2007), I will be grateful if you could start extending the necessary support of the United Nations on the above-mentioned issues at your earlier convenience.

I would like to take this opportunity to express sincere appreciation and gratitude of the Government of Nepal to the United Nations and to you personally for the consistent support for a democratic process and continued interest in the peace-building in Nepal.

Please accept Excellency the assurances of my highest consideration.

Girija Prasad Koirala
Prime Minister

H. E. Kofi Annan
Secretary-General
The United Nations
New York

ANNEXURE-X

CPN-Maoists Chairman Prachanda's Letter to the UN Secretary-General

H.E. Mr. Kofi Annan
Secretary-General of the United Nations
New York

Dear Mr. Secretary-General,

This is to draw your attention to the letter sent to you by the Government of Nepal on July 2, 2006 and to register our strong protest and disagreement over certain crucial points of the letter.

Firstly, the letter was written and sent unilaterally and secretively without any consultation with us in utter violation of the spirit of ongoing negotiation between the Government of Nepal and the CPN (Maoists). We came to know about the letter through the media after nearly three weeks, and hence this delay to register our disagreement over it.

Secondly, and more importantly, the content of the letter, particularly as stated in points nos. 3 and 4, is in complete violation of the 12-point Understanding of November 22, 2005 and eight points Agreement of June 16, 2006 reached between the two sides. For your kind recollection, clause-3 of the eight points Agreement clearly states: 'To request the United Nations to assist in the management of the armies and arms of both sides (emphasis added) and to monitor it for a free & fair election to the constituent assembly'. Against this, the said letter self-professedly and provocatively talks of 'Assist in the monitoring of the combatants of the Maoists and decommissioning of their arms' and 'Monitor to assure that the Nepal Army is inside barracks' etc. Such arbitrary and unilateral application of two different yardsticks to the two armies is highly objectionable and totally unacceptable to us. Particularly any talk of 'decommissioning' of arms of only the PLA before the elections to the Constituent Assembly is just unthinkable. As everybody knows, the so-called Nepal Army is still loyal to the autocratic monarchy and its democratic restructuring and keeping under credible international monitoring is more imperative and important for free and fair elections to the Constituent Assembly.

We would like to reiterate our appreciation to the United Nations and to you personally for the positive role played so far in favour of democracy, peace and progress in Nepal and expect the same in future. We shall be happy to co-operate in any manner with the UN team planning to visit Nepal soon.

Please accept, Excellency, the assurances of our highest consideration.

Prachanda
Chairman
Communist Party of Nepal (Maoists)

July 24, 2006

ANNEXURE- XI

Six-points Agreement SPA-Maoists on November 7, 2006

Respecting people's aspiration for democracy, peace and progress expressed through repeated historic People's Movement and struggles since 1951,

Reaffirming commitments to the 12-points and eight-points agreements, and 25-points Code of Conduct between the SPA and the Maoists along with other agreements, understandings, code of conducts and letter sent to the United Nations stating similar perspectives by the Maoists and the Nepal government,

Pledging for progressive restructuring of the state by resolving prevailing problems related with class, ethnicity, regional and gender differences,

Reiterating commitments to competitive multiparty democratic system, civil liberties, fundamental rights, human rights, complete press freedom, rule of law and all other norms and values of democratic system,

Guaranteeing the fundamental rights of the Nepalese people to cast their votes in the Constituent Assembly polls without any kind of fear,

By putting democracy, peace, prosperity, progressive social and economic transformation, independence, integrity, sovereignty and prestige of the state in the centre-stage and to implement the commitments made by both the sides to hold the elections to Constituent assembly by mid-June 2007 in a free and fair manner, the following decisions have been taken from the meeting of the top leaders of the SPA and the Maoists today, November 8, 2006.

I. Relating to the Implementation of the Past Agreements

Implement all the agreements, Understandings and Code of Conduct signed earlier—fully, sincerely and strongly.

Form a high-level commission to investigate and publicize the whereabouts of citizens stated to have been disappeared by the state and the Maoists in the past.

Accelerate the process of returning the houses, land and properties confiscated in the past. Ensure the environment so that displaced people would be able to return to their villages. For this purpose, committees would be formed in districts comprising representatives from both the sides. Complete all these works within one month.

Make public announcement regarding the withdrawal of all accusations and charges leveled by the state at the leaders and the cadres of the CPN (Maoists) and release all political prisoners from both the sides.

II. Relating to Management of Arms and Army

In order to hold the elections to constituent assembly in a peaceful, free and fair environment and for democratization and restructuring of the Nepali Army as per the feelings expressed in 12-points agreement, eight-points understandings, 25-points Code of Conduct and five-points letter sent to the United Nations, the following works would be carried out:

Relating to Maoists army

As per the commitments expressed in the letter sent to the United Nations by the Nepal government and the Maoists on August 9, the combatants of the Maoists would be sent to following cantonments. The United Nations would do the necessary verification and monitoring of them.

Main camps would be in the following places

1. Kailali, 2. Surkhet, 3. Rolpa, 4. Palpa, 5. Kavre, 6. Sindhuli 7. Ilam. There would be three smaller camps located in the periphery of each of these main camps.

All the arms and ammunitions would be securely stored in the camps except those needed for providing security of the camp after the Maoist combatants are sent to the cantonments. They will be put under a single lock system and the concerned side would keep the key of this lock. For the UN to monitor it, a device with siren as well as recording facility will be installed. When there is need to examine the stored arms, the UN would do so in the presence of the concerned side. Prepare the details of technology including camera for monitoring as per the agreement among the Nepal government, the Maoists and the United Nations.

On completion of cantonment of the Maoists combatants, Nepal government would take up the responsibility for providing ration and other facilities to them.

The interim cabinet would form a special committee to carry out monitoring, integration and rehabilitation of the Maoist combatants. Make arrangement for the security of the Maoist leaders as per the agreement with the Nepal government relating to Nepali Army.

The Nepali Army would be confined to the barracks as per the commitments of the letter sent to the United Nations. Guarantee that its arms would not be used for or against any side. Keep similar quantity of arms of the Nepali Army in the store, seal it with single-lock system and give the key to the concerned side. For the UN to monitor it, a device with siren as well as recording facility will be installed. When there is need to examine the stored arms, the UN would do so in the presence of the concerned side. Prepare the details of technology including camera for monitoring as per the agreement among the Nepal government, the Maoists and the United Nations.

The cabinet would control, mobilize and manage the Nepali Army as per the new Military Act. The interim cabinet would prepare and implement the detailed action plan of democratization of the Nepali Army by taking suggestions from the concerned committee of the interim parliament. This includes works like determination of the right number of the Nepali Army, prepare the democratic structure reflecting the national and inclusive character, and train them on democratic principles and human rights values.

Continue the works of the Nepali Army such as border security, security of the conservation areas, protected areas, banks, airport, power house, telephone tower, central secretariat and security of VIPs.

III. Relating to the subjects of the interim constitution

1. Relating to interim constitution

Finalize the interim constitution presented by the interim constitution drafting committee as per the agreements reached today.

The reinstated House of Representatives would promulgate the interim constitution and the newly formed interim legislature would endorse it.

2. Relating to the monarchy

No rights on state administration would remain with the king.

Bring the properties of the late King Birendra, late Queen Aishwarya and their family members under the control of the Nepal government and use it for the welfare purposes through a trust.

All properties acquired by King Gyanendra by the virtue of him being the king (like palaces of various places, forests and conservation areas, heritage having historical and archeological importance) would be nationalized.

Determine the fate of the institution of monarchy by the first meeting of the constituent assembly through simple majority vote.

3. Relating to interim legislature (Parliament)

The interim legislature would be unicameral of the following type:

i. There would be 209 members of the SPA and others who are members of the present lower and upper House (excluding those who opposed the People's Movement). Since the Left Front does not have its representation in the current parliament, its representation in the interim parliament would be determined based on understanding.
ii. 73 members from the side of the Maoists.
iii. 48 members from among the sister organizations and professional bodies, oppressed ethnic communities and regions and political personalities (to be nominated based on understanding) (total number:330).

But those who stood against the People's Movement would not

be given membership in the interim parliament.

The reinstated House of Representatives and national assembly would be dissolved once the formation of the interim Parliament is complete.

The people's government, people's court run by the CPN (Maoists) would be dissolved on the day of the formation of the interim Parliament.

Run the interim Parliament as per the political understanding.

4. Relating to interim government

Form the interim cabinet as per the understanding.

Determine the work division and structure of the interim parliament as per understanding.

The interim government would work as per the aspiration of the People's Movement, political understanding and culture of cooperation.

5. Relating to judiciary

Follow the norms and values and concept of the independent judiciary.

Make the judiciary committed to the aspiration of the People's Movement, democracy and interim constitution.

Institute a constitutional court to finalize disputes regarding the constituent assembly.

6. Relating to constitutional bodies

A new constitutional council will be formed that will include the Prime Minister, Chief Justice and the Speaker of the interim parliament, which will recommend appointments at the constitutional bodies. Such appointments will be based on specific criteria.

The appointments in the Election Commission will be completed on the basis of understanding.

7. Relating to local bodies

Interim local bodies will be formed in district, city and village level on the basis of agreement between the SPA and the Maoists.

8. Relating to citizenship problem

Distribute citizenship to all Nepalis who have been deprived of their citizenship certificate before the elections of the Constituent Assembly.

Considering mid-April 1990 as the base (cut off) year, all Nepalese citizens who were born before that date and have been continuously living in Nepal since then will be provided with citizenship certificate.

Other provisions regarding citizenship will be according to the provisions mentioned in the law.

9. Regarding the elections of the constituent assembly

The interim cabinet will be given the authority to ascertain the date to hold the elections of the Constituent Assembly by mid-June 2007.

The elections of the Constituent Assembly will be based on mixed electoral system. 205 members will be elected through First-Past-The-Post system. 204 members will be elected as per the proportional representation system on the basis of votes won by the political parties. A law in this regard will be made after consultation with the Election Commission.

While appointing the candidates, the political parties should ensure proportional representation of oppressed groups, region, Madhesi, Women, Dalits and other groups. 16 members will be nominated by the interim Council of Ministers from among distinguished persons.The total number of members of the constituent assembly will be 425.

Nepalese who are 18 years or above at the time when the interim constitution is promulgated will be eligible to vote.

Monitoring of the election of the Constituent Assembly will be done by the United Nations.

10. Structure of the state

To end discriminations based on class, ethnicity, lingual, gender, cultural, religion and region and to deconstruct the centralized and unitary structure of the state and to reconstruct it into an inclusive, democratic and forward looking state.

A high level commission will be formed to suggest on the restructuring of the state.

Final decision regarding the restructuring of the state will be made by the Constituent Assembly.

11. Directive principles of socio-economic transformation

To end all forms of feudalism, a common minimum program will be prepared for socio-economic transformation on the basis of mutual agreement and they will be implemented.

Formulate policies to implement scientific land reform program by doing away with the feudal land ownership. To adopt policies that will protect and promote national industries and resources.

To ascertain the rights of the citizens on sectors like education, health, shelter, employment, and food security.

Policies will be adopted to provide land and socio-economic security to backward groups like landless, bonded laborers, tillers, Haruwa-Charuwa and other such groups, which are socio-economically backward.

To adopt policies to take strict actions against the people who have worked in government positions and have amassed huge amount of properties through corruption.

Prepare a common development concept that will help in socio-economic transformation of the country and will also assist in ensuring the country's prosperity in a short period of time.

Follow policies ascertaining the professional rights of workers and increase investment on sectors like promoting industries, trade and export and increase employment and income generating opportunities.

IV. Relating to the management of the conflict victims

1. Provisions will be made for providing proper relief, respect and resettlement for the family members of the people who have died due to the conflict and for the ones who have been disabled.
2. Provide relief to the family members of the people who have been disappeared on the basis of the report presented by the investigation commission.

3. Carry out special programs to rehabilitate the people who have been displaced due to the conflict; to provide relief in case of destruction of private and public properties; and to reconstruct the destroyed infrastructures.
4. Conduct investigation about those who were involved in gross violation of human rights at the time of the conflict and those who committed crime against humanity. Form a high level Truth and Reconciliation Commission to create an environment for social reconciliation.

V. Miscellaneous

1. A high-level committee will be formed as per understanding to monitor if the agreement have been implemented.
2. The government will take action against anyone involved in acting against the Code of Conduct, agreement and laws.
3. At the time of the elections of the Constituent Assembly, the political parties will be free to present their policies regarding republic, socio-economic transformation, referendum, election system and other such issues in which an agreement has not been reached now.

VI. Time Schedule

1. To conclude comprehensive peace agreement between Nepal government and the CPN (Maoists) by November 16, 2006.
2. That all the Maoist combatants would gather into the camps by November 21, 2006 as stated in 2(1) and store the arms. The United Nations would do their verification and monitoring.
3. As stated in 2(5), the Nepali Army would remain confined in barracks by November 21, 2006, keep the specified number of arms in the store and the United Nations would conduct its monitoring.
4. To complete the interim constitution by November 21, 2006.
5. To promulgate the interim constitution by November 26, 2006,

establish the interim legislature and dissolve the House of Representatives and National Assembly.

6. Form the interim cabinet by December 1, 2006.

Prachanda
Chairman, CPN (Maoists)

Girija Prasad Koirala
Prime Minister and President of the Nepali Congress

Madhav Kumar
Nepal General-Secretary of CPN (UML)

Sher Bahadur Deuba
President of Nepali Congress (Democratic)

Amik Sherchan
Deputy Prime Minister and Chairman of People's Front Nepal

Bharat Bimal Yadav
Vice President of NSP (Anandi Devi)

Narayan Man Bijukchhe
President of NWPP C. P. Mainali Chairman of Left Front

November 8, 2006

Note of dissent by the UML

Agreeing for the implementation of the subjects stated above as all other parties have agreement on those, our party has following differences:

1. The UML believes that the issue of whether to keep the monarchy or not should be determined through the referendum along with the election to Constituent Assembly
2. The UML believes that it would be most democratic to adopt the proportional system for elections to the Constituent Assembly.

ANNEXURE- XII

Comprehensive Peace Accord held between Government of Nepal and CPN (Maoists) in 2006-11-22]

Preamble

Respecting popular mandate of Nepali people expressed in favor of democracy, peace and progression through the historical struggles and people's movements, time and again, from 2007 BS and even before till now;

Reaffirming the full commitment towards the 12-points agreement reached between SPA, CPN (Maoists), eight-points consensus, 25-points Code of Conduct held between Government of Nepal and CPN (Maoists), decision made in the meeting held between apex leaders of SPA and CPN (Maoists) held on November 8, 2006 including all agreement, consensus, Code of Conduct reached between Government of Nepal and CPN (Maoists), and letters of similar viewpoints sent to United Nations;

Expressing determination for progressive restructuring of the state to resolve existing problems in the country, based on class, caste, region, sex;

Reiterating the full commitment towards democratic value and acceptance including competitive multiparty democratic system of governance, civil liberty, fundamental rights, human rights, full press freedom and concept of rule of law;

Remaining committed towards Universal Declaration of Human Rights, 2048, international humanitarian laws and basic principles and acceptance relating to human rights;

Keeping democracy, peace, prosperity, progressive economic and social change and independence, indivisibility, sovereignty, and self-respect of the country at center;

Expressing commitment to hold elections to Constituent Assembly in free and fair manner till the end of the month of Jeth 2064 BS;

Declaring the beginning of a new chapter of peaceful collaboration by ending armed struggle continued in the country from 2052 BS through political consensus between the two parties to ensure sovereignty of Nepali people through Constituent Assembly, forward-looking political resolution, democratic restructuring of the state and economic-social and cultural transformation;

This comprehensive peace agreement has been reached between Government of Nepal and CPN (Maoists) with commitment to transform ceasefire between Government of Nepal and CPN (Maoists) into sustainable peace.

1. Preliminary

1.1. The name of this agreement is 'Comprehensive Peace Agreement'. In short the agreement shall be called Peace Agreement.

1.2. The agreement shall come into force after public declaration by the government and Maoist side.

1.3. Both the sides shall give necessary directives to all the agencies under their control for immediate implementation of this agreement and to abide by it and implement it and get it implemented.

1.4. All the agreement, consensus and decision reached between SPA, the government and Maoists that are enclosed in annex shall be integral part of this agreement.

1.5. The consensus and agreement to be reached hereafter for the implementation of this agreement shall also be the integral part of this agreement.

2. Definition: Unless the subject and context mean otherwise, in this agreement

(a) 'Ceasefire' means the acts to negate all forms of aggressions, kidnappings, disappearances, taking into custody aimed at each other and between Government of Nepal and CPN (Maoists), mobilization and strengthening of armed forces, destruction in the society by any means including aggression and activities of violence and acts of incitement and instigation.

(b) 'Interim Constitution' means 'Interim Constitution of Nepal 2063' to be issued until drafting and enforcement of the new constitution by Constituent Assembly.

'Interim Council of Ministers' means 'Interim Council of Ministers 'to be formed according to Interim Constitution'.

'Both the Parties' mean the party of Government of Nepal and the party of Communist Party of Nepal (Maoists).

'Prevailing Law' means Interim Constitution of Nepal 2063 and prevailing Nepal Laws that are not inconsistent with it. But this definition shall not obstruct legal arrangement existed before enforcement of Interim constitution 2063.

'Verification' means the subject of verification and true record keeping of military, combatant and arms by United Nations.

3. Political-Economic-Social Transformation and Conflict Management

Both the parties are in agreement to adopt following policy and program for political-economic-social transformation and to affirmatively resolve existing conflict in the country:

3.1. To ensure forward moving political economic and social transformation on the basis of decision made in summit meeting between SPA and CPN (Maoists) held on November 8, 2006 (Annex-6).

3.2. To guarantee sovereignty inherent in Nepalese people in practice by forming interim legislature—parliament according to interim constitution and by holding elections to Constituent Assembly in free and fair manner till the Month of Jetha, 2064 BS by Interim Government.

3.3. To not allow any authority regarding affairs of governance of the country to remain with the king. To bring the properties of late King Birendra, late queen Aishwarya and their family under Government of Nepal and to make use of the property in the interest of the state by forming a trust. To nationalize all the properties (like palaces situated in different places, forest and parks, heritages with historical and archeological importance) received by King Gyanendra in his capacity as the king. To decide the issue of whether or not to retain the monarchy by simple majority in the first meeting of Constituent Assembly.

3.4. To adopt a political system that complies with universally accepted fundamental human rights, multiparty competitive democratic system, sovereignty inherited in people, supremacy of the people, constitutional check and balance, rule of law, social justice, equality, independent judiciary, periodic elections, monitoring by civil society, complete press freedom, people's right to information, transparency and accountability in the activities of political parties, people's participation, impartial, competent, and fair concept of bureaucracy.

3.5. To address the problems related to women, Dalits, indigenous people, Janajatis, Madhesi, oppressed, neglected, minorities and the backward by ending discrimination based on class, caste, language, sex, culture, religion, and region and to restructure the state on the basis of inclusiveness, democracy and progression by ending present centralized and unitary structure of the state.

3.6. To keep implementing at least programs of common consensus for the economic and social transformation to end all forms of feudalism.

3.7. To adopt the policy to implement scientific land reform program by ending feudalistic system of land holding.

3.8. To follow the policy for the protection and promotion of national industries and resources.

3.9. To adopt policy to establish rights of all citizens in education, health, housing, employment and food reserve.

3.10. To adopt policy to provide land and other economic protection to landless squatters, Kamaiya, Halia, Harwa, Charwa and economically backward sections.

3.11. To adopt policy to severely punish people amassing properties by means of corruption while remaining in government posts.

3.12. To form common development concept for economic and social transformation and justice and to make the country developed and economically prosperous, at the earliest.

3.13. To follow the policy to increase investment in industries, trade and export promotion in order to increase opportunities for income generation by ensuring professional rights of the laborers.

4. Management of Army and Arms

In order to hold elections to Constituent Assembly in free and fair manner and for the democratic restructuring of the army to proceed with the following works according to12-points agreement, eight-points consensus, 25-points Code of Conduct, five-points letter sent to United Nations and decision taken by summit meeting held on November 8:

Relating to the Maoists' Army

4.1. As per the commitment expressed in the letter sent on behalf of the Government of Nepal and the CPN (Maoists) to the United Nations on August 9, 2006, the Maoists' Army combatants shall remain within the following cantonments. The UN shall verify and monitor them.

The main cantonments shall remain in the following locations: 1. Kailali 2. Surkhet 3. Rolpa 4. Nawalparasi 5. Chitwan 6. Sindhuli 7. Ilam

Three sub-cantonments shall be placed in the periphery of each of these main cantonments.

4.2. After placing the Maoist combatants within the cantonments, all the arms and ammunition except those required for providing security to the cantonments shall be securely stored and the keys to the single lock shall remain with the side concerned. The UN shall monitor the process of placing the weapons under the single lock by keeping records and fitting a device along with siren. In case of need to examine the weapons placed under the single lock, the UN shall do so under the presence of concerned side. All the technical details along with camera monitoring shall be prepared under the joint agreement of the UN, CPN (Maoists) and the Government of Nepal.

4.3. The Government of Nepal shall make all the necessary

arrangements including ration needed for the Maoist combatants after placing them within the cantonments.

4.4. The Interim Council of Ministers shall form a special committee in order to inspect, integrate and rehabilitate the Maoist combatants.

4.5. The government shall be taking care of security arrangements of the Maoist leaders.

Relating to the Nepali Army

4.6. As per the commitment expressed in the letter sent to the UN, the Nepali Army shall be confined within the barracks. Guarantee that the arms shall not be used for or against any side. The Nepali Army shall store the same amount of arms in accordance with that of the Maoists and seal it with single-lock and give the key to the concerned side. In case of need to examine the stored arms, the UN would do so in the presence of the concerned side. Prepare the details of technology including camera for monitoring as per the agreement among the Government of Nepal, the Maoists and the UN.

4.7. The Council of Ministers shall control, mobilize and manage the Nepali Army as per the new Military Act. The Interim Council of Ministers shall prepare and implement the detailed action plan of democratization of the Nepali Army by taking suggestions from the concerned committee of the interim parliament. This shall include tasks such as determining the right number of the Nepali Army, preparing the democratic structure reflecting the national and inclusive character and training them as per the democratic principles and values of the human rights.

4.8. Nepali Army shall be giving continuity to tasks such as border security, security of the conservation areas, protected areas, banks, airport, power house, telephone tower, central secretariat and security of VIPs.

5. Cease fire

5.1. Termination of military action and armed mobilization:

5.1.1. Both sides shall express commitment to refrain from carrying out following activities:

a. Direct or indirect use of any type of weapon or acts of attack against each other.

b. Searching or confiscating weapons belonging to other side with or without weapons at the place where the arms have been stored as per the understanding reached between both sides.

c. Hurt or render mental pressure against any individual.

d. Set up ambush targeting any side.

e. Involve in murder or violent activities.

f. Involvement in kidnap/detention/imprisonment/ disappearance.

g. Arial attack or bombardment.

h. Mining and sabotaging.

i. Spying military activities of any side.

5.1.2. Both sides shall not recruit additional armed forces or conduct military activities, including transporting weapons, ammunitions and explosives.

However, the security forces deployed by the interim government shall have authority to conduct routine patrol, explore in order to prevent illegal trafficking of the weapons, explosives or raw materials used in assembling weapons at the international border or custom points and seize it.

5.1.3. No individual or group shall bear any illegal weapons, ammunitions or explosives while traveling.

5.1.4. Both sides shall assist each other to mark the landmines and booby-traps used during the time of armed conflict by providing necessary information within 30 days and defuse and excavate it within 60 days.

5.1.5. Armies of both sides shall not bear arms or show their presence wearing combat fatigue during any public program, political meeting or civil assembly.

5.1.6. Nepal Police and Armed Police Force (APF) shall give continuity to the task of maintaining legal system and law and order along with criminal investigation as per the norms and sentiments of the Janandolan and peace accord as well as prevailing law.

5.1.7. Both sides shall issue circular to its respective armed bodies or personnel to stop addressing any armed personnel of opposite side by the term 'enemy' or behave in similar manner.

5.1.8. Both sides agree to maintain a record of the government, public, private building, land and other property seized, locked up or not allowed to use in course of the armed conflict and return them back immediately.

5.2 Situation Normalization Measures:

5.2.1. Collection of cash or kind and tax collection against one's wish and against the existing law shall not be allowed.

5.2.2. Both sides agree to make public the status of the people under one's custody and release them within 15 days.

5.2.3. Both sides also agree to make public within 60 days of signing of the agreement the real name, caste and address of the people made 'disappeared' or killed during the conflict and also inform the family members about it.

5.2.4. Both sides agree to constitute a National Peace and Rehabilitation Commission and carry out works through it to normalize the adverse situation arising as a result of the armed conflict, maintain peace in the society and run relief and rehabilitation works for the people victimized and displaced as a result of the conflict.

5.2.5. Both sides agree to set up a High-level Truth and Reconciliation Commission as per the mutual consensus in order to probe about those involved in serious violation of human rights and crime against humanity in course of the armed conflict and develop an atmosphere for reconciliation in the society.

5.2.6. Both sides pledge to abandon all types of war, attack, counter-attack, violence and counter-violence in the country with a commitment to ensure loktantra, peace and forward-looking change in the Nepali society. It is also agreed that both the sides would assist one another in the establishment of peace and maintaining of law and order.

5.2.7. Both sides guarantee to withdraw accusations, claims, complaints and under-consideration cases leveled against various individuals due to political reasons and immediately make public the state of those imprisoned and immediately release them.

5.2.8. Both sides express the commitment to allow without any political prejudice the people displaced due to the armed conflict to return back voluntarily to their respective ancestral or former residence, reconstruct the infrastructure destroyed as a result of the conflict and rehabilitate and reintegrate the displaced people into the society.

5.2.9. Both sides agree to take individual and collective responsibility of resolving, with also the support of all political parties, civil society and local institutions, any problems arising in the aforementioned context on the basis of mutual consensus and creating an atmosphere conducive for normalization of mutual relations and for reconciliation.

5.2.10. Both sides express the commitment not to discriminate against or exert any kind of pressure on any member of the family of the two sides or on the basis of being related to one another.

5.2.11. Both sides agree not to create any kind of obstacle and allow any kind of obstruction to be created in the independent traveling, assuming of duties and executing of work by the Government of Nepal and Public Bodies' employees and assist them in their work.

5.2.12. Both sides agree to allow unrestricted traveling as per the law within the state of Nepal to the United Nations,

International Donors Agencies and Diplomatic Missions based in Nepal, National and International Non-Government Organizations, Press, Human Rights Activists, Election Observers and foreign tourists.

5.2.13. Both sides are committed to operating publicity programs in a decent and respectable manner.

6. End of conflict

6.1. On the basis of the historical agreement reached between the SPA and the CPN (Maoists) on November 8, 2006, we declare an end to the armed conflict ongoing in the country since 1995 by giving permanency to the ongoing ceasefire between the Government and the Maoists.

6.2. The decisions taken by the meeting on November 8, 2006 of the senior leaders of the SPA and the CPN (Maoists) would be the main policy basis for long-term peace.

6.3. Following the arrival of the Nepali Army in the barracks and the Maoist Army combatants in temporary camps, holding, display and use of violence and arms for creating fear and terror and in any form against the agreement and law would be legally punishable.

6.4. Army of both the sides would not be allowed to publicize for or against any side and support or protest any side. But they shall not be deprived from their right to vote.

7. Human Rights, Fundamental Rights and Adherence to Humanitarian Law

By remaining committed to the Universal Declaration of Human Rights, 1948, the International Humanitarian Law and fundamental principles and standards of human rights, both sides expressed their agreement to the following issues:

7.1. Human Rights:

7.1.1. Both sides reiterate their commitment to the respect and protection of human rights and to international humanitarian law and accept that nobody should be discriminated e,g, on the basis of color, gender, language, religion, age, race, national and social origin, wealth, disability, birth and other status, thought or belief.

7.1.2. Both sides agree to create an atmosphere where the Nepali people can enjoy their civil, political, economic, social and cultural rights and are committed to ensuring that such rights are not violated under any circumstances in the future.

7.1.3. Both sides express the commitment that impartial investigation and action as per the law would be carried out against the people responsible in creating obstructions to the exercising of the rights envisaged in the letter of agreement and guarantee not to encourage impunity. Apart from this, they shall also guarantee the right to relief of the families of the conflict and torture victims and the disappeared.

7.1.4. Both sides would not be involved in the acts of torture, kidnapping and forcing the civilians in any work and take necessary action to discourage such acts.

7.1.5. On the basis of norms and values of secularism, both sides shall respect the social, cultural, religious sensitivity, religious rite and the religious faith of the individual.

7.2. Right to Live:

7.2.1. Both sides respect and protect the fundamental rights to live of an individual. Nobody shall be deprived of these fundamental rights and no law shall be formulated to award death penalty.

7.3. Right to Individual Dignity, Freedom and Mobility

7.3.1. Both sides respect and protect the right to individual dignity. In this connection, no person including those deprived of enjoying freedom as per the law would be subjected to torture or any other cruel, inhuman or degrading behavior or punishment. The citizens' right to confidentiality shall be respected.

7.3.2. Both sides shall fully respect the individual's right to freedom and security and shall not be allowed to keep anyone under arbitrary or illegal detention, kidnap or hold captive. Both sides agree to make public the status of every individual made 'disappeared' and held captive and inform about this to their family members, legal advisor and other authorized person.

7.3.3. Both sides shall respect and protect the citizen's right to free mobility and the freedom to choose within legal norms the location of one's residence and express the commitment to respect the right of the people displaced by the conflict and their families to return back to their homes or to settle in any other location of their choice.

7.4. Civil and Political Rights

7.4.1. Both sides are committed to respect the individual's freedom of speech, expression, setting up organizations and holding peaceful gatherings and right to freedom of exploitation.

7.4.2. Both sides respect the right of every citizen to take part directly or through one's selected representative in issues of public concern, to vote, to be elected and equality in joining of public services.

7.4.3. Both sides are committed to respect the individual's right to be informed.

7.5. Economic and Social Rights

7.5.1. Both sides are committed to respect and protect the individual's right to livelihood through employment of their choice or acceptance.

7.5.2. Both sides are committed to respecting and guaranteeing the rights of food security of all the people. They guarantee that there would be no interference in the transportation, use and distribution of food, food products and foodgrains.

7.5.3. Both sides identify with the fact that the citizens' right to health should be respected and protected. Both sides will not create hurdles in the supply of medicines and in health assistance and campaigns, and express commitment for treatment and rehabilitation of the people injured in course of the conflict.

7.5.4. With the realization of the fact that the right to education should be guaranteed and respected, both sides are committed to maintaining a conducive academic environment in the educational institutions. Both sides agree to guarantee that the right to education would not be impeded. They agree to put to an end, on an immediate basis, activities like taking the educational institutions under control and using them, abducting teachers and students, taking them under control and making them to disappear, and to not to establish barracks in a way that it would impede them.

7.5.5. Both sides agree that the private property of any individual would not be seized or usurped, except permitted by the laws.

7.5.6. Both sides believe in the fact that the industrial climate in the country should not be disturbed and production should be given continuity and that the right of collective bargaining and social security should be respected. They also believe in the fact that if any problem arises between the business houses and laborers, they should be encouraged to resolve the problem in a peaceful manner. Both sides respect the right to work prescribed by the International Labour Organisation.

7.6. Women and Child Rights

7.6.1. Both sides fully agree to protect the rights of the women and children in a special way, to immediately stop all types of violence against women and children, including child labor as well as sexual exploitation and abuse. They also fully agree not to include or use children who are 18 years old and below in the armed force. Children thus affected would be instantaneously rescued and necessary and suitable assistance would be provided for their rehabilitation.

7.7. Right of Personal Liberty

7.7.1. Both sides agree to the freedom of opinion and expression; freedom to assemble peacefully and without arms; freedom of movement; freedom to practice any profession, or to carry on any occupation, industry or trade; press and publication rights; the freedom to take part in peaceful political activities; the right of equality before the law; and to implement and have a tolerable system of justice implemented.

8. Dispute Settlement and Implementation Mechanism

8.1. Both sides agree to become responsible and accountable in a personal and collective way and not to repeat in future mistakes committed in the past and also to correct these mistakes on a gradual basis.

8.2. The National Peace and Rehabilitation Commission can set up mechanism as per the need for making the campaign for peace successful. The composition and working procedures of the Commission would be as determined by the Interim Council of Ministers.

8.3. Both sides are committed to settle all kinds of present or possible future mutual differences or problems through mutual talks, understanding, consensus and dialog.

8.4. Both sides express commitment that the Interim Council of Ministers can constitute and determine the working procedures of the National Peace and Rehabilitation Commission, the Truth and Reconciliation Commission, the High-level State Restructuring Recommendation Commission and other mechanisms as per the need to implement this agreement, the Interim Constitution and all the decisions, agreements and understandings reached between the SPA, the Government of Nepal and the CPN (Maoists).

9. Implementation and Follow-up

Both sides have agreed to make the following arrangements for the implementation of the understandings mentioned in this agreement and for their follow-up:

9.1. Both sides agree to give continuity to the task of monitoring of the human rights provisions mentioned in this agreement by the United Nations Office of the High Commissioner for Human Rights, Nepal.

9.2. Both sides agree for the monitoring of the management of arms and the armies by the United Nations Mission in Nepal as mentioned in the five-points letter send to the UN earlier and in the present agreement.

9.3. Both sides agree to get the United Nations supervise the elections to the constituent assembly.

9.4. The National Human Rights Commission shall also carry out works related to the monitoring of human rights as mentioned in this agreement together with the responsibility assigned to it as per the laws. In connection with carrying out its works, the Commission can take the help of national and international human rights organizations after maintaining necessary coordination with them.

9.5. Both sides agree to accept the reports submitted by the above-mentioned bodies, to provide the information requested by them, and to implement the suggestions and recommendations given by them on the basis of consensus and dialog.

10. Miscellaneous

10.1. Both sides agree not to operate parallel or any form of structure in any areas of the state or government structure as per the letter of the decisions of November 8 and the spirit of the peace agreement.

10.2. Both sides accept to sign any complementary agreements, as necessitated, for the implementation of the present agreement.

10.3. This agreement can be revised any time with the consent of both sides. Both sides agree to provide to each other prior written information if they wish to make any changes. The amendments could be made to the agreement with the consent of both sides after receiving the information. The provisions to be made by such an amendment would not be below the minimum standards of the accepted international human rights and humanitarian laws.

10.4. If any disputes arise in any interpretation of this agreement, a joint mechanism comprising both sides shall make the interpretation on the basis of the preamble and the documents included in the schedule of this agreement, and this interpretation would be final.

10.5. The concept of 'two sides' as mentioned in this agreement would automatically cease to exist after the constitution of the Interim Legislature-Parliament. Thereafter, all the responsibility of implementing the obligations stated in this agreement shall be as per the arrangements made by the Interim Council of Ministers. It would be the duty and responsibility of all the political parties to extend cooperation in the compliance and implementation of the agreement.

10.6. We heartily appeal to one and all to extend cooperation for resolving their problems and demands through talks and dialog and for holding the elections to the Constituent Assembly and maintaining the law and order, at a time when the entire country is focused on the main campaign of the election of the Constituent Assembly.

10.7. We heartily appeal to the civil society, the professional groups, the class organizations, the media, the intellectual community and all the Nepali people to actively participate in this historic campaign of building a new Nepal and establishing lasting peace through the elections of the Constituent Assembly by ending the armed conflict.

10.8. We heartily urge all the friendly countries and the United Nations, as well as the International Community to extend support to Nepal in this campaign of establishing full democracy and lasting peace.

Cognizant of the responsibility of the future of the country and the people, and becoming fully committed to this comprehensive peace agreement, we, on behalf of the Government of Nepal and the Communist Party of Nepal (Maoists), hereby make public this comprehensive peace agreement after signing it.

Prachanda President Communist Party of Nepal (Maoists)	Girija Prasad Koirala Prime Minister Government of Nepal

Signed on November 21, 2006

ANNEXURE- XIII

Agreement on Monitoring of Management of Arms and Armies on November 28, 2006

Preamble

In keeping with the letters to the United Nations (UN) Secretary-General of August 9 and the Comprehensive Peace Accord of November 21, 2006;

Guaranteeing the fundamental right of the Nepali people to take part in the Constituent Assembly elections in a free and fair environment without fear;

Declaring the beginning of a new chapter of peaceful democratic interaction by ending the armed conflict taking place in the country since 1996, based on the Comprehensive Peace Accord between the two parties in order to accomplish, through the Constituent Assembly, certainty of sovereignty of the Nepali people, progressive political outlet, democratic restructuring of the state, and social-economic-cultural transformation; and,

Affirming the will to fully observe the terms of this bilateral agreement witnessed by the United Nations;

The parties agree to seek UN assistance in monitoring the management of the arms and armies of both sides by the deployment of qualified UN civilian personnel to monitor, according to international norms, the confinement of Maoist Army combatants and their weapons within designated cantonment areas and monitor the Nepali Army (NA) to ensure that it remains in its barracks and its weapons are not used against any side.

Modalities of the Agreement

Principles

Neither of the parties shall engage in movement or redeployment of forces resulting in tactical or strategic advantage.

Any claims or reports of violations of this agreement will be reported to UN monitors, substantiated or not substantiated, and subsequently reported to the parties through the appropriate representative of the UN Mission in Nepal.

The security forces deployed by the interim government shall have authority to conduct routine patrol, explore in order to prevent illegal trafficking of the weapons, explosives or raw materials used in assembling weapons at the international border or custom points and seize them.

Both parties agree to allow the United Nations, International Donor Agencies and Diplomatic Missions based in Nepal, National and International Non-governmental Organizations, Press, Human Rights Activists, Election Observers and Foreign Tourists to travel unrestricted according to law in the state of Nepal. The parties will respect the security, freedom of movement and well-being of UN Mission and associated staff, goods and services in all parts of Nepal.

The parties shall immediately take all necessary measures to cooperate with efforts aimed at controlling illicit trafficking of arms and the infiltration of armed groups.

Both parties fully agree to not include or use children who are 18 years old and under in the armed forces. Children thus affected would be immediately rescued and necessary and appropriate assistance will be provided for their rehabilitation.

Definitions

The following definitions are accepted:

1. *Cantonment* (*Maoist army*) is a temporarily designated and clearly defined geographical area for encampment and provision of services for the Maoist combatant units including weapons, ammunitions and equipment. The cantonments are provided for all echelons of the Maoist Army.
2. *Barracking* (NA) is the deployment of Nepal Army units to barracks, including weapons, ammunitions and equipment. No units below a company level will be independently deployed unless for activities specified elsewhere in this agreement or otherwise mutually agreed by the parties.
3. *Secure arms storage areas* are either military barracks

with regular armory stores used for storage of weapons, ammunitions and explosives, or storage containers established in special perimeters at cantonment sites controlled and guarded by the responsible unit.

4. '*The parties*' refers to the party of Government of Nepal (including the Nepal Army) and the party of the Communist Party of Nepal (Maoists), (including the Maoist Army).
5. *UN Monitoring* refers to all efforts by the United Nations to determine relative compliance with the terms spelled out in this agreement and to report to all the parties and others concerned its findings.
6. *The Joint Monitoring Coordination Committee (JMCC)* is the monitoring, reporting and coordinating body chaired by the UN with membership of the parties. The JMCC is responsible for supervising compliance by the parties to this agreement.
7. *Joint Monitoring Teams (JMTs)* are the bodies which will assist in monitoring the cessation of hostilities. The JMTs will be active at the regional and local level and in mobile teams. Each team will be comprised of one UN monitor serving as team leader, one monitor from Nepal Army and one monitor from the Maoist Army. JMTs will not be used for weapons storage inspections. Inspections at Maoist army cantonments will take place with a UN monitoring team and a representative of the Maoist Army. Inspections at Nepal Army barracks will take place with a UN monitoring team and a Nepal Army representative.
8. *Maoist Army combatants:* For purposes of this agreement this will include regular active duty members of the Maoist Army who joined service before May 25, 2006, who are not minors and who are able to demonstrate their service, including by CPN(M) identity card and other means agreed by the parties.

Promotion

The parties shall promote awareness of this agreement, and

adherence to its provisions, among their commanders, members and affiliated groups.

The parties, Government of Nepal, Nepal Army (NA), CPN(M) and the Maoist Army, shall design, in cooperation with the UN Mission, an awareness program to ensure that local communities and the parties' commanders, members and affiliated groups understand the mandate of the UN Mission and all of the obligations of the parties spelled out in this agreement. The information programs shall include the use of meetings and print and electronic media in local languages.

Phases

This agreement shall come into force upon signing. These phases shall occur in the following sequence:

1. Reporting and verification;
2. Redeployment and concentration of forces;
3. Maoist Army cantonment, NA barracking and arms control; and,
4. Full compliance with the agreement.

A full and practical timeline will be established by the parties for all of these activities to take place in consultation with the UN.

Reporting and verification

The parties will report detailed information about their troops and this information will be treated with appropriate confidentiality by the United Nations. The parties will provide maps and sketches showing current dispositions, including:

1. Order of battle/military structure, organization, deployment and number of troops;
2. Minefields, landmines, unexploded ordnance, standard explosives, improvised explosive devices and exact location of such items;
3. All necessary information about roads, tracks, trails and passages related to encampments;

4. Information regarding armed or unarmed groups working along with the parties, the Nepal Army (NA) and the Maoist Army, including their responsibilities; and,
5. Other information required by the UN for proper monitoring of the disposition of arms and armies.

The UN Mission shall check this information immediately after monitors are deployed.

Redeployment and concentration of forces

Comprehensive plans, timelines and routes for the redeployment and concentration of forces will be provided by both the NA and Maoist Army to the UN Mission.

The redeployment and concentration of all combatants in Nepal—with the NA in barracks and the Maoist Army moving in to cantonment sites—shall be carried out in consultation with the UN. The redeployment and cantonment of forces will be monitored by the UN monitors after they are deployed.

Both sides express an understanding to create a record of government, public and private buildings, land and other properties and return them immediately.

The parties will withdraw all military and paramilitary checkpoints (unless explicitly permitted in this agreement) to promote and guarantee free movement and create an environment free of fear and intimidation.

The Nepal Police and Armed Police Force shall continue the task of maintaining law and order and conduct criminal investigations as per the spirit and sentiment of the *Jana Andolan* and Peace Accord as well as the prevailing law. Both parties agree not to operate parallel or other forms of mechanism in any areas of the state or state machinery as per the spirit of the decisions of November 8, 2006 and the essence of the Peace Accord. All sides agree to let employees of Nepal government and public agencies travel freely to any part of the country, to fulfill their duties and not to create any obstacle or obstruction while executing their work or not to let obstructions to arise and to facilitate their work.

Maoist Army cantonment, barracking of the NA and arms control

Maoist Army cantonment

In accordance with the commitment expressed in the letter sent to the United Nations, Maoist Army combatants and their weapons shall be confined within designated cantonment areas. The cantonment shall be based on comprehensive planning and preparation before implementation. After the Maoist Army combatants stay in the temporary cantonments, the Government of Nepal will provide food supplies and other necessary arrangements. When implemented, the comprehensive concept shall ensure good communications and proper logistics. UN monitors will have access to any and all cantonment sites for purposes of monitoring.

Commanders' responsibilities

The normal Maoist Army chain of command, control, communication and information will be utilized to control the Maoist Army cantonment, using the normal Maoist Army structure in administration of the sites.

There will be seven main cantonment sites and 21 satellite cantonment sites of three per main cantonment site. The satellite sites will be clustered no more than two hours driving distance from the main sites unless otherwise agreed by the parties.

The designated seven main sites will be under command, control, communication and information of the Maoist Army site commander and the satellite sites by the designated satellite commanders. The site commanders shall provide the following information in detail for each site to the UN Mission:

1. Command structure for the unit and sub-units plotted on a map;
2. Names of commanders down to company level;
3. Communication system;
4. Complete list of personnel;
5. Complete list of weapons, i.e. types, numbers, serial number

and calibre under storage at the main cantonment sites;

6. Ammunition inventory type, lot number and amount; and,
7. List of names for the site security guards detachment, and complete list of weapons and ammunition for the detachment (main and satellite cantonment levels).

Site commanders' responsibilities include:

1. Camp security, including access control to the site;
2. Respect of the security, freedom of movement and well-being of UN and associated staff, goods and services;
3. Providing information in cooperation with the UN Mission;
4. Maintenance of discipline, morale and normal training in the spirit of the Comprehensive Peace Accord, excluding live fire exercises;
5. Daily routines and control of troops; and,
6. Logistics and camp services (in cooperation with the Government of Nepal and other assisting agencies).

Weapons storage and control

The parties agree upon the safe storage of all Maoist Army weapons and ammunitions, in the seven main cantonment areas under UN monitoring, except as provided below for perimeter security purposes. Both sides shall assist each other to mark landmines and booby-traps used during the time of armed conflict by providing necessary information within 30 days and to defuse and remove/lift and destroy them within 60 days. All improvised explosive devices will be collected at designated sites a safe distance from the main cantonment areas. Unsuitable devices will be destroyed immediately. Stable devices will be stored safely and under 24-hour armed guard. The parties, in consultation with the UN, will determine a timeline and process for the later destruction of all improvised explosive devices. To ensure the safety of both monitors and Maoist Army personnel, no improvised explosive devices or crude bombs will be brought inside the cantonment sites.

In the main cantonment sites the weapons and ammunitions storage area will be secured by the following system:

1. A solid fence will surround the specified area, including a gate with a lock. There will be signs on the fence clearly identifying the restricted area.
2. The weapons storage depot will be composed of storage containers painted white and furnished with shelves for safe weapons storage and easy control, and with a complete inventory (weapon type, calibre and serial number).
3. A single lock provided by the UN will secure each storage container. The key will be held by the designated main cantonment site commander. A 24-hour surveillance camera will cover the storage site and will be monitored from the UN office in the cantonment site. Floodlights will be switched on automatically during hours of darkness.
4. The UN will provide an inspection registration device mounted on each container door indicating when the storage container has been opened.
5. An alarm system will be connected to sirens in both the UN office and the camp commander's office. The system will be activated if the container door is opened without a 'safe button' having been switched off in connection with regular inspections.
6. UN monitors will carry out the inspections of the arms storage area and containers in the presence of a Maoist Army representative.

Each main cantonment site will be allowed 30 weapons of the same make and model to be used only for clearly defined perimeter security by designated guards, with each satellite allowed 15 such weapons under the same conditions. These weapons will all be properly registered with make and serial number and locked in a guardhouse when not in use. The parties, in consultation with the UN, will periodically review the number of weapons needed for perimeter security purposes on the basis of a shared threat assessment.

Security provisions will be made for CPN(M) leaders through understanding with the government.

The UN Mission shall monitor these commitments with a full-time presence at the Maoist Army main cantonment sites and through field visits and regular inspections. These inspections will be carried out randomly and without warning.

Registration of Maoist Army combatants at cantonment sites

All Maoist Army combatants will be registered at the main cantonment sites. This registration will include the provision of age, name, rank, responsibilities within unit/formation, date of entry into service and will provide the basis for a complete list of personnel. Maoist combatants will be registered regardless if they are in possession of weapons or not. If with weapon, the type and condition of weapon will be specified. The total number of weapons will be categorized by unit/formation. Only those individuals who were members of the Maoist Army before May 25, 2006 will be eligible for cantonment. The parties will agree as to how this pre-existing service is to be confirmed in consultation with the UN.

As part of this registration, all Maoist Army combatants will present their Maoist Army identity card to be marked by the UN. The process for marking the cards will be determined. This registration card will be the basis for any assistance received by Maoist Army members. Unregistered persons will not be eligible for assistance or permitted to remain in cantonments.

Only those Maoist Army combatants who have been properly registered at cantonment sites will be eligible for possible integration into the security forces fulfilling the standard norms. Any discharged personnel will be ineligible for possible integration. Those who are eligible for integration into the security forces will be determined by a special committee as agreed in the Comprehensive Peace Accord. This integration process will be determined in subsequent agreement with the parties.

Upon registration Maoist Army combatants, if found to be born after May 25, 1988, will be honorably and automatically discharged.

Discharged Maoist Army combatants must release all weapons, uniforms and other military gear; and, agree not to return to cantonment sites unless mutually agreed by UN monitors in consultation with the parties. The assistance packages to be provided to voluntarily discharged personnel will be agreed by the parties in advance of cantonment.

The Interim Council of Ministers will form a special committee to supervise, integrate and rehabilitate the Maoist Army combatants.

Barracking of the Nepal Army

General regulations

In accordance with the commitment expressed in the letter sent to the United Nations, the Nepal Army shall remain in its barracks and its arms are not to be used in favor of or against any side. UN monitors will have access to any and all NA barracks for purposes of monitoring whether Nepal Army forces or weapons are being used for or against any party. Upon visiting any Nepal Army barracks for inspection, the site commander will be duly notified, and UN inspections will relate only to matters regarding the disposition of forces and weapons.

The Council of Ministers will control, mobilize and manage the Nepal Army as per the Army Act of 2006 (*Sainik Ain* 2063) or its successor legislation. The Interim Council of Ministers to prepare and implement the detailed action plan of the Nepal Army's democratization by taking suggestions from the concerned committee of the Interim Parliament/legislature. Under this to carry out activities like assessing the appropriate number of the Nepal Army, to train the army in democratic and human rights values while developing democratic structure, national and inclusive character.

Commander responsibilities

The normal NA chain of command, control, communication and information will be utilized to monitor the NA deployment to barracks. The commanders shall provide the following information in detail to the UN Mission:

1. Command structure for the unit and sub-units plotted on a map;
2. Names of commanders down to company level;

3. Communication system;
4. Order of battle/military structure, organization, deployment and number of troops;
5. Minefields, landmines, unexploded ordnance, standard explosives, improvised explosive devices and exact location of such items; and,
6. Other information required by the UN for proper monitoring of the disposition of arms and armies.

The NA will respect the security, freedom of movement and well-being of UN and associated staff, goods and services, and provide information in cooperation with the UN Mission according to Section 2.

The UN Mission shall monitor these commitments through daily presence in selected NA barracks, field visits and regular inspections.

Weapons storage and control

The Nepal Army will remain within the barracks as per the commitment expressed in the letter sent to the UN to ensure that their arms are not used for or against any party. The Nepal Army to store arms in equal numbers to that of the Maoist Army, to seal it with a single-lock and give the key to the concerned party. In the process of installing the lock, to assemble a mechanism including a siren and register for the monitoring by the UN. While carrying out the necessary examination of the stored arms, the UN will do so under the presence of the concerned party. The barrack where NA arms will be monitored under the conditions spelled out in section 4.1.2 will be identified and agreed by the parties. The arms will be stored in storage containers.

Deployment and Concentration of Forces—NA permitted activities

In accordance with the spirit of the Comprehensive Peace Accord, continuity will be given to functions of the Nepal Army including border security, security of the conservation areas, protected areas, banks, airports, power houses, telephone towers, central secretariat and security of VIPs. A detailed list of these institutions and installations will be kept by the NA, along with the number and types of forces assigned to such duties. The list of such institutions and installations will be kept by the NA under seal, and this information will be made available to UN monitors when deemed necessary in a case-by-case basis.

Permitted NA activities include:

1. Routine military activities within the barracks and regular training in barracks and camps. The JMCC will be notified 48 hours in advance before undertaking limited live fire exercises at designated live firing ranges.
2. Participation in official ceremonies, parades, etc. as directed by the Government.
3. Provision of Border Security as directed by the government.
4. Relief of troops on a one-to-one basis, including transport as mentioned.
5. Regular maintenance and replacement of non-lethal equipment, including transport as mentioned. Maintenance and replacement of lethal weapons will take place only with the determination of the interim government or agreement by both parties.
6. Execution of development and construction tasks as directed by the civilian authorities, on central, regional and local levels.
7. Provision of support in relief work in times of natural and other disasters as directed by the government.
8. Participation in peacekeeping operations called for by the United Nations, and all preparations, transport, training, transfer of equipment, etc. connected to this.
9. Provision of security for VVIPs and VIPs.
10. Provision of security of vital installations as directed by the government.
11. Provision of security of transportation of Nepal Rastra Bank funds.

For all of the above activities the rules regarding notification of troop, air movements and exercises spelled out in section 5.2 apply.

Compliance with the Agreement

Prohibited Activities

In the spirit of the Comprehensive Peace Accord, and in light of this agreement, after the placement of the Nepal Army in the barracks and the Maoist Army combatants in cantonment, the parties shall scrupulously refrain from the following activities:

1. Holding and carrying arms is in violation of the law. Displaying arms, intimidation and any type of use of violence is prohibited, and use of arms is legally punishable.
2. Any type of arms and weapons targeted against each other in a direct or indirect way or any act of attack.
3. Harming or intimidating any person, including internally displaced persons, humanitarian and development workers and other non-combatants, and any seizure of their equipment and property.
4. Ambushes, murder or violent operations.
5. Kidnapping, unlawful detention or imprisonment, disappearances.
6. All offensive military flights in and over Nepal.
7. Damaging or seizing public/private/government, military or UN property and all attacks on UN personnel and installations.
8. Planting mines or improvised explosive devices, conducting sabotage or military espionage.
9. Recruiting additional armed forces or conducting military activities against each other, including transporting weapons, ammunitions and explosives (unless mutually agreed by the parties and notified in advance according to the terms of this agreement).
10. Collecting cash or goods and services or levying tax against one's wishes and against the existing law.
11. Any actions that impede or delay the provision of humanitarian assistance or protection to civilians.
12. Any restrictions on the safe, free and unimpeded movement of humanitarian or development agencies undertaking

activities approved by the interim government or its successor.

13. All acts and forms of gender-based violence.
14. Any restrictions on the free movement of people and goods.
15. All activities that obstruct the efforts of the UN Mission and amount to a failure to cooperate with the UN Mission, including the prohibition of the UN Mission patrols and flights over any location.
16. Any attempt by a party to disguise its equipment, personnel or activities as those of the UN Mission, other United Nations agencies, the International Committee of the Red Cross/Crescent or any other similar organization.
17. Any attempt to redeploy military forces and equipment or occupation of any positions out of their respective deployment positions without the consent of the Joint Monitoring Coordination Committee.
18. The use of children who are 18 years old and under in the armed forces.
19. All hostile propaganda and incitement to military action.

The parties shall also refrain from all activities that are prohibited elsewhere in this agreement.

Permitted activities

The key principle that shall underpin permitted activities for both sides shall be to alleviate the effects of the armed conflict on civilians and the war-affected areas and to galvanize popular support for peace. Permitted activities for both sides will be conducted as per the decisions of the interim government. Troop, air movements and exercises have to be properly notified and approved by the JMCC at least 48 hours in advance.

Permitted activities include:

1. De-mining and decommissioning of military hazards;
2. Development activities to include improvement and opening of roads, rehabilitation of bridges and passages and airstrips according to the decisions of the interim government;

3. Humanitarian relief;
4. Socio-economic activities such as assisting free movement of people, goods and services;
5. Free movement of unarmed soldiers in plain civilian clothes who are on granted leave, medical referrals, or visiting families—no more than 12 percent of the total retained force at a given cantonment or barracks will be on authorized leave at any given time unless mutually agreed by the parties;
6. Supply of non-lethal items to military units, food, water, medicine, petrol, oil and lubricants, stationery, uniforms etc; and,
7. Medical evacuation.

Violations

The following acts shall constitute violations of the agreement:

1. Any act that contravenes this agreement;
2. Unauthorized troop movements;
3. Unauthorized recruitment, conscription or mobilization;
4. Unauthorized replenishment of military equipment;
5. Violation of human rights, humanitarian law or obstruction of freedom of movement of people, goods and services;
6. Espionage, sabotage, air surveillance and acts of subversion; and,
7. Military flights, or military flights utilizing civilian aircraft, over cantonment sites without 48 hour notification to the parties and the UN mission, except in emergency situations or medical evacuations.

The United Nations Mission

The Joint Monitoring Coordination Committee

The Joint Monitoring Coordination Committee (JMCC), the chairman of which will be appointed by the UN Mission and the delegates from the parties determined by the parties themselves. The nine-member JMCC shall be composed of representatives from the UN, NA and Maoist Army. The neutral Chairman will be appointed by the United Nations. There will be two Vice-Chairmen, one each from the Maoist Army and the NA. The remaining six members will be two UN, two NA and two Maoist Army, all as selected by the parties.

The JMCC shall reach its decisions by consensus. In the event of a deadlock, the representative of the UN Secretary-General shall have final authority for reporting on the compliance of the parties with this agreement to the Secretary-General and to the interim government for resolution. The Chairman shall report regularly to the representative of the Secretary-General and to the designated representatives of the parties regarding the activities of the JMCC.

The JMCC shall serve three main functions:

1. To assist the parties in implementing this agreement. The JMCC shall be the central coordinating body for monitoring arms and armies in accordance with the terms of this agreement.
2. To serve as a dispute resolution mechanism. The JMCC shall resolve all disputes and military or operational difficulties, complaints, questions or problems regarding implementation of this agreement.
3. To assist in confidence building. The JMCC shall work to gain the trust and confidence of the parties and promote the overall goals of this agreement among the people in Nepal.

In order to achieve these goals, the JMCC shall operate according to the following basic principles:

1. Resolve all problems and disputes at the lowest possible level, i.e. delegation of authority to the JMTs;
2. Promote joint problem-solving and build trust and confidence through active efforts to appropriately investigate and report on all incidents of concern to the parties; and,
3. Build on lessons learned in the process.

The Joint Monitoring Teams (JMTs), will assist the JMCC at the local level and through site visits. The JMTs will comprise one international monitor as the team leader and one monitor from Nepal Army and one monitor from the Maoist Army. The number of JMTs and their deployment will be determined by the chair of the JMCC in consultations with that body.

The tasks of the JMTs will include:

1. Village and community visits and liaison with the civilian community;
2. Cooperation with other UN-agencies, and liaison with international organizations and non-governmental organisations;
3. Assistance to the parties in creating a favorable operational environment for the conduct of the ceasefire by information sharing and defusing local tension;
4. A pro-active concept for initiation of conflict management at the local level; and,
5. Investigation of complaints linked to possible alleged violations of the agreement, reference paragraph 5.1, and to recommend measures to ensure compliance.

Miscellaneous

This agreement can be revised at any time with the consent of both parties. Both parties agree to provide to each other prior written information if they wish to make any change. The amendments can be made to the agreement with the consent of both parties after receiving the information. The provisions to be made by such an amendment will not fall below the minimum standards of accepted international human rights and humanitarian laws.

Both parties consent to sign any complementary understandings, as necessary, for the implementation of the present agreement.

This agreement will be signed by both parties in Nepali and English. The United Nations will witness the English-language version of this agreement and, accordingly, the English-language version of this agreement will be considered as authoritative in matters of dispute.

The spirit of the Comprehensive Peace Accord shall guide the interpretation and implementation of this agreement by all the parties.

Done in Kathmandu, Nepal on the 28th day of November, 2006 *(12 Mangsir 2063 BS)*

Krishna B. Mahara
Coordinator
Negotiating team
CPN (Maoists)

Krishna P. Sitaula
Coordinator
Negotiating team
Government of Nepal

Witnessed by
Ian Martin
Personal Representative of the Secretary-General
United Nations

REFERENCES

Acharya, Baburam (2005), *Aba Yesto Kahilyi Nahos* (Let such thing never happens), Kathmandu: Prof. Sri Krishna Acharya (in Nepali language).

Adhikari, Indra (2006), "Women in Conflict: The Gender Perspective in Maoist Insurgency," in Lok Raj Baral (ed.), *Nepal: Facets of the Maoist Insurgency*, New Delhi: Adroit Publishers.

-------- , (2004), "Beni Attack and After," *The Kathmandu Post,* 9 November.

-------- , (2003), "Nepal : The Maoist War and Prospect of Peace," *Agni* (Delhi), 6 : 4 : January-April.

Althusser, L. (1979), "The Crisis of Marxism," in *Power and Opposition in Post-Revolutionary Societies*, London: Ink Links (translated by G Lock).

Ananta (2003), "People's War in the 21st Century and Prachanda Path," *Problems and Prospects of the Revolution in Nepal*, Nepal: Janadisha Prakashan, 2004.

Apter, David E. (1993), "Democracy, Violence and Emancipatory Movements: Notes for a Theory of Inversionary Discourse," *Discussion Paper*, No. 44. May.

-------- Apter, David E. (1997), "Political Violence in Analytical Perspective," in David E. Apter (ed.), *The Legitimation of Violence,* London: Macmillan Press Ltd.

Arya, S. P. (1988), "Social Movement: A Conceptual View," in S. K. Srivastava and A.L. Srivastava (eds.), *Social Movement for Development*, Allahabad: Chugh Publications.

Azar, Edward and Burton John (eds.) (1986), *International Conflict Resolution: Theory and Practice,* Boulder, Colorado: Lynne Rienner Publishers.

Bajracharya, Ranjana and Prem Kumar Khatry (2005), "Inter-Religious Dialogue: An Unbreakable Thread to Unite the Diverse Cultures of Nepal," in R.D. Bajracharya, K.B. Bhattachan, D.R. Dahal and P.K. Khatri *Cultural and Religious Diversity: Dialogue and*

Development (Monographs and Working Papers: No 6) Kathmandu: UNESCO.

Baral, Lok Raj (2003), "The Specter of Terror and Its Impact on the Democratic Process," in Sridhar Khatri, Gert W. Kueck (eds.), *Terrorism in South Asia: Impact on Development and Democratic Process*, New Delhi: Shipra.

-------- (2006), "Maoist Insurgency: A Prognostic Analysis," in Lok Raj Baral (ed.), *Nepal: Facets of the Maoists Insurgency*, New Delhi: Adroit Publishers.

Baral, Lok Raj, Krishna P. Khanal and Krishna Hachhethu (2002), "Responsiveness of Nepali Political System," (Unpuplished Report).

Bassiouni, M. Cherif (2004), "Terrorism: The Persistent Dilemma of Legitimacy" *Case Western Reserve Journal of International Law,* Vol. 36 (2 & 3).

Benerjee, Samanta (1980), *In the wake of Naxalbari: A History of the Naxalite Movement in India*, Calcutta: Subornarekha.

Bhattachan, Krishna Bahadur (2000), "Possible Ethnic Revolution or Insurgency in a Predatory Unitary Hindu State, Nepal," in Dhruba Kumar (ed.), *Domestic Conflict and Crisis of Governmentability in Nepal*, Kathmandu: CNAS.

Bhattarai, Baburam (2005), "Janayudda Ka Das Barsha Ra Krishi Kranti Ko Prasna (Ten Years of People's War and the Question of Agricultural Revolution)," in *Kishan Sandesh* Vol. 2, December.

Bista, Dor Bahadur (1991), *Fatalism and Development: Nepal's Struggle for Modernization,* Calcutta: Orient Longmans.

Blumer, H. (1969), "Collective behavior," in A McClung-lee (ed.), *Principles of Sociology*, New York: Barnes and Nobel cited in Crossley, Nick (2002), Making Sense of Social Movements, Buckingham: Open University Press.

Burghart, R. (1984), "The Formation of the Concept of Nation-State in Nepal," *Journal of Asian Studies* 44 (1): 101–125.

-------- , "The Political Culture of Panchayat Democracy," in Michael Hutt (ed.), *Nepal in Nineties*, New Delhi: Sterling.

Chauhan, R.S. (1971), *The Political Development in Nepal 1950-70: Conflict between Tradition and Modernity*, New Delhi: Associate

Publishing House.

-------- (1989), *Society and State Building in Nepal: From Ancient Times to Mid-Twentieth Century*, New Delhi: Sterling.

Collier, Paul (1999), "On the Economic Consequences of Civil War," in *Oxford Economic Papers*, 51.

Coser, K. (1956), *The Functions of Social Conflict*, Glencoe, IL: Free Press.

Dahrendorf, Ralf (1959), *Class and Class Conflict in Industrial Society*, Stanford: Stanford University Press.

DFID Report on Economic Cost of Conflict 2002.

Dhungel, Ramesh (2006), "Limbuka 'Sampriti' Ra 'Niti' Samuha: Gorkha Sasan Ko Den (Sampriti and Niti Groups of Limbus: Contribution of Gorkha Rule)," in *Himal Khabarpatrika* 28 February-13 March 2006 (in Nepali Language).

Diani, Mario (2000), "The Concept of Social Movement," in Kate Nash (ed.), *Readings in Contemporary Political Sociology*, Oxford: Blackwell Publishers Ltd.

DREFDEN (1992), *Report on the Study and Research on the Local Election in Nepal 1992*, Kathmandu: DREFDEN.

Escobar, Arturo and Sonia E. Alvarez (eds.) (1999), *The Making of Social Movements in Latin America: Identity, Democracy, and Democracy,* Boulder: West View Press.

Gaborieau, Marc (1972), "Muslims in the Hindu Kingdom of Nepal," *Contribution to Indian Sociology,* New Series, No. VI, December, pp. 84-105.

Galtung, John (1996), *Peace by Peaceful Means: Peace and Conflict, Development and Civilization*, London: Sage publications.

Gellner, David N. (1997), "Caste, Communalism, and Communism: Newars and the Nepalese State," in David N. Gellner, Joanna Pfaff-Czarnecka and John Whelpton (eds.), *Nationalism and Ethnicity in a Hindu Kingdom: The Politics of Culture in Contemporary Nepal,* Amsterdam: Harwood Academic Publishers.

Gellner, David N. (1997), "Ethnicity and Nationalism in the World's only Hindu State," in David N. Gellner, Joanna Pfaff-Czarnecka and John Whelpton (eds.), *Nationalism and Ethnicity in a Hindu Kingdom: The Politics of Culture in Contemporary Nepal*, Amsterdam: Harwood Academic Publishers.

Ghosh, Partha S. (2003), "Human Rights and Terrorism," in D.D. Khanna and Gert W. Kueck (eds.), *Conflict Resolution, Human Rights and Democracy,* New Delhi: Shipra.

Gladwin, Maree (1994), "The Theory and Politics of Contemporary Social Movements," *Politics*, Vol. 14, No. 2.

Goodwin, Jeff and James M. Jasper (2003), *The Social Movements Reader: Cases and Concepts*, Malden, MA: Blackwell.

Gurr, T. D. (1970), *Why Men Rebel*, Princeton: Princeton University Press.

-------- (1974), "Persistence and Change in Political Systems, 1800-1971," *Amer. Pol. Sci. Rev. 68.*

-------- (1993), *Minorities at Risk: A Global View of Ethno-Political Conflicts*, Washington: United States Institutes of Peace.

-------- (2000), "Ethnic Warfare on the Wane," *Foreign Affairs,* Vol. 79, No 1, May/June.

Gurung, Harka (1997), "State and Society in Nepal," in David N. Gellner, Joanna Pfaff-Czarnecka and John Whelpton (eds.), *Nationalism and Ethnicity in a Hindu Kingdom: The Politics of Culture in Contemporary Nepal,* Amsterdam: Harwood Academic Publishers.

Gurung, Harka (2003), "Trident and Thunderbolt: Culture Dynamics in Nepalese Politics," The Mahesh Chandra Regmi Lecture delivered at Conference on 'The Agenda of Transformation: Inclusion in Nepalese Democracy' Organized by Social Science Baha, Kathmandu, 24-26 April.

Gurung, Harka (2003), *Social Demography of Nepal,* Lalitpur: Himal Books.

Gurung, Harka (2005), Social Exclusion and Maoist Insurgency. Paper Presented at National Dialogue Conference on ILO Convention 169 on Indigenous and Tribal Peoples, Kathmandu, 19-20 January.

Gyawali, S. B. (1935 /1992 B.S.), *Prithvinarayan Shah*, Darjeeling: Gyawali (in Nepali).

Habermas, Jurgen (1987), *The Theory of Communication Action,* Cambridge: Polity Press. Vol. 2.

-------- (1995), *The Theory of Communication Action: Reason and the Rationalization of Society*, Cambridge: Polity Press.

-------- (1997), *Between Facts and Norms: Contributions to a Discourse Theory of Law and Democracy*, Cambridge: Polity Press.

Habermas, Jurgen (2003), "Toward a Cosmopolitan Europe," *Journal of*

Democracy, Vol. 14, No. 4, October.

Hachhethu, Krishna (2002), *Party Building in Nepal: Organization, Leadership and People*, Kathmandu: Mandala Book Point.

-------- (2003), "Democracy and Nationalism Interface between State and Ethnicity in Nepal," *Contributions to Nepalese Studies* 30(2) July.

Halliday, Fred (2001), "Terrorism," in Joel Krieger (ed.), *The Oxford Companion to Politics of the World*, New York: Oxford University Press.

Heberle, Rudolf (1951), *Social Movements; An Introduction to Political Sociology*, New York : Appleton-Century-Crofts.

Himal 14/5 May 2001.

Himal, May 2001.

Hoftun, Martin, Raeper, William and Whelpton, John (1999), *People Politics and Ideology: Democracy and Social Change in Nepal*, Kathmandu: Mandala Book Point.

Huntington, Samuel P. (1968), *Political Order in Changing Societies*, New Haven: Yale University Press.

-------- (1987), "The Goals of Development," in Myron Weiner and Samuel P. Huntington (eds.), *Understanding Political Development*, Boston: Little Brown.

ICG Report, October 27, 2005.

IIDS (2000), *The Fourth Parliamentary Election*, Kathmandu: Institute for Integrated Development Studies.

INSEC (1996), *Human Rights Yearbook*, 1995, Kathmandu: INSEC.

INSEC Report (2005), *Nepal: 300 Days of Royal Take Over*, Kathmandu: INSEC.

INSEC (2006), *Human Rights Yearbook*, 2005, Kathmandu: INSEC.

ISRSC (2004), *District Development Profile of Nepal*, Kathmandu: Informal Sector Research and Study Center.

Janadesh Year 15, Vol. (13) 2006.

Jelin, Elizabeth (ed.) (1990), *Women and Social Change in Latin America*, London: UN Research Institute for Social Development and Zed Books.

Johnson, Chalmers (1966), *Revolutionary Change*, Boston: Little Brown cited in Ghanashyam Shah (ed.) (2002), *Social Movements, and the State*. New Delhi: Sage Publication.

Joshi, Bhuwan Lal and Rose, Leo E. (1966), *Democratic Innovations in Nepal: A Case Study of Political Acculturation,* Berkeley and Los Angeles: University of California Press.

Kantipur, June 6, 2001.

Kantipur, May 3, 2006.

Karki, Arjun and Seddon David (eds.) (2003), *The People's War in Nepal: Left Perspectives*, New Delhi: Adroit Publishers.

Khanal, Krishna P. (2006), "The Maoist Agenda of Restructuring the State: An Appraisal," in Lok Raj Baral (ed.) *Nepal: Facets of the Maoist Insurgency,* New Delhi: Adroit Publishers.

Kisan Sandesh Vol. 2, December 2005.

Kumar, Dhruba (2006), "The Military Dimansion of Maoist Insurgency," in Lok Raj Baral (ed.) *Nepal: Facets of the Maoist Insurgency,* New Delhi: Adroit Publishers.

Kumar, Satish (1967), *Rana Polity in Nepal: Origin and Growth*, Bombay: Asia Publishing House.

Kwok-Sing Li (tr. Mary Lok), (1995), *A Glossary of Political Terms of the People's Republic of China,* Hong Kong.

Laclau, Ernesto and Moufte, Chantal (1985), *Hegemony and Socialist Strategy*, London: Verso.

Lopez, George A. and Stohl, Michel S. (eds.) (1989), *International Relations*, USA: Co Press.

Louis, Prakash (2002), *People Power: The Naxalite Movement in Central Bihar*. Delhi: Wordsmiths.

Mahara, Krishan B. (2005), "*Janadisha Bare KehiKura* (some arguments about people's move)", *Kisan Sandesh* Vol. 2, December.

Malla, K. P. (1992) "Bahunbada's Myth and Reality" *Himal* 5 (3)

Mahat, Ram Sharan (2005), *In Defence of Democracy : Dynamics and Fault Lines of Nepal's Political Economy,* New Delhi : Adroit Publishers.

Marx, Karl and Angel, Frederick (1977), *Selected Works*, Vol. 1-3, Moscow: Press.

Marx, Karl and Angels, Friedrich (1988), *Manifesto of The Communist Party*, republished in Susan J. Ferguson (eds.), *Mapping the Social Landscape: Reading in Sociology* 1999 p. 450.

McAdam, Doug, Tarrow Sidney and Charles Tilly (1997), "Toward an

Integrated Perspective on Social Movements and Revolution," in Mark Lichbach and Alan Zuckerman (eds.), *Comparative Politics*, Cambridge: Cambridge University Press.

Mehden, Fred Von Der (1973), *Comparative Political Violence*, New Jersey: Prentice-Hall Inc.

Mehta, Ashok K. (2005), *The Royal Nepal Army: Meeting the Maoist Challenges*, New Delhi: Rupa Co.

Merton, Robert K. and Robert A. Nisbet (1971), *Contemporary Social Problems*, 3rd edn., New York: Harcourt, Brace, Jovan ovich.

Mohanty, M. (1977), *Revolutionary Violence: A study of the Maoist Movement in India,* New Delhi: Sterling.

Moore, Barrington J. R. (1966), *Social Origins of Dictatorship and Democracy: Lord and Peasant in the Making of the Modern World*, New York: Penguin.

Mukherjee, P. N. (1977), "Social Movements and Social Change," *Sociological Bulletin 26*(26):1-38.

Nepal Human Development Report 2004, Kathmandu: UNDP.

Nepal Samachar Patra, June 15, 2001.

Nepal Samachar Patra, December 17, 2000.

Nepal, May 07, 2006.

NESAC (1998), Nepal: Human Development Report 1998, Kathmandu: Nepal South Asia Center.

Neupane, Govinda (2000), *Nepalko Jatiya Prasana* (Question of Caste/ Ethnicity in Nepal), Kathmandu: Centre for Development Studies.

Newsweek 10, September, 1973.

Nieburg, H. L. (1969), *Political Violence: The Behavioral Process*. New York: St. Martin's Press.

Oommen T. K. (1988), "Mobilization for Social Development: The Indian Situation," in S. K Srivastava and A.L. Srivastava (eds.), *Social Movement for Development*, Allahabad: Chugh Publications.

-------- (1990), *Protest and Change: Studies in Social Movements*, New Delhi: Sage Publications.

Oxford Dictionary of Sociology 2005 Oxford, United Kingdom: Oxford University Press.

Parson, Talkott (1972), *The Social System,* New Delhi: Amerind.

Parvati (2003), "The Question of Women's Leadership in People's War in Nepal," *Problems and Prospects of the Revolution in Nepal*, Nepal: Janadisha, 2004.

Ptaff-Czarnecka, Joanna (1997), "Vestiges and Vision: Cultural Change in the Process of Nation Building in Nepal," in David Gellner, Joanna Ptaff-Czarnecka and John Whelpton (eds.), *Nationalism and Ethnicity in a Hindu Kindom: The Politics of Culture in Contemporary Nepal*, Amsterdam Harwood Acadamic Publishers.

Phadnis, Urmila (1990), *Ethnicity and Nation-Building in South Asia*, New Delhi: Sage.

Philipson, Liz (2002), Conflict in Nepal: Perspective on the Maoist Movement. An Unpublished Paper Submitted to DFID in May 2002.

Pokhem, B. (1997), "Introduction," in B.Pokhem (ed.), *Insurgency in the Northeast*, New Delhi: Omsons Publications.

Polletta, Francesla and Jasmer, James M. (2001), "Collective Identity and Social Movements," *Annu. Rev. Sociol.* 27: 283-305.

Prachanda (1993), "Mao Tse-tung's Contribution in the Development of Universal Theory of People's War," *Problems and Prospects of the Revolution in Nepal*, Nepal: Janadisha, 2004.

Prachanda (1996), "War Policy of Nepalese New Democratic Revolution in the Context of Historical Development," *Problems and Prospects of the Revolution in Nepal*, Nepal: Janadisha, 2004.

-------- (1997a), "Some Ideological and Military Questions Raised by People's War," *Problems and Prospects of the Revolution in Nepal*, Nepal: Janadisha Publications, 2004.

-------- (1997b), "People's War and the Problem of Development of United Front," *Problems and Prospects of the Revolution in Nepal*, Nepal: Janadisha, 2004.

-------- (1999), "New Democratic Revolution and the Theory of People's War," *Problems and Prospects of the Revolution in Nepal*, Nepal: Janadisha, 2004.

-------- (2004), "Down with Parliamentarism! Long live new democracy!," *Problems and Prospects of the Revolution in Nepal*, Nepal: Janadisha, 2004.

-------- (2004), "The Problem of Ideological Deviation in the Nepalese People's Revolution," *Problems and Prospects of the Revolution in Nepal*, Nepal: Janadisha, 2004.

Prasad, Kamal (2005), "Adhibashi/janajati ra Bhumisambandha Bare (About the Relationship between the Ethnic/Native People and Land)," in *Kisan Sandesh* (2):17.

Pristhabhumi (Kathmandu), 21 March, 1991.

Pyakurel, Uddhab (2005), *2046 Ko Paribartan ra Nyayapalika* (1990 Change and Judiciary), Kathmandu: Nepal Center for Contemporary Studies.

-------- (2006), "Identity Politics in Nepal," *Research Journal* Vol. 1 (1), January-July.

-------- (2006), "*Rajyako Punarsamrachana Ra Pahichanko Prasna* (Restructuring of the State and Question of Identity)," *Kantipur,* 16 November.

Raj, Sebasti L. and Chaudhary Arundhauti Roy (1998), *Contemporary Social Movements in India: Achievements and Hurdles,* New Delhi: Indian Social Institute.

Rao, M. S. A. (ed.) (1978), *Social Movements in India*, Vol 1-2, New Delhi: South Asia Books.

Raeper, William and Hoftun, Martin (1992), *Spring Awakening: An Account of the 1990 Revolution in Nepal*, New Delhi: Viking.

Rijal, Dhruba and Yokota, Yozo (2006), *Understanding Development, Conflict and Violence: The Cases of Bhutan, Nepal, North-East India and Chittagong Hill Tracts of Bangladesh,* New Delhi: Adroit Publishers.

Rose, Leo E. and John T. Scholz (1980), *Nepal: Profile of a Himalayan Kingdom,* New Delhi: Selectbook Service Syndicate.

Rudolf, Heberle (1951), *Social Movements: An Introduction to Political Sociology*, New York: Appleton-Century-Crafts.

Runciman, W.G. (1966), *Relative Deprivation and Social Justice*. Berkeley: University of California.

Sales, Anne de (2003), "The Kham Magar Country, Nepal: Between Ethnic Claims and Maoism," in Deepak Thapa (ed.), *Understanding the Maoist Movement of Nepal*, Kathmandu: Martin Chautari.

Samay, 30 December 2004.

Scott, Alan (1990), *Ideology and the New Social Movements*, London: Unwin Hyman.

Seddon, David (2002), The Maoist Insurgency in Nepal: Revolutionary Theory and Practice. Paper presented at 'Symposium on South Asia-Conflict in South Asia' organized by Research Group on South Asia in the School of Development Studies, University of East Anglia, 18 June.

Shah, Ghanashyam (1990), *Social Movements in India: A Review of Literature*, New Delhi: Sage Publications.

Shah, Ghanashyam (ed.) (2002), *Social Movements and the State*, New Delhi: Sage Publications.

Shah, Rishikesh (1990), *Modern Nepal: A Political History, 1769-1955,* 2 Vols. New Delhi: Manohar .

-------- ,(1992), *Ancient and Medieval Nepal,* New Delhi: Manohar.

Sharma, Prayag Raj (1997), "Nation-Building, Multi-Ethnicity, and the Hindu State," in David N. Gellner, Joanna Pfaff-Czarnecka, and John Whelpton (eds.), *Nationalism and Ethnicity in a Hindu Kingdom: The Politics of Culture in Contemporary Nepal*, Amsterdam: Harwood Academic Publishers.

Sharma, Sudheer (2002), The Ethnic Dimension of the Maoist Insurgency. Unpublished Paper, May.

Sharma, Sudheer (2003) "The Maoist Movement: An Evolutionary Perspective," in Deepak Thapa (ed.), *Understanding the Maoist Movement of Nepal*, Kathmandu: Martin Chautari and CSDR.

Shuman, Frederick (1967), "Insurgency," in Encyclopedia of Social Sciences, New York cited in Anil Kumar Singh, "Insurgency in India: Internal and External Dimensions," *Aakrosh* (Delhi), October 2004, p. 51.

Singh, Anil Kumar (2004), "Insurgency in India: Internal and External Dimensions," *Aakrosh* (Delhi), October.

Singh, Mohan Bikram (2003), "The Royal Palace Massacre and the Maoists' Pro-King Political Line," in Arjun Karki and David Seddon (eds.), *The People's War in Nepal : Left Perspectives,* New Delhi: Adroit Publishers.

Singh, N. Joykumar (2005), *Social Movement in Manipur*, New Delhi: Mittal Publications.

Thapa, Deepak (ed.), (2003), *Understanding the Maoist Movement of Nepal,* Kathmandu: Martin Chautari.

Thapa, Deepak with Sijapati, Bandita (2003), *A Kingdom Under Siege: Nepal's Maoist Insurgency 1996 to 2003*, Kathmandu: The

Printhouse.

The Constitution of the Kingdom of Nepal 2047 (1990), Kathmandu: HMG, Ministry of Law, Justice and Parliamentary Affairs, Law Books Management Board.

The Himalayan Times, July 16, 2004.

The Hindu, February 8, 9 and 10, 2006.

The Kathmandu Post, May 21, 2005.

The Kathmandu Post, August 31, 2004.

The Worker, no 2, June 1996.

Thompson, E. P. (1968), *The Making of the English Working Class*, Hammondsport: Penguin

Tilly, Charles (1978), *From Mobilization to Revolution*, New York: Random House

UK Government Website: http://www.homeoffice.gov.uk/security/terrorism-and-the-law/terrorism-act/proscribed-groups

Upendra, Yadav (2003), *Nepali Jan Andolan aur Madhesi Mukti ka Sabal*, Nepal: Madhesi People's Right Forum (in Hindi).

URPC Press Statement, November 26, 2001.

Warner, M. (2001), Complex Problem-Negotiated Solutions: Strategies and Tools for Reducing Conflict as an Obstacle to Sustainable Rural Livelihood, London: Overseas Development Institute.

Weinstein, Jay (1997), *Social and Cultural Change: Social Science for a Dynamic World*, Boston: Allyn and Bacon.

Whelpton, John (1997), "Political Identity in Nepal: State, Nation and Community," in David N. Gellner, Joanna Pfaff-Czarnecka, and John Whelpton (eds.), *Nationalism and Ethnicity in a Hindu Kingdom: The Politics of Culture in Contemporary Nepal*, Amsterdam: Harwood Academic Publishers.

Wilkinson, Paul (1971), *Social Movements*, London: Pall Mall.

Wilson, Paul (1973), *Introduction to Social Movements*, New York: Basic Books.

Wolfenstien, E. Victor (1971), *The Revolutionary Personality: Lenin, Trotpky, Gandhy*, USA: New Jersey.

Wolff, K. H. (ed.) (1959), *George Simmel 1858-1918: A Collection of Essays with Translations and a Bibliography*, Columbus; Ohio State University Press.

World Fact Book 2002.

Yami, Hisila and Bhattarai, Baburam (1996), "Nationality Question in Nepal", in *Problems and Prospect of Revolution in Nepal,* Nepal: Janadisha Publications.

Yogi, Narahari Nath, and Acharya, Baburam (1953), "Rastrapita Shri 5 Bada Maharaja Prithvi Narayan Shah Ko Divyopadesh (Divine Counsel of the Great His Majesty the King Prithvi Narayan Shah)", *Prithvi Jayanti Samaroha Samiti* (Prithvi Birthday Celebration Committee) 2nd edition, rev, Kathmandu: Bageswari Press.

Zwi, A. and A. Ugalde (1991), Political Violence in the Third World: A Public Health Issue, *Health Policy and Planning*, 1991, 6(3):203-217.

INDEX

Active Organisations 96
Active Stage of Disagreement 21
Adhikari, Manmohan and Pushpa Lal Shreshtha 61
Advent of Indo-Aryan and Mongolian Elements 33
Agreement on Monitoring of Management of Arms and Armies 192
Agricultural Development Bank 102
Aim of *RIM* 62
Ajatsatru 29
Amatya, Tulsi Lal 62
Ambitious Lichhvi Kings 29
April 24, 2006, 158
Apter 22
Arun River 32
Autocratic Monarchy in Nepal 155
Autocratic Panchayat System 54
Autonomos Indigenous Tribal Area 36

Baral 18, 24
Barracking of Nepal Army 20
Basnyat Conspriracy 42
Bassiouni 19
Bernstain 68
Bhattarai, Baburam 63-66, 68, 96, 97, 104, 106, 109, 112
Blackwell 24
Brahmanas 37, 39, 40, 44, 37, 72, 75, 78

Caste/Ethnic Composition in 24 Districts with Maoist Influence 90
Ceasefire, Definition of 170
Central Military Commission 110
Chand, Lokendra Bahadur 115
Chhathar Ghar 38
Chaubise State 33, 34
Classification of Rana Family 45
Close Circuit Televisions 125
Communist History of Nepal 108, 127
______ Leaders 66
______ Party of China 17
______ Party of India 63
______ Party of Nepal 60, 62,-64
____ Leadership Struggle of 61
____ Maoist 13
Communists in Nepal 131
Community Study and Welfare Centre 13
Comprehensive Peace Accord 202, 204
______ Spirit of the 208
Comprehensive Peace Agreement 125
Concept of Land Bank 148
Constitution of the Kingdom of Nepal 81
Convention of CPN 61, 128
Credit of Unification 35

Dalits in the Hills 78
Declaration of 'Peoples War' 13
Delhi Compromise 61
Demad of Maoist 138-141
Democratic System in Nepal 54

Deuba government 66, 114, 117
______ Sher Bahadur 116
DFID Report 15
Dharmaditya Dharmacharya 46
Different Communities in 1990 Constitution 81
District Administrative Office 106
District of Mid-western Region 104
Dravya Shah 35
Durbhanga Plenum in 1961 62
Dullu Pillar 31

Eastern Parts of Nepal 32
Educational Status of Caste/Ethnic Groups and Regional Groups 79
Eight-Point SPA-Maoist Agreement 156

Election Manifestos of Six Major Political Parties in Nepal 84-88
Elements of Political Agenda 26
Emergence of Nepal as a Nation State 39
Essence of Nepal's Glorious History 151
Ethnic Activism 50
______ Communities 88, 131
_____ Elites in Nepal 57
______ Group 72
_____ Major 78, 79

Features of the Maoists Struggle 23
February 1, 2005 Coup 58
______, 2006 147
First Political Force 121
First World War 60
Five Radical Forces 63
Followers of Marxism-Leninism-Maoism 67
Founder of First Ruling Dynasty 26
Four
______ Layer Hierarchy 71
______ Party Alliance 117
______ Prominent Kshatriya Families
Front Organization of Maoist 96

Galtung 22
Garden of Four *Varnas* and 36 *Jatis* 38
Gautam, Shiva Raj 97
General Elections of Nepal 84-88
Gharti Purna Bahadur 89
Goal of Political Struggle 68
Gopalvamsi Dynasty 28
Gorkha House 32
______ Regime 35, 36
______ Ruler 35, 37
______ Ruling Elite of 38
Government of Nepal 162, 180
______ and CPN (M) 124, 179
_____ Comprehensive Peace Accord between 175, 176
______ 25 points Ceasefire Codes of Conduct 159-61
Guerilla War in Nepal—Condition for Success in 100
Gurr 22
Gurang, Dev 102
Gurang, Gopal 52
Guthi 39

Halliday 20
Heberle 25
Hierarchies of Relationship 71
High Caste Hindu Groups 39
High Caste Social Groups 42
Highlights of Nepali Congress Manifesto 48

Higher Caste Group 75
Hill High Caste 72
Hilly Region of Nepal 70
Hindu Fundamentalist Group of Nepal and India 55
Hindu Lichhvi Rulers 33
Hindu Religion 54
Hindu Varna System 44
Hinduism—Reforming Movement of 45
Histories of the Communist Parties in Nepal 60
History of Communist Movement in Nepal 16
Homeland of Shah King 49
Hudson 36
Human Rights Commission Report of Nepal 13

Indian Naxalite Movement 131
Indigeneons People 29
Inevitable Aspect of Democratic System 83
Influencial NC Leaders 105
Informal Sector Service Centre 13, 105
INIG 72
International Communist Movement 69
______ Cristis Group 94
______ Report 95
Internally Displaced People Project 14

Jang Bahadur 42, 43
Jayasthiti Malla 30, 31, 44
______ and Ram Shah of Gorkha 34
Jelin 26
Jhapa Movement 128
JMCC 205-208
Job of Ranas 46
Journalist and Media Personnel 117
Jumla, Powerful Principalities before Unification 37

Karnali Region 31
Kathmandu
______ Newars of 34, 41
______ Oldest Religion of 30
______ Valley 28-31, 39, 44, 49, 103, *et al*
Keshar Jung Raimajhi 61
Key Terms used in Armed Struggle 16-22
Khas and Magars 40, 41
King
______ Birendra 54, 125, 129, 169
______ Gyanendra 58, 114, 116, 121, 169
______ Mahendra 51, 52, 58, 61
______ Tribhuwan 58
______ and Ranas 61
King's Coup—Outcomes of 118
Kingdom of Nepal 123, 158
Kirants of Mongolian Stocks 28
Kipat Systems 46, 53
Koirala, B.P. 47, 48
______, G.P. 112, 129, 133
Koirala's Letter to UN-Secretary General 162
Kot Parva & Jang Bahadur 42

Lama Nirmal 62
Land of Nepal 70
Lands of Mallas in India 30
Leadership Struggle of CPN 61
Lichhvi Period 30, 33
Lichhvis 29
Local Rulers and Elite 35
Lopez and Stohl 21

Mahakali Treaty 127
Mahara, Krishna Bahadur 17
Mainstay of Economy 14

_____ Elements of the 67
Mainstream of Nepali Politics 142
Major Parties in Nepal 97
Major Palitical Forces 127
Major Racial Stains 33
Malla Dynasty—External Attacker to the 30
Malla Kingdom of 11th to 14th Century 32
Malla Period 31
Mandeva 29
Maoist
_____ Advocate 102
_____ Army 197
_____ Combatants 200
_____ Guerilla
_____ Insurgency 13
_____ Insurgents 142

Maoist Mcvement 108, 113, 118, 120, 122, 132
_____ Elements of the 67
_____ in Nepal 15, 16, 23, 26, 67, 120 *et al*
_____ Initiating Area of the 104
_____ Origin Growth and Spread of the 102
_____ SPA and 124
Maoist of Nepal 67, 69, 70
Maoist Paty—Policy & Programme 88
Maoist Struggle in Nepal 16
Mao-TSe-Tung 17
_____ Marxism-Leninism—Principles of 62
Marxism-Leninism-Maoism
_____ Fallowers of 67
_____ Ultimate Aim 60
May 25, 2006 124
Mechi River 62
Mehta, Ashok K. & Sadip Bahadurshah 94
Merton and Nisbet 19
Migrant Landlords 69
Minority Religious Groups 55
Mohan Nirmal Singh and Bikram Rana 62
Monarchy in Nepal Democracy 58
Muluki Ain 1854 44

Nagadaha 28
Nascent Communist Movement 60
National Symbols and National Anthem 53
Native People 69
Naxlites of India 107
NCDN 88
Nehru Government's Toy 61
Nehru, Jawaharlal 61
Nepal Police and Armed Police Force 196
Nepal National Education and Planning Commission 48
Nepal Trade Union Federation 96
Nepal's Democratic System 58
_____ Foreign Policy 150
_____ Maoist 93
_____ Present International Boundaries 28
Nepali Army 180
_____ Functions of 220
Nepalese Population 70, 71
_____ Society 99
Nepali Congress 49-51, 61, 117
_____ and CPN (UML) 55, 57
_____ and ULF 68
Nepali Economy 14
Newar of Gorkha 38
Newars 72
NGOs and other Organisations 50
Nieburg 22
Non-Hindu Indigenons Group 46
Norwegian Refugee Council 38

November
______ 7, 2006 166
______ 28, 2001 142
______ 28, 2006 134, 192, 208

Occasion of Nepali New Year 122
Official and Literary Language of Nepal
Old Form of Hinduism and Buddhism 33
'Operation Romeo' 65
Organizational Structure of the CPN (Maoist) 98
Orthodox Hindu Religion 36
Other Marginalized Group in Nepal 80

Panchayat 68, 127
Panchayat Regime (1960-90) 51
Panchayat System 52, 117
Panchayati Slogan 51
Party-Breaking Trend 63
People of Tibetan Origin 70
People's Democratic Forum 96
______ Liberation Army 94, 133
______ Republic of China 96

Phadnis 23
Policy on Armed Struggle 99
Policy and Programme of Maoist Party 88
Political Situation of Nepal 122
Political Violence 23
Polletta and Jasmer 26
Population of Dalits 135
Position of Dalits in the Hills 28
Present Territory in Nepal 32
Primary Goal of Nepalization 52
Prithvi Naraian Shah 35-39, 52
______ Demise of 42
Process of Hinduization and Gorkhaization 27, 39
______ Hallmark of 30
Process of Ranaization 44
Progeny of Brahmanas and Kshatriyas 40
Pseudo-Democratic Period (1951-60) 47
Prachanda 68, 69, 93, 99, 100, 109
______ Letter to UN Secretary General 164
Prachanda Path—Principles Expressed in 101
Raimajhi, Keshar Jung 61
______ and others 67
Rana
______ Colonel SJB 95
______ Heriditary System 42
______ Oligarchy 43, 47, 60
______ in Nepal and Shah Dynasty 45
______ Political System 43
______ Integral Part of 50
______ Regime 41-43, 44, 47
______ Initiator of 42, 45
______ Ruler 43

Rana's Religions Orthodoxy 45
Ranas 28
Rashtriya Sankritic Samiti 56
Rapti Zone—Poverty in 104
Redeployment and Concentration of all Combatants in Nepal 196
Region-Based Frontier Organization of the Maoist and its Leadership 91
Regional Autonomons Government the CPN (Maoist) 92
Regionally Backward Groups 102

Regmi, Achut Raj 55
Rijal and Yokota 21, 22, 23
RNA 118, 124

Roots of Social Movements 19
Rose and Scholz 33
Royal Massacre 121
Royal Order of 1846 37

Saint Simon 18
Security Forces 14
Sen Dynasty of Palpa 32, 35
Seven Main Cantonment Sites 197-199
Seven Parliamentary Alliance 58, 59, 122, 123
______ and CPN 152
______ Government and Maoist 124
______ and Maoist 126
Shah 26
______ Dynasty 41, 49
______ Family 51
______ and Rana Regime 46
______ Regime 35
Share of Caste/Ethnic Groups in Prestigious Occupation 75
Shaivism 30
Shrestha
______ Krishna Mohan 115
______ Pushpa Lal 61, 62
Singh, Mohan Bikram 62, 63, 108
South Asian Himalayan Country 13
Split of CPN-UML 121
Small Farmer Development Programme 102
State of Emergency in Nepal 96, 115
Strategy and Tactics of War 100
Sugauli Treaty of 1816 28
Suppressed and Marginalized People of Nepal 88
Supreme Legal Framework 81

Tarai Congress 50
______ Dalits 72
Thapa, Surya Bahadur 115
Tharu and Tarai Communities 104
Theory of 'People's War' 68
Three Fold Maoist Organization 93
Traditional Homeland of Tribal People 70
Traditional Homeland of Tarai People 70
Tripartite Agreement on Monitoring the Arms and Armies 134
Twin Agenda of Secular State 89

Ultimate Goal of Communism through Socialism 70
UML 116, 117, 125
Unification of Nepal 48
______ Post 35
______ Pre 28
Universal Declaration of Human Rights 175
UN Mission 197, 199, 201, 205
UPFN 64-66, 97, 103, 105, 130
______ Main Demand of 63
URPC 95, 96, 112

Vaishnavas and Buddhist Sects 30
Vaishnavism and Shaivism 34
Vaishali Dynasty 20
Village Development Committes 102, 104, 110, 114

Violations of Agreement 206

Warner 20
Whelpton 38
Wilkinson 24, 26
Wilson 25
Works of Nepali Army 168

Yamini, Hisila 96
Yogi and Acharya 38
Youth Communist Leaders 62

Zwi and Ugalde 23